LEGENDS AND LIES
The American Revolution

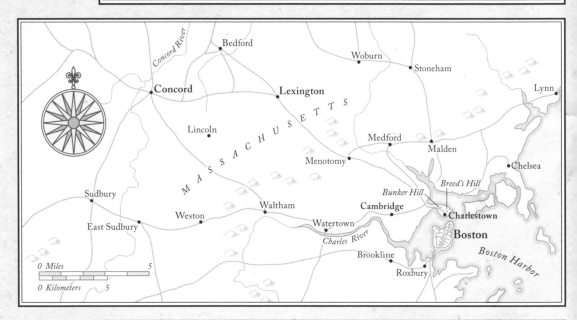

Halifax

NOVA SCOTIA

MASSACHUSETTS

Concord River
Bedford
Woburn
Stoneham
Concord
Lexington
Lynn
Lincoln
Medford
Malden
Menotomy
Chelsea
Sudbury
Bunker Hill
Breed's Hill
Waltham
Cambridge
Weston
Charlestown
East Sudbury
Watertown
Boston
Charles River
Brookline
Boston Harbor
Roxbury

0 Miles 5
0 Kilometers 5

NEW JERSEY

NEW YORK

Weehawken
Hudson River
Bayard's Hill
East River
Gowanus Creek
New York
"The Battery"
Brooklyn
Long Island

0 Miles 5
0 Kilometers 5

Staten Island

Atlantic Ocean

D1212897

BILL O'REILLY'S

BILL O'REILLY'S

LEGENDS & LIES

The Patriots

WRITTEN BY DAVID FISHER

Henry Holt and Company
New York

Henry Holt and Company, LLC
Publishers since 1866
175 Fifth Avenue
New York, New York 10010
www.henryholt.com

Henry Holt® and ® are registered trademarks of Henry Holt and Company, LLC.
Copyright © 2016 by Warm Springs Productions, LLC and Life of O'Reilly Productions
All rights reserved.
Distributed in Canada by Raincoast Book Distribution Limited

Library of Congress Cataloging-in-Publication Data is available.

ISBN: 978-1-62779-789-4

Henry Holt books are available for special promotions and premiums.
For details contact: Director, Special Markets.

First Edition 2016

Designed by Nancy Singer
Endpaper map by Jeffrey L. Ward
Photo research by Liz Seramur of Selected Shots Photo Research, Inc. with
assistance from Nancy Singer and Olivia Croom

Printed in the United States of America

1 2 3 4 5 6 7 8 9 10

CONTENTS

Having just finished writing another *O'Reilly Factor* script, I am thinking about the people who made my program possible: the American revolutionaries. This day the Factor is packed with opinion and robust debate that would be unthinkable on television in, say, China and many other countries.

Having lived in Boston for some years, I immersed myself in New England history. Back in the mid-eighteenth century, life was hard in the Massachusetts Bay Colony. Few people had any luxuries at all—they lived week to week trying to feed their families and ward off fatal disease.

The climate was harsh and the labor hard.

Thus many British subjects living in the colonies were in no mood to share what little they had with a corrupt king thousands of miles away. As King George's financial demands grew, so did rebellion and sedition against the Crown. It was almost all about money.

The leaders of the rebellion were a very mixed crew. Led by tough working-class guys, the Sons of Liberty roughed up the king's men and eventually sent an unforgettable message by dumping English tea, the source of a hated tax, into the cold, murky waters of Boston Harbor. Others, like John Hancock, were patricians who had a lot to lose by defying London but did so anyway because they believed in freedom and fairness.

The actual American Revolution began soon after the Tea Party and is filled with thrilling stories of bravery and deceit, brilliance and stupidity.

This book will bring some of those stories to life while telling the reader the truth about Benjamin Franklin, George Washington, John and Samuel Adams, and other American icons.

Along the way, we debunk some of the lies attached to the legends, which I always find fascinating. As a former high school history teacher,

I am often shocked to find that some Americans know virtually nothing about the origins of the place where they currently live and therefore believe most anything.

How many of us know the story of the Francis Marion—the Swamp Fox? What a guy he was—a fearsome fighter who used the thickets of South Carolina to terrorize British forces. Marion's guys were tough outdoorsmen who openly mocked the king's men dressed in their elaborate "red coats."

The Swamp Fox used guile and guerrilla tactics to hammer a much more powerful opponent. He exemplifies the true American spirit; self-sacrifice and goal oriented.

How much more opposite could Francis Marion be from, say, Benjamin Franklin, the crafty inventor turned diplomat who guided the Independence movement? Talk about two different worlds: Franklin at home in the salons of Paris; Marion camping out in desolate backwaters!

This book chronicles both men, demonstrating the diversity that was present in colonial America, even as it is today in modern times.

My life has been directly affected by those who forged rebellion against England and won freedom. I have made my living for over forty years by using my freedom of speech and working in a free press. No other country on earth has so many liberties in the marketplace of ideas in which I traffic every working day.

So I owe the original patriots a deep debt and hope to repay it by writing the truth about them and bringing their courageous deeds to millions of readers. It is a mission that is worthy and necessary in this age of declining knowledge about how America became the land of the free.

As always in my books of history, there is no political message other than stating the facts. The American revolutionaries were men and women of differing opinions, united against what they saw as an unbearable oppressor—King George.

But not every colonial was a rebel. About half the population, called Tories, did not want separation from the Crown. That caused a bitter divide that lasted for decades after independence was finally won. In fact, if you travel to Cambridge, Massachusetts, today, you can visit Brattle Street and see some of the large homes that colonists loyal to the king inhabited. To this day, that neighborhood is called "Tory Row."

So what side would you have taken? Most of us now would most likely say "the patriots!" But back in 1775, the decision was not an easy one. Few thought George Washington and his ill-equipped army could defeat the powerful, well-trained British regulars. And the Brits were vengeful—the lives of all rebels were definitely on the line, as they say.

Still, the allure of freedom intoxicated many colonists. But it was the extraordinary leadership provided by the subjects of this book that made our present freedoms possible.

Their stories demand to be told accurately. We don't need false legends or propaganda. The truth is simply too compelling.

Hopefully, you will enjoy the following pages and visualize the intense struggle that gave all contemporary Americans a chance at living a free and worthwhile life. Reading this book will be educational and enjoyable; my favorite formula. We write for you, the reader, in a fast-paced, action-packed way. But please don't forget how important these stories really are as you get caught up in the drama.

So let's go, and thanks for taking the time to learn about the patriots.

Bill O'Reilly

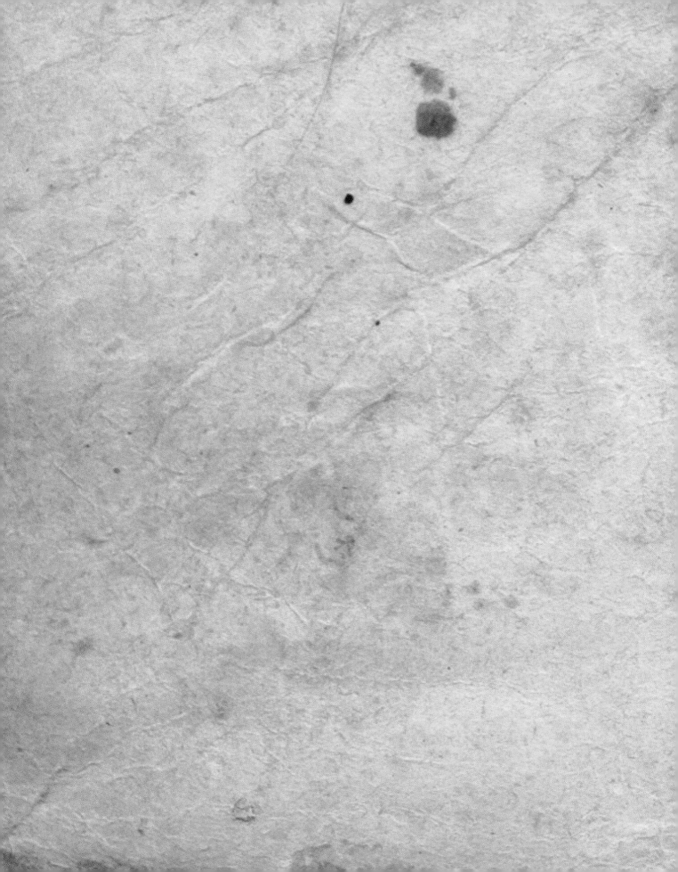

INTRODUCTION

It took slightly more than four decades from the first rumblings of discontent for the thirteen loosely aligned colonies comprising New England to be transformed into one of the largest and most prosperous nations on earth. It started with a simple idea, that all men deserve to be treated equally, and became the great experiment that would change the world.

The American Revolution was born in the town meetings of Massachusetts, when ordinary people stood up and spoke passionately to their neighbors about their common interests. It did not begin as a quest for freedom but rather as citizens' simple desire to have their rights respected. It was a war of ideas as much as a fight over economics.

When the first shots were fired at Lexington and Concord, it is probable that the British believed this was more of a nuisance than a war. Would the colonies really dare fight the greatest military power ever assembled? The British army was well equipped, well trained, and highly professional. The British navy controlled the oceans. The colonials had no army and no navy, just poorly equipped and untrained local militias.

At first the British tried to contain the revolt within Massachusetts, believing they might end it by occupying Boston. That strategy failed at Bunker Hill, when the redcoats were stunned by the ferocity of the colonists' defense. When the cannons Washington had retrieved from abandoned Fort Ticonderoga put the British troops in jeopardy, the British withdrew to Canada to reinforce their army. It was time to take this uprising seriously.

No man did more for the cause of American freedom than George Washington, who was, wrote Henry Lee, "First in war, first in peace and first in the hearts of his countrymen." At top, his celebrated entry into New York City in November, 1883. Below, General Horatio Gates accepts the surrender of General Burgoyne at Saratoga, New York, in October 1777, marking the turning point of the war.

In 1776 the largest military offensive in history captured New York, forcing Washington to retreat. The colonial army had been reduced to only six thousand men when Washington launched an extraordinary Christmas Night attack on the Hessians in Trenton, providing the colonies with a great military victory—and hope.

A year later the strategy changed once more; this time the British intended to isolate the northern colonies. To accomplish this, they split their army in half—and were stunned when five thousand troops were captured at the Battle of Saratoga. The war had become incredibly costly, causing many people in England—and Parliament—to question the value of continuing the fight.

Everything changed when France entered the war on the colonial side in 1778, forcing the British to protect their possessions scattered around the world. Once again the British objectives had changed, and they launched an invasion of the American south, where they expected to be supported by Loyalists. At the beginning of 1780 there were more than sixty thousand British and German troops fighting Washington's twelve-thousand-man army. While at first the southern strategy worked and the British successfully captured South Carolina, the attempt to move north was defeated by small, highly mobile guerrilla bands using hit-and-run tactics. The result was that Lord Cornwallis's army was trapped at Yorktown, Virginia, by American and French forces and ultimately surrendered, effectively ending the fighting in America.

The colonies won the war. The question became: What kind of nation would emerge from the victory? The founding fathers battled over lofty ideals and harsh realities, and slowly a new form of government was carefully molded. It was tested in numerous and unexpected ways, but, with the Louisiana Purchase, a vast new democratic nation was born.

What follows is not a complete retelling of the war and its aftermath but rather an investigation into the truth behind many of the legendary stories from the time, the stories of the heroes and the traitors, the leaders and the ordinary soldiers, who together forged one of the most exciting narratives in all of history.

David Fisher
January 2016

The midnight rides of Paul Revere, William Dawes, and others alert colonists that British troops are marching

ᛣ

The shots heard round the world are fired at Lexington and Concord

ᛣ

The Second Continental Congress meets and appoints George Washington commander in chief

ᛣ

The Battle of Bunker Hill is the first major conflict of the war

ᛣ

Lord Dunmore offers freedom to slaves who fight for the British

After more repressive laws are passed, Samuel Adams begins organizing the colonies

ᛣ

The first British troops are sent to Boston

1768

Washington's army suffers several devastating defeats and is in jeopardy of being disbanded

ᛣ

The British army is defeated at Saratoga

ᛣ

The Marquis de Lafayette arrives

ᛣ

The Continental army settles in Valley Forge for the winter; Baron von Steuben arrives and begins training Washington's troops

British Parliament passes the Sugar and Currency Acts

ᛣ

The first Committees of Correspondence are formed

1764

The Boston Tea Party and similar antitax protests are held throughout New England

1773

1775

1777

1770

The protests turn violent with the Boston Massacre

1776

Henry Knox completes an amazing journey carrying cannons from Fort Ticonderoga to Boston

ᛣ

The British army evacuates Boston

ᛣ

The Declaration of Independence is signed

ᛣ

British troops capture New York

ᛣ

Washington inspires the colonies by crossing the Delaware River on Christmas Night to capture more than a thousand Hessians in Trenton

1765

Parliament imposes the Stamp Act on the colonies

ᛣ

In Massachusetts, the Sons of Liberty are formed

1774

Parliament imposes the Intolerable Acts

ᛣ

The First Continental Congress meets in Philadelphia

1778

France enters the war

ᛣ

British troops withdraw from Philadelphia

The Treaty of Paris
ending the Revolutionary
War is signed

1783

George Washington is
elected America's first
president

1789

The Alien and
Sedition Acts are
passed

1798

The British
southern offensive
is thwarted by
guerrilla fighters,
among them
Francis Marion

꒰

Benedict Arnold's
betrayal is
discovered

1780

The Constitutional
Convention
meeting in
Philadelphia creates
the American
Constitution

1787

The Whiskey
Rebellion takes
place

1794

The Louisiana
Purchase doubles
the size of America

1803

1781

The Articles of
Confederation, binding
the colonies in a nation,
are ratified

꒰

Cornwallis surrenders his
British army at Yorktown

1788

The Constitution is
ratified

1796

John Adams is elected
as the second president;
Thomas Jefferson becomes
vice president

1804

Aaron Burr
kills Alexander
Hamilton in a duel
and eventually is
arrested

1786

Daniel Shays
leads a rebellion
against taxation;
Washington
returns to military
command to put it
down

1791

The Bill of Rights is
adopted

꒰

The First Bank of the
United States is given a
charter

1800–1801

In the presidential
election, Thomas
Jefferson and
Aaron Burr tie
in the electoral
college; the House
eventually elects
Jefferson president

CHAPTER 1

Samuel Adams AND Paul Revere

THE REBELLION BEGINS

The flame that would ignite the American Revolution was lit on a Thursday morning, February 22, 1770, when, according to the *Boston Gazette*, "a barbarous murder . . . was committed on the body of a young lad of about eleven years of age."

Earlier that morning Christopher Seider and a crowd of young men had marched defiantly through Boston's cobblestone streets to the merchant Theophilus Lillie's shop. In addition to a cart overflowing with rotten fruit, they carried painted papier-mâché figures of Lillie and three other importers who refused to respect the colonists' boycott on all British goods. As the protesters stained the shop windows with rubbish, the greatly despised customs collector Ebenezer Richardson tried to stop them. Richardson, described by the *Gazette* as "a person of a most abandoned character," had been forced to leave the Massachusetts town of Woburn after impregnating his sister-in-law and blaming the local minister. Richardson tried to knock down the rioters' papier-mâché figures. When his attempt was thwarted, he threatened to "blow a lane through this mob" until finally retreating the hundred paces to his own home.

☞ The Boston Massacre, March 5, 1770.

The growing crowd, numbering as many as sixty boys, turned its whole attention to him. The morning was dark. More nasty words were exchanged. "By the eternal God," Richardson swore, "I will make it too hot for some of you before night." At first only rubbish was thrown into Richardson's yard and was thrown back by Richardson and his wife, Kezia, but soon rocks were being hurled and the Richardsons retreated into their secure home. Windows were shattered as the barrage grew in intensity. Seconds after an egg or a stone struck his wife, Ebenezer Richardson appeared defiantly at a second-story window, holding high a musket loaded with swan shot.

He fired once. It was intended to be a warning, he later swore, but two boys were struck. Sammy Gore was wounded in both thighs and his hand but would survive. Christopher Seider was hit in his breast and abdomen by eleven pieces of shot "the bigness of large peas."

"The child fell," reported the *Boston Evening-Post*, "but was taken up and carried into a neighboring house, where all the surgeons within call were assembled, and speedily determined the wounds mortal, as they indeed proved about 9 o'clock that evening."

Richardson and his alleged accomplice, George Wilmot, were taken to Faneuil Hall. As more than a thousand people stood watching, they told their story to three magistrates. Richardson was charged with murder. The crowd pressed forward, its intentions clear, and, as the newspapers reported, "had not gentlemen of influence interposed, they would never have reached the prison." There is reason to believe one of those gentlemen may well have been Samuel Adams, who by then was well established as a leader of the protests.

The whole of Boston was invited to attend the boy's funeral, "when all the friends of Liberty may have an opportunity of paying their last respects to the remains of this little hero and first martyr to the noble cause." More than two thousand of the city's approximately twenty thousand citizens marched in an extraordinary procession, which caused John Adams to write in amazement, "My eyes never beheld such a funeral. The procession extended further than can be well imagined."

The fervor in the city continued to grow until a few days later it finally exploded in battle between the colonists and British soldiers. To the English this was called the Incident on King Street, but Americans have always known it simply as the Boston Massacre.

The names and events of the American Revolution are the foundation on which this great nation is built. But contrary to what is often believed, it did not begin as a quest for freedom but rather as a protest to ensure that colonists enjoyed their rights as citizens of the British Empire. How had relations between Great Britain and the colonists come to this kind of violence? Until the early 1760s, the estimated two million free white men and women living in America—or "the best poor man's country," as it was known to Europeans—enjoyed

News was interpreted by artists and published in newspapers and pamphlets, which often served as propaganda.

a mostly peaceful and prosperous relationship with Great Britain. While each of the thirteen colonies was mostly self-governed by elected assemblies that made and enforced laws, controlled land ownership, and levied taxes, the cultural, economic, and political ties to the empire remained strong. While some colonists had risked their lives crossing the ocean for personal or religious freedom, many more of them had come for the economic opportunity; the colonies were known as a place where a hardworking man could eventually lay claim to his own piece of land or establish a business.

While colonists proudly called themselves Americans, even those people born in North

America remained loyal to the Crown. Their goal was not to become an independent nation. The first sign of trouble came on November 16, 1742, when riots erupted in the streets of Boston after Royal Navy sailors impressed, or kidnapped, forty-six men, intending to force them to serve aboard British naval ships in the long war against France. While impressment was common in other parts of the world, until that night both tradition and the law had protected Massachusetts's men. The riots lasted three days; the city was paralyzed and colonists took several British naval officers hostage, then attempted to storm the State House.

The commodore of the British fleet anchored in Boston Harbor ordered his ships to load twenty-four cannons and threatened to bombard the city. He never had to make good on his threat, as Governor William Shirley soon arranged a trade of the impressed men for hostages held by the rioters. A day later the fleet sailed.

But the seeds of discontent had taken root. A pamphlet signed by "Amicus Patriae," an

anonymous American patriot, was distributed during the crisis. This "Address of the Inhabitants of the Province of Massachusetts" defended the "natural right" of the people to be free in the streets and band together for defense against impressment if necessary. Evidence suggests that the author of that pamphlet was a young brewer named Samuel Adams.

By that point in his life, Samuel Adams had proved to be a remarkably unsuccessful businessman. After being dismissed from his first job at a countinghouse, he borrowed a small fortune from his father to open his own merchant business, which failed. He then began working in the family's successful malt business, becoming known somewhat derisively as "Sam the maltster." His problem, according to historian Pauline Maier, was that he was "a man utterly uninterested in either making or possessing money." His true passion was politics, and that perhaps was his greatest inheritance: his father, Samuel Adams Sr., was a wealthy merchant, church deacon, and a leader in Boston politics, eventually being elected to the Massachusetts House of

Representatives. Samuel Adams Jr. entered politics in 1747, being elected to the post of clerk in the Boston market. He also served as the local tax collector—and failed miserably at that job, too. According to British law, he was personally responsible for taxes he failed to collect. To settle that debt, the sheriff announced an auction of Adams's property, including the family brewery. Adams's reputation, and perhaps the fact that he threatened to sue any purchaser, allowed him to keep his property. In 1748 Adams joined several men to found a newspaper, the *Independent Advertiser*, and wrote in its first issue, "Liberty can never exist without equality." It was an attack on both the wealthy mercantile class and the growing threats on individual freedom from England.

By 1760, 130 years after being founded by the Puritans, Boston was a thriving, growing seaport. While in theory its commerce was regulated by British navigation and trade laws called the Navigation Acts, in fact those laws were rarely strictly enforced. Instead, a system of common laws had developed based on the local practices that had served to encourage business. That changed in 1761, when London ordered its customs officials in Boston to begin aggressively cracking down on smugglers who were depriving the government of taxes needed to finance the Seven Years' War or, as it was known in America, the French and Indian War. Suddenly the Navigation Acts, so long ignored, were to be enforced. It seemed only fair that the Americans should help pay for the ten thousand British troops who were protecting them from the French. But rather than reducing the flow of smuggled goods, these duties had the opposite effect, enticing more people to take risks.

To assist the tax collectors, the newly appointed chief justice of the Massachusetts Superior Court, Thomas Hutchinson, issued writs of assistance, warrants that allowed the taxmen to enter any premises in the city without cause in order to search for smuggled goods and seize whatever they found. Years later Samuel Adams would write that it was in Hutchinson's courtroom that "the child independence was then and there born" as the men of Boston were "ready to take up arms against writs of assistance."

Behind the power of these laws, English customs agents ransacked homes and businesses searching for smuggled goods. Angry colonists joined together and formed raucous political parties to fight these new laws. They didn't demand independence from Great Britain; the colonists simply wanted to be treated with respect and have a voice in their own government. As Samuel Adams wrote, "If taxes are laid upon us in any shape without our having a legal representation . . . are we not reduced . . . to the miserable state of tributary slaves? . . . We claim British rights, not by charter only; we are born to them."

Several leaders emerged from this turmoil, among them John Adams and John Hancock. John Adams was the wealthy second cousin of Samuel Adams, who had drawn him into the cause. He and his cousin were said to be a curious sight when walking together, the wealthy

Stylized portraits like these of John Adams (top) and John Hancock were intended to convey a strong unemotional image.

This 1774 anti-British engraving of Samuel Adams, which appeared in the short-lived *Royal American* magazine, showed Parliament trampling on the colonists rights.

John Adams turned out as a proper gentleman while his admittedly poorer cousin reflecting the manners of a lesser class. By all accounts John was arrogant and cantankerous; he was also respected for his powerful intellect and was happy to lecture at length about his opinions. A fifth-generation descendant of Puritans who had settled in the Massachusetts Bay Colony in 1632, he was the first member of his family not to join the militia, instead becoming a lawyer. Under the pseudonym Humphrey Ploughjogger, in 1763 he began publishing essays supporting the legal rights of Americans.

John Hancock was only seven years old when his father died and he was sent to live with his wealthy uncle, the revered shipping tycoon Thomas Hancock. John was raised a child of great privilege, and after graduating from Harvard he traveled to Britain to attend the coronation of twenty-two-year-old King George III. When his uncle died, the then twenty-six-year-old Hancock took control of his import-export empire and became the second-richest man in the colonies. He was known as a generous man who gave easily and often to causes and friends, among them Samuel Adams—and would eventually become one of the primary financiers of the freedom movement. But he also was impossibly vain with the expected arrogance of the very wealthy, and at times his ambition seemed to extend farther than his capabilities. But like the other towering figures who would join with him to found the United States of America, he also had the extraordinary courage to risk his life and his fortune for a cause in which he deeply believed.

These men were brought into the fight in the early 1760s, when the British Parliament began passing new and more onerous trade laws. The British victory in the Seven Years' War had been costly; England's national debt had almost doubled to 145 million pounds, and the government was desperate for increased revenue. In 1764, the Sugar Act modified an existing but rarely enforced law and added new goods—including sugar, certain wines, coffee, and calico—to the growing list of taxable items, as well as limiting exports of lumber and iron. The Currency Act completely banned the New England colonies from issuing their own paper currency. These new restrictions crippled the colonial economies. But it was the widely vilified Stamp Act that finally led to rebellion.

The Stamp Act imposed a duty on all legal and commercial documents, newspapers, almanacs, liquor licenses, college diplomas, playing cards, and even pairs of dice. Essentially every printed document, except books, was taxed. Harsh penalties were in store for those who defied this act; in addition to large fines, people caught counterfeiting stamps "shall be adjudged a felon, and shall suffer death as in cases of felony without the benefit of clergy." This was the first attempt by Parliament to impose a direct tax on all of the colonies. And it was not at all prepared for the reaction.

For the first time, colonists began actively resisting British rule. In Boston the group that eventually became known as the Sons of Liberty was formed. Led by shoemaker Ebenezer McIntosh, it consisted of shopkeepers, workingmen, students, and artisans, including the noted silversmith Paul Revere—every one of them affected by this tax—and eventually numbered as many as two thousand people.

It was not long before their peaceful protests erupted into violence. Lieutenant Governor Hutchinson had arranged for his brother-in-law, Andrew Oliver, to be appointed to the lucrative post of stamp tax collector. On the morning of August 14, 1765, these Sons of Liberty hung an effigy of Oliver from "the Liberty Tree," a large elm tree at the corner of Essex and Washington Streets, steps from the Boston Common. Hutchinson ordered the sheriff to cut it down, but a crowd gathered in front of the tree to prevent him from doing so. This was among the very first public acts of defiance against the king. The day grew into a celebration as the colonists felt the first surge of their power. When night fell, the mob cut down the effigy and marched with it to the South End wharves, where they destroyed a brick building that had been built to distribute the stamps. They marched with timbers from that building to Oliver's grand home. In a bonfire fueled by those timbers they beheaded Oliver's effigy, then ransacked his home and stable house. The next day Oliver resigned his post.

Twelve days later a group of emboldened colonists attacked Hutchinson's home, venting years of frustration at being casually dismissed by the wealthy classes as "rabble," and within hours they had reduced the mansion to rubble. Hutchinson offered a $300 reward, several years' income for many of these people, to anyone providing information that would help convict the leaders of the attack. Although their identities were well known, no one stepped forward to claim that reward. McIntosh and several other rioters were indicted and jailed, but they were quickly released when angry crowds gathered in front of the jail.

The spirit of protest spread rapidly to the other colonies, from Newport, Rhode Island, to "Charlestown," South Carolina (as it was then spelled). A rudimentary communications network developed, creating new, stronger links among the colonies. Crowds marched through cities along the Eastern Seaboard shouting, "Liberty and no stamps!" In Virginia's House of Burgesses Patrick Henry introduced seven resolutions demanding repeal of the Stamp Act. Sons of Liberty groups were formed; the specter of what happened in Boston caused stamp agents to resign, convinced local tradesmen to ignore the Stamp Act, and led to an effective boycott of British goods. Four days after Hutchinson's house was destroyed, New York City's stamp distributor, merchant James McEvers, also resigned, fearing his "house would have been pillaged, my person abused and His Majesty's revenue impaired."

Smugglers flourished throughout the colonies; among those men accused of that crime was the New Haven merchant Benedict Arnold, who was accused by a hired deckhand of failing to pay duty on goods brought in from the West Indies. There was little sympathy for informers. Arnold responded by organizing a mob that tied his accuser to a whipping post and gave him forty lashes. After being fined 40 shillings for disturbing the peace, Arnold hanged the judge in effigy! Parliament, caught off guard, did not know how to respond. But something had to be done—the colonial boycott of imported English goods had rippled through the British economy, causing considerable unemployment and unrest. British citizens were demanding an end to this disruption. Benjamin Franklin of Pennsylvania sailed to London and warned the House of Commons that any attempt to use troops to enforce the Stamp Act would lead to a violent rebellion. England saw no sense in sending troops across the Atlantic, as the act had been passed to pay for the troops already there. Repealing the act seemingly would reward the protesters and encourage increased defiance in the future. But there was little alternative. In March 1766 Parliament repealed the Stamp Act.

An unintended movement had been born from the protests. "The people have become more attentive to their liberties," wrote John Adams in his diary, ". . . and more determined to defend them. Our presses have groaned, our pulpits have thundered, our legislatures have resolved, our towns have voted; the crown officers have everywhere trembled."

Speaking to Parliament in 1767, the statesman and philosopher Edmund Burke

THE REPEAL. Or the Funeral Procession, of MISS AMERIC-STAMP.

The repeal of the Stamp Act in 1766 marked a significant colonial victory and, as the *Boston Gazette* (bottom) announced, was celebrated with "public rejoicing." It also was celebrated with the publication of *The Repeal or the Funeral of Miss Americ-Stamp*, which was widely reprinted and became one of the best-known satirical cartoons of the entire period.

acknowledged that a movement had been started and no one might predict the eventual outcome, saying ruefully, "The Americans have made a discovery that we mean to oppress them;
we have made a discovery that they intend to raise a rebellion against us. We know not how
to advance; they know not how to retreat."

Parliament failed to pay heed to Burke's warnings, instead passing new duties on glass,
lead, paints, paper, and tea. They believed that these Townshend Acts—as they were known
because they were proposed by the chancellor of the exchequer, Charles Townshend—would
be acceptable because they were indirect taxes. This time they were not going to allow mob
actions to force their hand; instead British commander in chief Lieutenant General Thomas
Gage ordered many of the soldiers who had been fighting the French in rural outposts to the
coastal cities, and with additional troops now sent from England, eventually two regiments
of redcoats were posted in Boston to maintain order.

Townshend was wrong. The colonists were fighting not only against the cost of these new
laws but even more so against the principle that the government in England had the right to
levy taxes on them without their consent. Boston, the main port of entry for British goods,
remained the center of this growing resistance to British rule. Samuel Adams, now forty-six
years old and clerk of the Massachusetts House, emerged as the leader of the opposition. It
was becoming increasingly obvious to him that the colonists, if they didn't want to be treated
as second-class British citizens, would eventually have to strike out on the incredibly risky
and seemingly impossible path to independence.

The taxes devastated the local economy. Silversmith Paul Revere, for example, turned to
performing dental work to make up for some of the losses he had suffered. Among his patients
was the highly respected and debonair physician Joseph Warren, who had become well known
in the city for bravely opening an inoculation hospital during the smallpox epidemic of 1763.
Both men had joined the Sons of Liberty, and their relationship would prove to be vital in the
ensuing years. Among Revere's accomplishments was the creation of a younger generation of
patriots called the Liberty Boys, several of whom conveniently served as apprentices in his shop.

As the situation deteriorated, the colonies looked at the bonds that had tied them to
"Mother England" for so long and now only saw chains. In the early spring of 1768 Lord
Hillsborough, the brusque cabinet officer responsible for the colonies, ordered the colonial
assemblies to be dissolved. Once again the American people took to the streets, attacking
customs agents. Parliament responded by ordering additional troops to Boston. Even more
ominous, their officers were granted permission to take whatever actions deemed necessary.

Under the protection of these soldiers, previously cowed customs agents began strictly
enforcing the Townshend laws. In June, John Hancock's small sloop, the *Liberty*, arrived in

port carrying a cargo of Madeira wine. Traditionally, shipowners and customs agents nego-
tiated an accommodation, resulting in only part of a cargo being declared and taxed. It was
mutually beneficial: the owner profited from the untaxed portion and the agent received some
remuneration for his goodwill. But this time, the customs agent insisted that duty be paid on
every bottle aboard the *Liberty*. The sloop's captain responded by locking the customs agent
Samuel Adams in the brig while the entire cargo was unloaded. The next day the British navy
seized the ship. As it was being towed out of Boston Harbor by the fifty-gun warship HMS
Romney, a mob gathered on the dock; colonists beat two customs agents badly and vandalized
their homes. When John Hancock was accused of smuggling, he hired lawyer John Adams to
defend him; the charges were dropped but Hancock was not able to recover his sloop.

While Adams had attempted to raise a force to meet the arriving redcoats, there was
still no appetite for direct, organized conflict. The reasons were not just sentimental—few

Independent groups known as the Sons of Liberty fomented revolution in colonial cities
using any possible means: demonstrations, petitions, speeches, handbills, and, when necessary,
violence. In this popular engraving, John Lamb is stirring up more than two thousand New
York Sons of Liberty in December *1773* to prevent two shiploads of tea from landing.

colonists were foolish enough to believe that an untrained and poorly armed militia could resist the powerful British army.

The 1765 Quartering Act forced colonists to shelter British troops in both public buildings and unoccupied houses and barns—but not private homes, although the Colonial government was required to pay for all food and drink. The British army was no longer in America to protect the colonists; it had become an occupying force. Eventually it proved impossible to find appropriate housing for all of the troops that been marched into the city, and tents were set up in the very heart of the city, on the Boston Common.

The presence of a thousand redcoats in the city made an impression. In 1768, alarmed Boston merchants voted to boycott British goods. To their surprise, other colonies did not immediately join them. Only after Boston merchants voted to suspend trading with colonies that refused to participate did New York, Philadelphia, and others reluctantly join the boycott. A popular ditty titled "The Mother Country. A Song," which is often attributed to Ben Franklin and was written at some point during this period, explained the colonists' stance:

> We have an old Mother that peevish is grown,
> She snubs us like Children that scarce walk alone;
> She forgets we're grown up and have sense of our own;
> Which nobody can deny deny; Which nobody can deny.
>
> If we don't obey orders, whatever the case;
> She frowns, and she chides, and she loses all patience,
> and sometimes she hits us a slap in the face,
> Which nobody can deny deny; Which nobody can deny.
>
> Her orders so odd are, we often suspect
> That age has impaired her sound intellect:
> But still an old Mother should have due respect,
> Which nobody can deny deny; Which nobody can deny.

But should any nation question the colonists' loyalty to the Crown, Franklin concluded:

> Know too, ye bad neighbours, who aim to divide
> The sons from the Mother, that still she's our Pride;
> And if ye attack her we're all of her side,
> Which nobody can deny deny; Which nobody can deny.

The boycott was sustained with some difficulty for almost two years; while patriots were expected to avoid British-made goods, merchants needed the trade in British products to survive. But those merchants—men like Theophilus Lillie, who refused to honor the boycott—were publicly ridiculed and, in a few cases, physically attacked. Meanwhile, the women of the city organized into a group called the Daughters of Liberty. To reduce the demand for British textiles, they threw spinning and weaving parties and wore homespun clothing as a symbol of their devotion to the growing protest movement.

Members of Parliament were divided on how to handle this dissent among the colonists. Some demanded harsh penalties for Americans who defied the legal authority of the Crown and wanted to bring their leaders to England for trial, while others pushed to reestablish the traditional relationship that had long benefited both sides. "There is the most urgent reason to do what is right, and immediately," wrote Secretary of War Lord Barrington in 1767, "but what is right and who is to do it?"

The uneasy peace, enforced by the redcoats when necessary, lasted until 1770. The boycott agreement among the colonies was set to expire that January. Many merchants, whose storehouses were overstocked with British-made goods, were pleased to see it end. But when they finally offered those goods for sale, many colonists organized protests and began threatening them.

Those protests turned deadly on the twenty-second of February when Ebenezer Richardson shot eleven-year-old Christopher Seider. The boy's funeral became a great political event in which leaders of the Sons of Liberty attempted to rally the people of Boston to their cause. The coffin was inscribed with phrases in Latin: "The serpent is lurking in the grass" and "innocence itself is nowhere safe." As the increasingly bitter lieutenant governor wrote, "If it had been in their power to have brought him to life again, [they] would not have done it but would have chosen the grand funeral, which brought many thousands together, and the solemn procession from Liberty Tree."

During the days following the funeral, numerous fights broke out between soldiers and bands of Liberty Boys. As one British officer later stated, "The insolence as well as utter hatred of the inhabitants to the troops increased daily." On March 2 an employee of rope maker John Gray asked an off-duty soldier if he wanted work; when the soldier said he did, the workman replied, "Well then go and clean my shithouse!" That soldier came back later with about a dozen men and a great brawl ensued. The next day, a British sergeant disappeared and was believed to have been murdered. The soldiers spread word that many of the colonists "carried weapons concealed under their clothes" and would use them with little provocation. A handbill warned that soldiers would defend themselves when attacked, and the wife of a grenadier was heard to say that soon the soldiers "would wet their swords or bayonets in New England people's blood."

Rumors spread like wildfire across the city, among them the warning that the British

In August 1765, angry colonists gathered at the Liberty Tree, a large elm near Boston Common, to protest the Stamp Act by hanging an effigy of the royal stamp distributor.

intended to cut down the Liberty Tree. On the night of March 5, less than two weeks after Seider had been buried, an angry, boisterous mob roamed through the streets taunting soldiers and pelting them with snowballs. Some of them may have enjoyed at least one merry pint. Men broke into two meetinghouses and began ringing the alarm bells usually rung to alert the citizenry of a fire. This time it was a call to assemble. The city was alive with danger. At eight o'clock that evening two British soldiers were attacked and beaten. A small group of colonists descended on the 29th Regiment barracks but was repulsed without bloodshed. A larger crowd, as many as two hundred strong and armed with clubs, gathered in Dock Square. Slightly more than an hour later the Boston Massacre began with the exchange of a few nasty words.

As with so many historic confrontations, the Boston Massacre is remembered quite differently from both sides. Americans view it as a cold-blooded slaughter; the English consider it a terrible accident that escalated into a tragedy, an accident they had taken great steps to avoid.

What is agreed is that it began on King Street when a wig maker's apprentice named Edward Garrick publicly accused a British officer named John Goldfinch of failing to pay a bill. Captain Goldfinch did not respond, but a lone sentry guarding the customhouse named Hugh White spoke up and said, "He is a gentleman, and if he owes you anything he will pay it." Garrick replied that there were no gentlemen left in the regiment, causing White to leave his post to stand up for the honor of the troops. White struck Garrick with the butt of his musket, knocking him to the ground. A crowd quickly gathered, "mostly lads," the newspapers reported, and some of them started hurling pieces of ice at the guard. White retreated to the safety of the customhouse.

British captain Thomas Preston led twelve men and a noncommissioned officer to the customhouse "to protect both the sentry and the King's money." About a hundred colonists armed with clubs and other weapons had gathered in front of the customhouse, Preston later testified at trial, and were threatening "to execute their vengeance" on White. A townsman had told him that the mob intended to carry White off and murder him. Preston claimed he had been desperate to avoid conflict, testifying that "so far was I from intending the death of any person that I suffered the troops to go to the spot where the unhappy affair took place without any loading in their pieces; nor did I ever give orders for loading them."

According to eyewitness reports, Preston lined his men by twos in a column and, with empty muskets but fixed bayonets, moved smartly across King Street to rescue the beleaguered sentry. After White fell into the ranks, Preston attempted to march the men back to the barracks, but the mob that now numbered as many as three hundred blocked their way. The soldiers formed a rough skirmish line, standing in a semicircle about a body length apart. The crowd continued screaming threats and bombarding the troops with snowballs, pieces of coal, ice, oyster shells, rocks, and sticks.

But the patriots' account was very different. As the *Boston Gazette* reported a week later, "Capt. Preston with a party of men with charged bayonets, came from the main guard to the commissioner's house, the soldiers pushing their bayonets, crying, make way! They took place by the custom house and, continuing to push to drive the people off, pricked some in several places, on which they were clamorous and, it is said, threw snow balls."

As Preston claimed, "The mob still increased and were more outrageous, striking their clubs or bludgeons one against another and calling out, 'Come on you rascals, you bloody backs . . . fire if you dare, G-d damn you, fire and be damned, we know you dare not.' At this time I was between the soldiers and the mob, endeavoring all in my power to persuade them to retire peacefully, but to no purpose. They advanced to the points of the bayonets, struck some of them and even the muzzles of the pieces, and seemed to be endeavoring to close with the soldiers." One of the crowd asked Preston if he intended to order his men to fire. No, he replied, pointing out that he was at that moment standing in front of his men's muskets and "must fall a sacrifice if they fired."

What happened next changed the course of history, but we'll never know the exact chain of events. As the crowd pressed closer, according to the *Boston Gazette*, "the Captain commanded them to fire; and as more snow and ice balls were thrown he again said, 'Damn you, fire, be the consequences what it will.' One soldier then fired, and a townsman with a cudgel struck him over the hands with such force that he dropped his firelock; and, rushing forward aimed a blow at the captain's head. . . . However, the soldiers continued to fire successively till seven or eight or, as some say, eleven guns were discharged."

Captain Preston's version of events was different. "One of the soldiers having received a severe blow with a stick, stepped a little on one side and instantly fired, and on turning to and asking him why he fired without orders, I was struck with a club on my arm. . . . A general attack was made on the men by a great number of heavy clubs . . . by which all our lives were in imminent danger, some persons at the same time from behind calling out, 'Damn your bloods—why don't you fire?' Instantly three or four of the soldiers fired, one after another, and directly after three more in the same confusion and hurry. On my asking the soldiers why they fired without orders, they said they heard the word fire and supposed it came from me. This might be the case as many of the mob called out fire, fire."

According to several accounts, a forty-seven-year-old mulatto sailor named Crispus Attucks, who may have been an escaped slave who had found freedom working on the oceans, grabbed the musket held by a soldier and knocked the man to the ground. The soldier, Hugh Montgomery, scrambled to his feet and shouted, "Damn you, fire!" and triggered a blast into the crowd. Seconds later the other soldiers began firing. Other reports claim Montgomery was "jostled" and, in panic, fired his musket aimlessly but other troops, hearing that shot and thinking they heard a command to fire, began shooting.

What slim chance there might have been of preserving the peace between England and the colonies disappeared in those few seconds. Crispus Attucks was struck by two bullets in his chest and thus became the first casualty of battle in the Revolutionary War. By the time the shooting ended, three colonists were dead. Two others would die later that night, and another six men were injured. In addition to Attucks, among the dead were Samuel Gray, "killed on the spot, the ball entering his head and beating off a large portion of his skull," James Caldwell, shot in the back, and two other seventeen-year-olds.

The entire confrontation lasted no more than twenty minutes, but it resonated throughout the colonies and the British Empire. No one knows for certain which leaders of the Sons of Liberty were in that crowd that night. There has long been speculation that Samuel Adams and

Paul Revere were among them, but this was a mob beyond the powers of any leader to control.

Adams and Revere, and certainly Dr. Warren, were on the scene immediately, as was Lieutenant Governor Hutchinson, who ordered Preston and his men to return to their barracks. In an effort to prevent further violence, Hutchinson then went to the Old State House to meet with Boston Council leaders, assuring them that he would see justice done. Finally, stepping out onto a balcony overlooking the still-bloody streets, the lieutenant governor asked for calm, promising, "Let the law have its course. I will live and die by the law."

Within hours a warrant was issued for the arrest of Captain Preston. Two justices interrogated him for more than an hour about the shooting, then removed him to jail, probably as much for his own security as for punishment regarding the events.

Under most circumstances, the deaths of these five men barely would have been noted, but the patriot leaders understood that they could be used to further their political aims. A massive funeral was held for the five men; an estimated twelve thousand Bostonians turned out for the

On March 5, 1770, sailor and former slave Crispus Attucks became the first casualty of the Revolution when outnumbered and frightened redcoats began shooting into a crowd in what has become known as the Boston Massacre.

In 1768, the Sons of Liberty commissioned
silversmith Paul Revere to create this bowl to
honor the courage of the Massachusetts House
in standing up to demands from Parliament.

solemn procession. They were buried in a large vault in the same burying ground on Tremont
Street as Christopher Seider. Samuel Adams erected a marker with the words "as a memento
to posterity to that horrid massacre," thereby giving it the name that has lived in history.

According to Adams, in the days following the funeral John Hancock called on patriots
to tell the story of the massacre to their children until "tears of pity glisten in their eyes, and
boiling passion shakes their tender frame."

Many of the events leading to revolution were celebrated in art by Paul Revere, who was
among the leading engravers and silversmiths of the time. In 1767, for example, to honor the
ninety-two legislators who defied King George and Parliament by refusing to rescind a letter
sent to the other colonies protesting the Townshend Acts, he created the beautiful Sons of
Liberty or Rescinders' Bowl. Decorated with symbols of liberty, the classic silver bowl became
a symbol of freedom to the colonists. When General Gage marched his newly arrived troops
in a show of force in 1768, Revere's engraving depicting this occupying army, titled *The Insolent
Parade*, was widely distributed. And within three weeks of the Boston Massacre Paul Revere
also created and sold an engraving titled *The Bloody Massacre in King Street, March 5, 1770*, an
effective propaganda piece that contributed significantly to the rising fervor for independence.

The storied engraving, which relied heavily on a drawing done by the uncredited artist
Henry Pelham, bears little resemblance to the actual facts of the event. Rather than a chaotic
scene on a snowy winter's night, Revere portrayed an orderly, taut line of redcoats firing in
unison into an unarmed crowd on a bright blue-sky-lit afternoon, apparently responding
to orders from an officer standing behind them. The blood of the patriots spurts from their
bodies; the sign BUTCHER'S HALL is affixed to the building behind the troops and a puff of
gun smoke makes it appear as if a sniper is firing from that building. Below the engraving is
a poem apparently written by Revere, which includes the lines: "While faithless P—n and his
savage bands, / With murd'rous rancor stretch their bloody hands; / Like fierce barbarians
grinning o'er their prey, / approve the carnage and enjoy the day."

The journey to independence had begun.

Paul Revere's sensationalized engraving *The Bloody Massacre in King Street*, considered one of the most effective pieces of propaganda in American history, went on sale only three weeks after the event.

CHAPTER 2

John Adams

Ready for War

The morning after the Boston Massacre, the city was reeling. Shops were closed and church bells tolled. Captain Preston and his men had been detained and were being held and closely guarded. One of their victims, Patrick Carr, an Irish immigrant about thirty years of age, lay mortally wounded. Samuel Adams, Hancock, Revere, and other leaders of the Sons of Liberty were meeting to prepare their demand that all British troops be immediately removed. The representatives of the Crown also were meeting, discussing ways to stem the violence. Many customs commissioners were packing their belongings and preparing to flee, now fearful for their lives. Coroner Thomas Dawes was preparing the bodies of the dead men for their funeral and burial. And thirty-four-year-old lawyer John Adams was at work in his office when a prosperous merchant named James Forest knocked on his door. "With tears streaming in his eyes," as Adams wrote years later, the Loyalist Forest asked Adams to defend Captain Preston and his men against the murder charges.

Protests against the Stamp Act, like this Boston rally in 1765, ignited the bonfires of revolution.

Forest admitted that Adams was not his first choice; he had tried to retain other lawyers, but none of them would risk their standing in the city to take the case. It was an extraordinary request, but it was natural that Forest eventually would come to him. Adams's legal career had begun twelve years earlier. His first year of practice was a struggle. He made errors in preparing the documents for his only case, representing a farmer suing for damages to his crops caused by a neighbor's loose horse, and lost. His practice had grown slowly after this initial defeat, and he had received great recognition in the city only a year before when he successfully defended four sailors who had killed a British naval officer.

In the case of *Rex v. Corbet*, the British frigate *Rose* had stopped the American cargo vessel *Pitt Packet* returning from Spain with a hold full of salt. British navy lieutenant Henry Panton and several sailors boarded the brig and found four seamen hiding in the cargo space. As Adams told the story years later, Michael Corbet and the three other men, fearing they were being impressed into British service, had armed themselves with a fish gig, a musket, a hatchet, and a harpoon. Corbet swore he had drawn a line of salt and warned Panton that if he crossed that line, it would be an admission that he intended to impress the men and he would resist "and by the Eternal God in Heaven, you are a dead man." When Panton took a step forward, Corbet plunged his harpoon into the lieutenant's jugular vein.

But a different story was told during the trial. In that testimony, supposedly a marine had fired his pistol in the crowded brig and during the fight that ensued, Corbet had thrown his harpoon and killed Panton.

It was John Adams's first murder trial. Corbet's fate was not all that was at stake—the case put the laws governing the relationship between England and her colonies on trial. No one disputed that Corbet had killed Panton. But larger issues had to be adjudicated: By what legal right had Panton boarded the *Pitt Packet*? And was Corbet acting in self-defense, believing he was to be impressed?

While other patriots, like Adams's cousin Samuel, John Hancock, and Paul Revere, were ready to take the fight for their rights to the streets, Adams made the intellectual argument for each man's natural rights. He was said to value logic and reason far above strength and cunning, and he believed rights might be won more easily in the courtroom. His essays had made him well known to the citizenry of pre-Revolutionary Boston.

A large crowd had turned out for the trial. After three days of testimony and questioning, John Adams rose for the defense. The question that must be resolved, he argued, "is, whether impresses in any cases, are legal." If they were not, then the sailors had the right to resist and therefore must be acquitted. He had spent several weeks researching his case and had found a

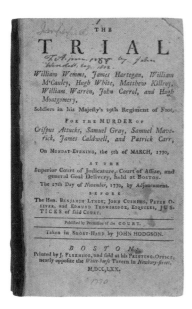

John Adams risked his reputation—and his life—to defend the British soldiers who had killed colonists at the Boston Massacre. The controversial trial resulted in the acquittal of the soldiers and proved that justice for all existed in the colonies.

statute specifically prohibiting British naval officers from impressing American seamen. But he had barely begun his argument when Lieutenant Governor and Chief Justice Hutchinson declared a recess. Adams was perplexed. When the trial resumed four hours later, Hutchinson announced a verdict of justifiable homicide and set the prisoners free.

No explanation was ever given for the abrupt decision, and Adams would wonder about it for the rest of his life. The most likely explanation is that rather than give Adams the opportunity to speak eloquently about the rights of man and further increase tensions between the Crown and the colonists, Hutchinson chose to end the trial quickly.

The verdict assured Adams's reputation as one of Boston's most respected lawyers and political leaders. So it was considered curious that he would now risk his reputation and perhaps even his own safety and that of his beloved wife, Abigail, and their young son John Quincy Adams, by agreeing to defend men who were seen as the cold-blooded killers of American patriots. And yet agree he did. His only stipulation was that his friend Josiah Quincy join him as cocounsel. Some historians believe the ambitious Adams took the case in exchange for an understanding that he would receive a seat in the Boston legislature when it became available. Indeed, three months after the trial, this is what happened. John Adams himself never directly explained why he had accepted this challenge. In his dotage he proudly described his defense of Preston and the other soldiers "one of the most gallant, generous, manly and disinterested actions of my whole life, and one of the best pieces of service I ever rendered my country." It might well have been a moral decision, based on his passion for equal justice for all under the law. His cousin, Samuel Adams, it was said, was not against his cousin defending the men—he expected him to give them a fine defense to show Boston's commitment to justice—after which all of the soldiers would be convicted.

But Samuel Adams was building a movement and undoubtedly saw the trial as an opportunity to gather greater support. Paul Revere's engraving of the massacre was widely circulated. When Patrick Carr died nine days later, his obituary, perhaps written by Samuel Adams, emphasized, "This is the fifth life that has been sacrificed by the rage of the soldiery, but it is feared it will not be the last" and was accompanied by a Paul Revere drawing of a coffin. A pamphlet titled "A Short Narrative of the Horrid Massacre in Boston," much of it written by Joseph Warren, was published several days after the event. Supposedly drawn from testimony given by ninety-six eyewitnesses, it described a cold-blooded, point-blank murder.

At the strong suggestion of General Thomas Gage, commander of British forces in North America, Hutchinson agreed to delay the trial for several months, giving Adams sufficient time to prepare his defense while allowing the colonists' white-hot anger to cool. Meanwhile, the British government took steps to calm the tension in the city. Within days, both of the regiments occupying the city were moved offshore to a fort on Castle Island in Boston Harbor—regiments that Parliament referred to sarcastically as the "Samuel Adams regiments." And less than two months later, in a decision that was as much economic as it was political, Parliament repealed the hated Townshend duties—with the exception of the tax on tea. It was estimated that the colonial boycott had cost British exporters as much as £700,000, while only £21,000 in duties had been collected, a staggering loss for those traders. Local merchants were pleased to resume selling imported British goods and even patriotic colonists were quite happy to buy them. Much of the unrest was slowly dissipating.

Five colonists died and six others were injured at the Boston Massacre, which became the rallying cry for colonists. This illustration, with the initials of the victims, accompanied reports of the funerals.

As he prepared for the trial, John Adams's defense was bolstered by the deathbed account of Patrick Carr, who lingered for several days before succumbing to his wounds. Carr told his doctor, Samuel Hemmingway, that the soldiers had shown great restraint and only after the mob began bombarding them with dangerous projectiles did they fire their muskets. He acknowledged that they acted in self-defense and told Dr. Hemmingway that he bore no malice to the man who had shot him. Adams knew this eyewitness testimony could possibly save his clients from the rope, but he also knew that the court might not admit the evidence. The prosecution would have no opportunity to cross-examine a dead man.

The trial of Captain Preston began on October 24 at Boston's new courthouse on Queen Street. Adams had successfully separated the officer's trial from that of his men. Josiah Quincy's Loyalist brother Samuel and patriot Robert Treat Paine prosecuted the case. Adams managed to seat a jury composed of men mostly from outside the city, and at least five of them were Tories, men who remained loyal to the Crown.

But it still would require all of Adams's legal skills to prove beyond a doubt that Captain Preston never ordered his men to fire their muskets. And doing so successfully would pit John Adams in direct opposition to his cousin and the patriotic movement. It is fair to assume that more than once Adams was asked to consider his loyalties, but it appears he remained steadfast in his commitment to justice above politics.

In his opening statement to the court, John Adams said, "I am for the prisoners at the bar, and shall apologize for it only in the words of the Marquis Beccaria: 'If I can but be the instrument of preserving one life, his blessing and tears of transport, shall be a sufficient consolation to me, for the contempt of all mankind. . . .' We are to look upon it as more beneficial, that many guilty persons should escape unpunished, than one innocent person should suffer. The reason is, because it's of more importance to community, that innocence should be protected, than it is, that guilt should be punished. . . . But when innocence itself, is brought to the bar and condemned, especially to die, the subject will exclaim, it is immaterial to me, whether I behave well or ill; for virtue itself, is no security. And if such a sentiment as this, should take place in the mind of the subject, there would be an end to all security what so ever."

Preston pleaded not guilty and Adams chose not to put him on the stand. The trial lasted six days, the first criminal trial in the colony's history to extend more than a single day. In a highly unusual step, the jury was sequestered for the duration of the trial. The prosecution presented fifteen witnesses, but several of them gave conflicting testimony. One, William Wyatt, for example, told the court, "I heard the officer say fire. The soldiers did not fire. His back was to me. I heard the same voice say fire. The soldiers did not fire. The officer then stamped and said Damn your bloods fire be the consequences what it will. Immediately the first gun was fired." But Theodore Bliss recalled, "I saw the people throw snow balls at the soldiers and saw a stick about 3 feet long strike a soldier upon the right. He sallied [moved forward] and then fired. . . . Then the other[s] fast after one another. . . . I know not whether he sallied on account of the stick or stepped back to make ready. I did not hear any order given by the captain to fire. I stood so near him I think I must have heard him if he had given an order to fire before the first firing."

Adams produced twenty-three witnesses to prove his contention that the soldiers had been provoked and Preston had not given an order to shoot. Newton Prince, a free black man who had responded to the ringing of the fire bells, swore, "The people whilst striking on the guns cried fire, damn you fire. I have heard no orders given to fire, only the people in general cried fire." A merchant, Richard Palmes, was close to Preston. "The gun which went off first had scorched the nap of my surtout [overcoat] at the elbow." Palmes testified that he said to Preston, "I hope you don't intend the soldiers shall fire on the inhabitants. He said by no means. The instant he spoke I saw something resembling snow or ice strike the grenadier on the captain's right hand. . . . He instantly stepped one foot back and fired the first gun. . . . After the gun went off I heard the word fire. . . . I don't know who gave the word fire."

After considerable deliberation, the jury found Captain Preston not guilty. He was released and awarded £200 in compensation. Then he sailed to England.

The trial of Preston's troops began on November 27. Apparently before it began, there was a heated debate between Adams and Josiah Quincy, who wanted to show that this terrible event was planned by patriots to drive British soldiers out of the city. Adams threatened to withdraw from the defense if Quincy insisted on employing that strategy. Rather than casting blame on the Sons of Liberty and perhaps antagonizing patriots on the jury, Adams suggested placing that blame on the distant and despised government in London, which had put these troops in an untenable position. Quincy finally agreed.

At trial they intended to show, in Adams's own words, that the soldiers had been attacked by "a motley rabble of saucy boys, negroes and mulattoes, Irish teagues [an epithet meaning a Roman Catholic] and outlandish jacktars [seamen] . . . throwing every species of rubbish they could pick up in the street" and therefore had the right to defend themselves. Admittedly they had fired their muskets, but only after being attacked and in fear for their safety.

Adams and Quincy kept residents of Boston off the jury. This trial lasted nine days. Samuel Adams was outraged that the court allowed jurors to hear the secondhand testimony of Patrick Carr, arguing that Carr's testimony was not to be trusted, as he was an Irish "papist" and a

Catholic, and this was his deathbed confession. Justice Peter Oliver told the jurors, "This Carr was not upon oath, it is true, but you will determine whether a man just stepping into eternity is not to be believed, especially in favor of a set of men by whom he lost his life." This notable exception to the inadmissibility of hearsay evidence has remained an important part of the American legal code.

Adams's brilliant summation lasted more than a day. He re-created the hectic scene of terrified soldiers under attack by a mob. How else could those soldiers respond, he wondered, "when the multitude was shouting and huzzaing, and threatening life, the bells all ringing, the mob whistle screaming and rending like an Indian yell, the people from all quarters throwing every species of rubbish they could pick up in the street, and some who were quite on the other side of the street throwing clubs at the whole party"?

Ironically, the person generally celebrated in American history as the first casualty of the Revolution, Crispus Attucks, is the person Adams blamed for inciting the soldiers to shoot. It was Attucks, Adams claimed, who "had hardiness enough to fall in upon them, and with one hand took hold of a bayonet, and with the other knocked the man down: this was the behavior of Attucks; to whose mad behavior, in all probability, the dreadful carnage of that night is chiefly to be ascribed."

And finally, Adams drew upon his own passion for the law, reminding jurors in a statement that has echoed throughout American courtrooms for longer than two centuries: "Facts are stubborn things; and whatever may be our wishes, our inclinations, or the dictates of our passions, they cannot alter the state of facts and evidence: nor is the law less stable than the fact; if an assault was made to endanger their lives, the law is clear, they had a right to kill in their own defense." It was not only the soldiers he was defending but the law itself, which had to remain free from shifting beliefs. Whatever politics or passions the jurors might hold, it is their sole job to uphold the law; as he told them, "The law, in all vicissitudes of government, fluctuations of the passions, or flights of enthusiasm, will preserve a steady undeviating course; it will not bend to the uncertain wishes, imaginations, and wanton tempers of men."

In instructing the jury, Judge Oliver addressed the complexities of the case when he told them, "If upon the whole ye are in any reasonable doubt of their guilt, ye must then . . . declare them innocent." It marked the first known time a judge had used the phrase "reasonable doubt" in an American courtroom.

The jury deliberated only two and a half hours before finding six of the soldiers not guilty. Only the two redcoats proved to have deliberately fired into the crowd were convicted of manslaughter. Adams pleaded for an ancient form of leniency by invoking an old tenet of

English law known as the "plea to clergy." Both men had an *M* for "murderer" branded on their thumbs, which meant they could never use that appeal again, then departed Boston with their entire regiment.

A satisfied Adams later wrote in his diary, "Judgment of death against those soldiers would have been as foul a stain upon this country as the execution of the Quakers or witches, anciently. As the evidence was, the verdict of the jury was exactly right."

When talk of a revolution against England began in earnest only a few years later, John Adams's defense of Preston and his troops served to give him credibility as the moral leader. Although the verdict was not received favorably by the patriots, he had emerged from the trial as a man of honor.

The king's government continued to make an effort to reduce the friction with the colonies, hoping to find a path to return to the respectful relationship, while contending with other challenges and opportunities across the ocean. Under the reign of George III, the debate over how far to extend the rights to free elections, freedom of the press, and free speech continued without resolution. In 1770, Captain James Cook sailed into Botany Bay and claimed Australia for Britain. In 1771 the "factory age" began when the first cotton mill was opened. A year later the abolitionist movement took hold, marking the first significant step toward outlawing slavery. New coal-powered inventions and canals were greatly improving transportation throughout the country.

A period of calm was interrupted in 1772 when the schooner HMS *Gaspee* ran aground in Rhode Island's Narragansett Bay. It had been chasing a small packet attempting to smuggle goods through customs. While the ship lay helpless in the shallows, members of the Providence Sons of Liberty boarded, wounded its captain, and burned the ship to the waterline. Lord Dartmouth ordered the royal governor of Rhode Island to identify and indict the men responsible. After an investigation, a commission of inquiry was set up to determine if there was enough evidence to arrest those men and send them to England to be tried for treason, an act that would deprive them of the right to trial by a jury of their peers.

In response to the *Gaspee* affair, as well as a rumor that the royal governor and superior court judges were to be paid directly by the royal treasury, making them less sensitive to local realities, Samuel Adams proposed the formation of a Committee of Correspondence in Boston with the stated purpose of determining other Massachusetts towns' sentiments toward the Crown. In fact, it was a desperately needed system to enable colonial leaders to communicate quickly and directly with each other. This first twenty-one-member committee was charged with determining "the rights of the colonists, and of this province in particular, as men, as

BURNING OF THE GASPEE SCHOONER.

In June 1772 the British customs ship *Gaspee* ran aground near Warwick, Rhode Island, while chasing smugglers. Patriots boarded the ship and looted and burned it.

Christians, and as subjects; to communicate and publish the same to the several towns in this province and to the world as the sense of this town." Six hundred copies of this document, titled *The Votes and Proceedings of the Freeholders and Other Inhabitants of the Town of Boston,* but more generally known as the "Boston Pamphlet," were printed and distributed to more than 250 towns. It enumerated twelve ways the British government was violating the colonists' rights, among them taxing and legislating without representation, the quartering of standing armies during peacetime, and enforcing trade policies that restricted economic growth. More than one hundred towns and villages formed their own committees and responded.

While the commission of inquiry eventually ruled that there was insufficient evidence to

In 1772, *The Votes and Proceedings of the Freeholders and Other Inhabitants of The Town of Boston, In Town Meeting assembled, According to Law* or as it became known, *The Boston Pamphlet,* described in detail how the rights of the colonists as English citizens were being violated.

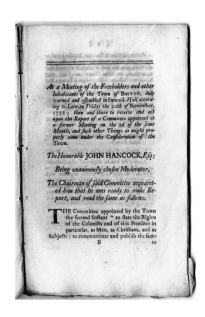

bring anyone to trial for the burning of the *Gaspee,* the Committee of Correspondence had become firmly entrenched. Eventually a single such committee representing the entire colony and chaired by Samuel Adams was formed. Other colonies followed that example and within two years a viable communications network was established. The patriot leaders had no great plan—there was not yet a strategy or even a stated goal—but the spirit of freedom had been born. In taverns and inns, in the safety of private homes, in churches, and in shops, newspapers, pamphlets, and broadsides were being distributed and debated, voices were being raised, sermons were being given, poems were read, and songs were sung. The idea that the colonies should be independent of England, an idea only a few years earlier too impossible to even imagine, had become real, and the fight was about to begin.

The job of transforming stirring words into actions began on the night of December 16, 1773. To save the financially troubled East India Company, Parliament had passed the Tea Act, which granted the failing company and its chosen distributors the exclusive rights to sell tea in America. The colonists, especially those merchants excluded from this monopoly, were furious—more by the haughty manner by which Parliament imposed its will than by the actual tax that, ironically, lowered the price of tea. But in paying that lesser price for tea, colonists would be accepting the right of Parliament to tax them.

Rather than facing the temptation of a favored beverage at a fine price, the colonies banded together to prevent the East India Company from landing its teas. In Boston, Philadelphia, and New York, tea-laden cargo ships were stopped from unloading. On December 16 an estimated seven thousand Bostonians gathered at the Old South Meeting House and resolved that the three vessels in the harbor, the *Dartmouth*, the *Eleanor*, and the *Beaver*—each carrying 114 chests of tea—be given safe passage to return to England with their cargoes intact. But when the king's customs collector refused to allow the ships to depart until the duty was paid, the colonists knew that it was time to show their grit.

That night, as thousands of people stood watching from the dock, approximately 116 men, most of them members of the Sons of Liberty, marched to Griffin's Wharf and boarded the ships. To protect their identities, they disguised themselves as Indians, wearing rudimentary war paint, cloths wrapped around their brows, and blankets around their shoulders, and they all carried hatchets and axes. The captains handed over the keys to their holds without fuss and the invaders smashed open every chest of tea and emptied the contents into the harbor waters. "The destruction of the tea," as it was called by the newspapers—it would not become celebrated as the Boston Tea Party for another fifty years—took about three hours. Contrary to the historical image of chaos, the raid was well organized and great care was taken to ensure that no one was hurt. There was no damage done to the ships, which actually were American-owned but carrying British cargo. The single lock broken by the patriots was replaced, and before departing the raiders took time to sweep the decks clean. Although there were several British warships in the harbor, no effort was made to stop the men. The financial loss was the equivalent of more than a million dollars.

The Sons of Liberty sent its best horseman, Paul Revere, to New York and Philadelphia to carry news of this rebellion. Eventually similar "tea parties," in which tea was dumped or burned, took place in New York, Annapolis, and Charlestown—and in March the Boston raid was repeated as sixty men tossed thirty chests into the water.

"This is the most magnificent movement of all," proclaimed John Adams. "This destruction of the tea is so bold, so daring, so firm, intrepid and inflexible, and it must have so important consequences, and so lasting, that I can't consider it but an epocha [momentous event] in history." And to demonstrate his support, Abigail Adams later reported, John Adams tossed all the tea in his cupboard into the fire.

This grave insult to the Crown demanded a response. "We are now to establish our authority," said Lord North, "or give it up entirely." The repercussions were harsh. Because Boston was acknowledged as the heart of colonial dissent, Parliament believed that by cracking down hard on that city, it would show the other colonies the potential consequences of their actions.

Americans throwing the Cargoes of the Tea Ships into the River, at Boston

The Destruction of the Tea at Boston Harbor depicts the 1773 Boston Tea Party, showing crowds on the docks cheering as the disguised patriots dump a British cargo into the bay.

The commander of the British army, General Thomas Gage, replaced Governor Hutchinson and immediately ordered his troops to occupy Boston. Parliament passed a series of new laws known collectively in England as the Coercive Acts, but became known in America as the Intolerable Acts. Under these new laws Boston Harbor was closed to all goods with the exception of food and firewood until the East India Tea Company was reimbursed. All town meetings and gatherings were prohibited, essentially eliminating self-government. Royal officials were granted increased authority, including the ability to force citizens to shelter soldiers in their homes. In defending these acts before the House of Commons, Lord North warned, "The Americans have tarred and feathered your subjects, plundered your merchants, burnt your ships, denied all obedience to your laws and authority. . . . Whatever may be the consequences, we must risk something; if we do not, all is over."

Virginia's Richard Henry Lee described the Intolerable Acts as nothing less than "a most wicked system for destroying the liberty of America." The meaning of these acts was clear to all the other colonies: the fate of any one colony foretells the future of all of them; they must stand together or fall separately. They immediately made preparations to send the necessary supplies—all of the vittles they would need to survive—to Massachusetts. And for the first time in a decade, representatives of twelve of the colonies agreed to meet in Philadelphia to debate a united resistance to continued British oppression. Only Georgia, which relied on its British soldiers for protection from hostile Cree Indians, did not send representatives.

At risk of being arrested for treason, Samuel and John Adams joined Thomas Cushing in representing Massachusetts at this First Continental Congress in Philadelphia. As the patriots passed through each town, the residents turned out to show support. Security along their route was provided by America's first intelligence network, Paul Revere's "Mechanics." Consisting of about thirty men drawn from the Sons of Liberty, the network had been created "for the purpose of watching British soldiers and gaining every intelligence on the movements of the Tories."

The Congress was called into session in Carpenter's Hall on September 5 and would meet through the end of October. This was the first time the colonies were attempting to form a united organization. But there was no common goal. There were as many representatives who wanted to negotiate a peaceful reconciliation with England, recommending the establishment of a continental parliament, as there were people who advocated a complete break from the Crown. What did become clear, though, was that should it become necessary, the other colonies would provide strong support for Massachusetts. In his diary of the First Continental Congress, John Adams wrote of being told that George Washington, a Virginia

Colonists believed the firm policies of British Prime Minister Lord North gave them no choice but to fight for their independence.

Clyde Osmar DeLands's romanticized 1911 oil painting shows delegates to the First Continental Congress outside Philadelphia's Carpenter's Hall in 1774.

earistocrat and planter who had gained renown for his courage during the French and Indian War, had vowed to the Virginia Convention that he "would raise 1,000 men, subsist them at my own expense, and march myself at their head for the relief of Boston." And on September 17, after the Congress had adopted a resolution basically renouncing allegiance to England so long as British troops remained in Boston, he added, "This day convinced me that America will support Massachusetts or perish with her."

The first links of unity were being forged. While this congress was unable to reach an acceptable compromise, on October 14 they did agree to send directly to the king, bypassing Parliament, a Declaration of Rights and Grievances. The inhabitants of the colonies "are entitled to life, liberty, and property," it read, "and they have never ceded to any sovereign power whatever, a right to dispose of either without their consent." After enumerating their rights, they threatened "to enter into a non-importation, non-consumption, and non-exportation agreement or association," a complete boycott of all British imports, if the Intolerable Acts were not repealed.

Following Boston's example, most of the cities and towns were by now being run by locally elected committees that made appointments, raised a militia, promoted trade, collected taxes, and administered the courts. There were some who were opposed to this development. Historically, political representatives had always come from the educated, wealthy class, and suddenly common folk were being appointed to important leadership positions. A wealthy South Carolina landowner complained bitterly about having to debate men who knew little more than "how to cobble a shoe" or "cut up a beast." The governor of Georgia was appalled by the fact that the great port city of Savannah was being run by a committee consisting of "a lowest parcel of people, chiefly carpenters, shoemakers, blacksmiths, etc., with a Jew at their head."

Change was inevitable and Parliament did not appear to know how to deal with it—other than by imposing its rule by force. The New England colonies began taking the next brave step toward independence: preparing for war. Massachusetts set out to train a twelve-thousand-man militia and requested the other colonies to provide an additional twenty thousand trained men. Under John Hancock's direction, Boston's Committee of Safety also formed an elite group known as the minutemen for their ability to respond to any provocation within minutes. Colonists hid muskets and balls in cellars and woodsheds and barns and carried out raids against British military stores; a hundred barrels of gunpowder and several cannons were captured at Portsmouth, New Hampshire, and forty-four pieces of artillery were taken at Newport, Rhode Island, and delivered to Providence.

As promised, throughout that winter the other colonies smuggled sufficient goods into Boston to avert starvation. When King George III was informed that the colonies had ignored his threats and were forming local governing assemblies, he ordered ports up and down the

American seaboard closed and forbade fishermen to cast their nets in the North Atlantic.

In March 1775, the Virginia Convention met in Richmond to consider raising its own militia. While many delegates to that convention urged patience, the matter was settled on March 23, when patriot Patrick Henry spoke eloquently about the many steps that had led them to this point, then concluded, "Is life so dear, or peace so sweet, as to be purchased at the price of chains and slavery? Forbid it, Almighty God! I know not what course others may take; but as for me, give me liberty, or give me death!" These precise words were not recorded, but those men inside St. John's Church who heard them said they could never forget them. They resulted in a resolution declaring the independence of the United Colonies from England. Henry himself was charged with building a militia.

The redcoats also began preparing for war. It is believed, though unproven, that early in 1775 Governor Gage issued warrants for the arrests of Samuel Adams and John Hancock, perhaps believing the rebellion could be stopped by containing its leadership. While that legal route proved tricky, another, more deadly solution was proposed: a plot to assassinate Adams, Hancock, and Dr. Warren. Although this story has never been completely proved, and the evidence remains sketchy, several hundred British soldiers reportedly volunteered to participate in the attempt. It was to be carried out on March 5 when thousands of Bostonians would be attending a rally at the Old South Meeting House to commemorate the fifth anniversary of the Boston Massacre.

As former governor Hutchinson wrote in his diary, he was told by Colonel James that about three hundred soldiers "were in the meeting to hear Dr. Warren's oration. If he had said anything against the King, etc., an officer was prepared, who stood near, with an egg to have thrown in his face, and that was to have been the signal to draw swords, and they would have massacred Hancock, Adams, and hundreds more; and he [Col. James] added he wished they had."

When the soldiers arrived at the meetinghouse, Adams asked the townsmen in the front rows to surrender their seats so as to reduce the tension, "inviting them into convenient seats," he wrote, "that they might have no pretense to behave ill." Warren concluded his remarks without incident, but when Adams rose to introduce the next speaker a soldier shouted, "Fire!" and the audience began fleeing the hall. People leaped from the windows and piled outside through the doors. The furious Adams and the soldier had to be held apart before order was restored. It was weeks later when the details of the plot were leaked. It failed, reported a newspaper, because "he who was deputed to throw the egg fell in going to the church, dislocated his knee, and broke the egg, by which means the scheme failed."

Boston was no longer a safe place for Samuel Adams and John Hancock. They secretly moved into the home of Reverend Jonas Clarke in the town of Lexington, twelve miles

This 1876 Currier & Ives lithograph captures the historic moment when Patrick Henry rose in the Continental Congress in *1775* and issued the call for freedom that has reverberated through the centuries: "Give me liberty, or give me death!"

outside Boston on the road to Concord. Meanwhile in London, Lord Dartmouth had decided to make a preemptive strike; he intended to end this rebellion before it could take root by seizing the rebels' arms, arresting their leaders, and reasserting royal authority. General Gage, told by Dartmouth to take whatever steps necessary to "re-establish government," ordered his troops to march to Concord to seize weapons and ammunition hidden there and "arrest and imprison the principle actors . . . in the Provincial Congress."

On the night of April 18, Joseph Warren learned from his spy network that as many as one thousand redcoats were preparing to march on Lexington and Concord. He knew that Samuel Adams and John Hancock were lodging in a tavern in Lexington and would be in grave danger. The source of the dashing Warren's intelligence may have been General Gage's winsome wife, Margaret Kemble Gage. Warren immediately summoned both Paul Revere and William Dawes, a tanner who was active in the militia, and sent them by different routes to give warning. Word of the redcoats' arrival spread rapidly throughout Boston, and numerous other riders were dispatched to alert the political leaders and the militias in the towns and villages surrounding the city. This British movement was not a surprise; in fact the militias had been preparing for a confrontation for months. They had been told exactly what to do, where to go, and whom to inform. In March, the Massachusetts Congress had declared that when Gage marched out of Boston with as many as five hundred armed troops, "it ought to be deemed a design to carry into execution by force the late acts of Parliament, the attempting of which . . . ought to be opposed." And, in response to warnings several days earlier, the cannons and powder had been moved out of the town. When the call to arms came, they were ready for it.

Few moments in American history are better known than "the midnight ride of Paul Revere." In preparation for this night, Revere had arranged a simple code for his men to use to relay information. When the troops began marching, they were to hang lanterns in the bell tower of the Old North Church, one lantern if the troops were proceeding by land from Boston Neck and two lanterns if they were rowing across the bay to march from Cambridge. After leaving

On April 18, 1775, Paul Revere was one of several patriots who risked their lives to warn that British troops were marching. This litho is as historically inaccurate as Longfellow's beloved poem about that night—it even appears that Revere is riding in sunny daylight.

The Midnight Ride of . . . Sybil Ludington?

While the concept of a lone man riding courageously through every Middlesex County village and farm warning colonists that the British are coming does make a wonderful story, the truth is that in addition to Revere, several other men and supposedly one legendary young woman rode through that April 18 night and several other nights to alert patriots that the British army was on the march. If Henry Wadsworth Longfellow had been slightly more accurate his classic poem, "The Midnight Ride of Paul Revere," actually would have read, "When the truth was known lamps were hung in the steeple, and the warning was spread by a large number of people." It was primarily due to Longfellow's poem that the patriot and master silversmith Revere emerged as the hero who aroused the countryside.

Best known among the other riders are William Dawes and Samuel Prescott. Like Revere, the tanner Dawes was sent by Dr. Joseph Warren to warn Hancock and John Adams to flee, and arrived in Lexington about a half hour behind the silversmith. Along the way Revere and Dawes met Prescott, who served as their guide, and after all three men were stopped by the British, Prescott became the only one of them to reach Concord.

Israel Bissell was a professional post rider, a postman, who may have made the longest journey, setting out along the Old Post Road on April 13 from Watertown, Massachusetts, and carrying a message from General Joseph Palmer 345 miles to Philadelphia in four days and six hours. Some historians believe he made it only to Hartford, where the news was passed to another post rider who continued the journey. But the oft-told story claims that along the way he warned militias and colonists that British troops had landed, announcing, "To arms, to arms, the war has begun." As General Palmer had published in a local newspaper to inform colonists that Bissell, who was mistakenly identified as Tryal Russell, was on a mission, "The Bearer, Tryal Russell, is charged to alarm the country quite to Connecticut and all persons are desired to furnish him with fresh horses as they may be needed."

But supposedly the most unusual person to make such a dangerous ride was sixteen-year-old Sybil Ludington. While this story has become firmly lodged in history, like many stories of the Revolution there is some doubt that it actually happened. According to legend, she made her forty-mile ride—twice the distance covered by Revere—from nine p.m. to dawn two years later, galloping through the rain on April 26, 1777, after her father, Colonel Henry Ludington, dispatched her to warn residents in Danbury, Connecticut, that the British were attacking. She carried a stick, which she used that night to prod her horse, beat upon closed doors, and defend herself when approached by a highwayman. The biography of her father, *Colonel Henry Ludington: A Memoir*, published in 1907, describes her ride: "Imagination only can picture what it was . . . on a dark night, with reckless bands of 'Cowboys' and 'Skinners' abroad in the land. But the child performed her task, clinging to a man's saddle, and guiding her steed with only a hempen halter, as she rode through the night, bearing the news of the sack of Danbury." According to the legend, while the four hundred men she roused arrived too late to save Danbury, which had been set on fire by men led by General William Tryon, at the Battle of Ridgefield they were able to drive the Loyalists back to Long Island Sound. In recognition of her effort, Alexander Hamilton wrote a letter of praise and General Washington visited the family mill to personally express his appreciation.

Several others risked their freedom to deliver warnings through those days of wartime. Nathaniel Baker, who was alerted by Revere and Dawes while visiting a lady friend, raced home spreading the alarm along his route. Samuel Prescott roused Sergeant Samuel Hartwell and requested he ride to inform Captain William Smith—instead his wife, Mary Hartwell, handed her five-month-old infant to a slave and took off down the road to tell the captain. Josiah Nelson was on alert, ready to spread the news throughout

Bedford when he heard men approaching. Assuming they were patriots, he shouted into the night asking if they had word that regulars were marching. Instead a British officer struck him in the head with a sword, opening a gash and making Nelson the first casualty of the war. After being bandaged by his wife, Nelson proceeded to Bedford to sound the alarm.

In reality there were dozens of brave men, and at least a few women, who rode to spread the word that "the British are coming!"

Two years after Revere's ride, sixteen-year-old Sybil Ludington rode twice the distance he covered to warn militiamen that the British were attacking Danbury, Connecticut. At left, William Dawes, who took a different route from Revere (bottom, right) that April night and avoided capture while raising the alarm.

Warren, Revere returned to his home to retrieve his boots and overcoat, then was rowed across the Charles River and waited for the signal. Two lanterns were hung in the tower and Revere took off on a borrowed horse to warn Adams and Hancock that the troops were coming by sea. It is said that as he passed each home on the road, he warned that the British were on the march.

As the British troops loaded into boats to be rowed to Cambridge, Revere rode the twelve miles to Lexington. As he neared Charlestown two redcoats on patrol tried to stop him, but he managed to escape at full gallop, and after chasing him three hundred yards, the redcoats returned to their post. He reached Clarke's home slightly before Dawes, and the sentry, Sergeant Monroe, cautioned him about making so much noise that he would wake everyone inside. Monroe later remembered that Revere responded, "Noise! You'll have noise enough before long! The regulars are coming out!"

While apparently John Hancock wanted to stay in Boston and join the fight, Samuel Adams convinced him that he would better serve the coming rebellion by going to Philadelphia, where the Second Continental Congress was scheduled to meet in just a few weeks.

Revere, joined by Dawes and Dr. Samuel Prescott, a doctor who had served as the liaison between Concord and the patriot leaders, set out to warn the militia in Concord. Riding into the dark night, they encountered a British scouting party. They split up, riding in different directions; Revere and Prescott were caught, and Dawes was said to have ridden into the yard of a home screaming that he was being pursued by two soldiers. Those redcoats, fearing an ambush, turned away. Prescott managed to escape his captors, disappearing into the forest, and continued on his mission until successfully reaching Lincoln and Concord.

Revere had previously carried many messages and had dealt with British patrols but, as he later recalled, he had never encountered such danger. "I saw four of them, who rode up to me with their pistols in their hands, said 'G-d d—n you, stop. If you go an inch further, you are a dead man.'" He was accused of being a spy and five different times the officers threatened to kill him; three times they promised to "blow your brains out." Revere identified himself and the officer in command recognized his name. Revere readily boasted that the warning had been spread and five hundred patriots were prepared to meet the British. The officer responded that fifteen hundred troops were marching. Four other men had been captured on the road, and they all rode as prisoners back toward Lexington. When they got close, they heard guns firing by the tavern. While the British assumed those shots meant the fight was beginning, later it was learned it was men emptying their muskets, as was tradition, before going into Buckman Tavern.

Revere and the others were released, although their horses were taken from them. After walking back to the house to retrieve papers left there by Hancock, Revere passed through fifty or sixty militia gathered on the green preparing to meet the British troops. As he did, he heard a commander telling his men, "Let the troops pass by, and don't molest them, without they begin first."

Paul Revere's night was done; the riders had raised the alert! Throughout Massachusetts, church bells rang, warning shots were fired, bonfires blazed, trumpets sounded, and drums were beaten. The minutemen were gathering in Lexington and Concord; the fight for freedom was about to begin.

No more than a hundred men awaited the British army on the common at Lexington.

Colonists fled from the green at Lexington when British troops fired "the shot heard round the world" on April 19, *1775* (above), but the patriots inflicted severe casualties on the confident British as they withdrew from Concord to Boston. (Following page) Seventy-three redcoats were killed, and 174 were wounded that day, causing British leader Lord Percy to proclaim, "Whoever looks upon them [the patriots] as an irregular mob will be much mistaken."

They were not blocking the road. Their commander, Captain John Parker, remained hopeful that the British would pass peacefully and, after discovering no cannons in Concord, would return to Boston. An advance guard of about 250 British regulars arrived in Lexington just before dawn. They made a rough attempt to surround the militia. While they maneuvered, Parker told his men, "Stand your ground; don't fire unless fired upon, but if they mean to have a war, let it begin here."

As Samuel Adams and John Hancock lay hidden in a nearby field, the redcoats and patriot militia confronted each other. A number of spectators stood to the side. An officer,

believed to be the commander of the British vanguard, Major John Pitcairn, rode forward waving his sword and ordering the patriots to disperse. Apparently Pitcairn also had ordered his troops not to fire. After a moment, Parker yelled to his men to go back to their homes. Some of the militia turned their backs and started moving away, but others didn't hear him.

Who fired the first shot, which has become known in history as "the shot heard round the world," has never been determined. Historians have identified several different men who might have fired that infamous first shot, but no one will ever know for certain that person's identity. Both sides believed the shots had come from the opposing force. A redcoat wrote

that there was no intention to attack the colonists, "but on our coming near them they fired on us two shots upon which our men without any orders, rushed upon them, fired and put them to flight." Yet in a deposition given, later signed by more than thirty men who had been there that morning, "whilst our backs were turned on the troops, we were fired on by them, and a number of our men were instantly killed and wounded, not a gun was fired by any person in our company on the regulars to our knowledge before they fired on us."

As Revere testified, "I saw, and heard, a gun fired, which appeared to be a pistol. Then I could distinguish two guns, and then a continued roar of musketry." Within seconds eight patriots suffered fatal wounds while another ten were wounded, while only one regular was slightly hurt. As these minutemen fled into the woods, the British continued their march toward Concord.

An estimated 250 men were waiting there for the British. When they finally arrived, the patriots' commander ordered his outnumbered men out of Concord, deciding to make the fight on his own terms. He would not give the British the static opponent they were trained

The Retreat

From Concord to Lexington of the Army of Wild Irish Asses Defeated by the Brave American Militia
M.r Deacon M.r Loeings M.r Mulikens M.r Bonds Houses and Barn all Plunder'd and Burnt on April 19.th
according to Act June 11 1775

This political cartoon, titled *From Concord to Lexington of the Army of Wild Irish Asses Defeated by the Brave American Militia,* was published by a newspaper in London two months after the battle at Lexington and Concord as a means of criticizing the conduct of Prime Minister North's government.

to fight. While the British searched houses for weapons, setting on fire several houses and whatever contraband they found, reinforcements from villages and towns arrived and swelled the militia. There is some evidence that the soldiers actually helped put out the fires they had set to prevent the homes of completely innocent people from being destroyed. By the time the British were ready to leave Concord, the patriots had taken positions behind barricades and in the woods. Led by Major John Buttrick, a small force attacked the redcoats guarding the North Bridge. After fire from the regulars killed two of his men, Buttrick ordered, "Fire, fellow soldiers, for God's sake, fire!" Two soldiers were killed, the first British casualties of the war.

The British withdrew without finding the cannons and powder they had come to destroy. During much of the sixteen-mile march back to Boston, the militia army fired continually at the retreating British army, picking them off relentlessly, one by one, as more and more militiamen joined the force. The colonists let loose their anger and resentment on the retreating redcoats. When the British reached Lexington, the militiamen waiting for them there had their revenge.

The British regulars did not know how to contend with this Indian-like strategy and, enraged, broke into houses along their route, setting many of them on fire and shooting anyone they suspected of being a sniper. The militia attacks ceased only when reinforcements from Boston reached the redcoats. On this first day of war, 73 regulars were killed and as many as 250 more were wounded, while 49 minutemen were killed. It was an extraordinary victory for the colonists. The lessons learned that day about how to fight a superior force would become the patriots' hallmark throughout the Revolutionary War.

The leaders of the rebellion successfully avoided capture and made their way to Philadelphia. When the Second Continental Congress convened there on May 10, 1775, thousands of patriots had encircled Boston. While the British army could be supplied by sea, this overwhelming American force prevented them from breaking out. Among the first tasks facing the congress was turning that disorganized militia into an army. It is believed that John Adams was the one to nominate as its commander the gentleman farmer from Virginia, George Washington.

Washington was well respected, although his military experience was limited to success in frontier fighting during the French and Indian War. But he accepted the limitations of his military knowledge and the enormity of the task facing him, telling his fellow delegate from Virginia, Patrick Henry, "Remember Mr. Henry, what I now tell you: from the day I enter upon the command of the American armies, I date my fall, and the ruin of my reputation." He then purchased several books about organizing and commanding large forces and set off to Boston to take command.

CHAPTER 3

❧

Benjamin
FRANKLIN

Inventing America

When sixty-nine-year-old Benjamin Franklin landed in Philadelphia on May 5, 1775, he seemed to be a man without a country. He had spent most of the last two decades living on Craven Street in London, working to find ways to keep the colonies and England bound together. His son William, the governor of New Jersey, was an outspoken Loyalist. And as Franklin himself had written several years earlier, "Being born and bred in one of the countries, and having lived long and made many agreeable connections of friendship in the other, I wish all prosperity to both sides; but I . . . do not find that I have gained any point in either country except that of rendering myself suspected for my impartiality; in England, of being too much an American, and in America of being too much an Englishman."

☞ The brutality of the hand-to-hand fighting during the Battle of Bunker Hill is depicted in Alonzo Chappel's 1859 oil painting.

Franklin stepped off a ship into the Revolution. The first shots had been fired while he was still at sea. He immediately accepted an appointment as one of Pennsylvania's five delegates to the Second Continental Congress, becoming the oldest and most famous representative. This must have made him quite happy: Benjamin Franklin was noted for his appreciation of Benjamin Franklin. And, indeed, few men accomplished more in their lifetime than Ben Franklin. Historian Walter Isaacson described him as "the most accomplished American of his age and the most influential in inventing the type of society America would become."

The founding fathers arrived at the conclusion that a free and independent United States was a just cause worth dying for by following very different paths. But Franklin was the one who traveled the greatest distance to finally arrive at that point.

There was little in Franklin's early childhood to suggest that he would become such a towering figure. He was born in what was then the Massachusetts Bay Colony in 1705, the fifteenth child of candle maker Josiah Franklin. Although he had a limited formal education, he learned by reading every book or pamphlet he found. His lifetime of inventing began when he was eleven, when he devised a pair of swim fins that fit his hands. Among his many later inventions were bifocals, the heat-efficient Franklin stove, a musical instrument called the glass armonica, and the lightning rod. As a twelve-year-old he was apprenticed to his brother's print shop, where he worked for five years. When his brother refused to publish his writing, Ben wrote witty letters that appeared under the pseudonym Mrs. Silence Dogood, who introduced herself as a woman with "a natural inclination to observe and reprove the faults of others, at which I have an excellent faculty. I speak this by way of warning to all such whose offences shall come under my cognizance, for I never intend to wrap my talent in a napkin."

After leaving his brother's employ he settled in Philadelphia, where he formed a partnership to open a printing shop. He was quite successful and in 1729 he was elected the official printer for Pennsylvania. That same year he purchased the *Pennsylvania Gazette*, which eventually became the most successful newspaper in the colonies; it was also the paper that printed America's first political cartoon—naturally drawn by Franklin. He had a reputation as a ladies' man, and an affair resulted in the birth of his illegitimate son, William Franklin. He published his first *Poor Richard's Almanack* in 1732. In addition to containing all of the information expected in almanacs—a calendar, weather predictions, poems, recipes, sayings, and wisdom—he included serial stories and characters, one of them being poor Richard, to entice readers to purchase the following year's edition. Many of the well-known sayings attributed to Franklin, among them "a penny saved is a penny earned" and "early to bed, early to rise, makes a man healthy, wealthy and wise," first appeared in those pages. *Poor Richard's*

By 1745, as this scene outside his bookstore and print shop is dated, Benjamin Franklin had become one of Philadelphia's best known and most successful residents. By then he had been publishing his wildly popular *Poor Richard's Almanack* for more than a decade.

was widely popular and was published annually for twenty-five years, selling as many as ten thousand copies each year.

A man of infinite interests, Franklin soon delved into civic affairs. He created America's first lending library, the Pennsylvania Hospital, an early insurance company, an academy that would become the University of Pennsylvania, and the first fire company in Philadelphia. (His reminder, "An ounce of prevention is worth a pound of cure," was intended to remind people to take care when using candles or the fireplace.)

His small printing shop had become a substantial enterprise, which included a publishing company, a newspaper, and partial control of the postal system. The books he published ranged from Bibles to the first novel published in America, a reprint of Samuel Richardson's British bestseller, *Pamela, or, Virtue Rewarded*, a racy tale of lust and morality. By forming partnerships to open print shops in several cities, from Newport to Charlestown, he became a wealthy man and was able to retire when he was forty-two years old to pursue his interests in science and politics. He spent a decade experimenting with electricity and created terms including "battery," "conductor," and "electrician." In 1753 he performed one of history's best-known experiments, flying a kite with a key attached to it in a thunderstorm; he put his hand near the key—and felt a spark of static electricity; he had demonstrated that lightning was also an electrical spark and could be attracted with a conductor. That discovery led to his invention of the lightning rod, which he described as "upright rods of iron, made sharp as a needle and gilt to prevent rusting, and from the foot of those rods a wire down the outside of the building into the ground; . . . Would not these pointed rods probably draw the electrical fire silently out of a cloud before it came nigh enough to strike."

In 1736, long before his legendary capture of lightning, Franklin began serving in Pennsylvania's colonial legislature. He led Pennsylvania's delegation to the Albany Conference in 1754, a meeting of several colonies called to find ways of bettering relations with Native Americans and forming a common defense against the French. At that session he presented his Albany Plan of Union, one of the first serious attempts to unite the colonies around their common interests; while the plan was approved by the conference, it was rejected by colonial legislatures, which were not ready to cede any power to a central government. Franklin did manage to convince the Pennsylvania Assembly to fund a militia, and he led an expedition into the Lehigh Valley to build forts to enable settlers to defend themselves against the French and Indians.

By then one of Pennsylvania's most respected citizens, Franklin was sent to England in 1757 by the assembly to represent the interests of the colony—primarily against its proprietors, the Penn family. William Penn had been given the land in 1681 in payment of a royal debt. He had governed the territory in accordance with his Quaker heritage, and it had become a place that welcomed people of all religions and beliefs. Upon his death, his sons, Thomas and Richard Penn, inherited all the land that had not been sold. They remained in London and contributed very little toward the welfare or progress of the people who lived on those lands. Part of Franklin's mission was to petition the king to impose taxes on the family, to raise money desperately needed to help pay for the defense of the colony during the French and Indian War.

Franklin settled happily in London with his son William; his wife feared sea travel and remained at home. He fit easily into British society; like him, the English valued education and culture, celebrated provocative ideas, respected and understood science, and found joy in the theater and the arts. He traveled to several countries, meeting the most respected men of the time, including economist Adam Smith and philosopher David Hume. He met Samuel Johnson at least once and spent time with political satirist William Hogarth; he visited Joseph Priestley's laboratory; the Royal Society of London honored him as the first non-British citizen to receive its highest award; and, after being given an honorary degree by the

This oil painting by an unknown American artists portrays Franklin in his early forties. "Most people dislike vanity in others," he once wrote, "whatever share they have of it themselves; but I give it fair quarter wherever I meet with it, being persuaded that it is often productive of good to the possessor."

University of St. Andrews, he enjoyed the prestige of becoming the esteemed "Dr. Franklin." He also managed to make important connections in the government and secured for his son the post of royal governor of New Jersey. As to his initial mission, he enjoyed only limited success; while the concept of taxing a proprietor was accepted, the tax generated only a very small amount of money.

He returned to Pennsylvania in 1762 but pined for London. He wrote to Polly Stevenson, the daughter of his landlady on Craven Street, "I envy most its people. Why should that petty island, which compared to America is but like a stepping-stone in a brook, scarce enough of it above water to keep one's shoes dry; why, I say, should that little island enjoy in almost every neighborhood more sensible, virtuous and elegant minds than we can collect in ranging 100 leagues of our vast forests?"

Certainly to his delight, the assembly sent him back to London in 1764 to petition the king to allow Pennsylvania to be free of rule by the Penn family and become a royal colony. This was entirely in keeping with Franklin's own beliefs. "King George's virtue," he had written a year earlier when advocating this change in government, "and the consciousness of his sincere intentions to make his people happy, will give him firmness and steadiness in his measures . . . after a few of the first years, will be the future course of His Majesty's reign, which I predict will be happy and truly glorious." He believed that the British people had mostly goodwill toward the colonies. "The popular inclination here is to wish us well, and that we may preserve our liberties." He was certain that eventually Parliament would bow to the wishes of the people where the colonies were concerned.

It was a year later, when Parliament passed the Stamp Act, that Franklin was faced with having to choose between the England he had come to love and his American homeland. Although initially he argued forcefully against the Stamp Act, once it was clear that the king intended to impose it, he urged the colonists to be realistic, telling them, "A firm loyalty to the Crown . . . is the wisest choice."

Perhaps because it had been so long since he had truly lived in Philadelphia, Franklin wasn't aware of the hardening attitude toward the Crown. From his viewpoint in England, the alternatives to the tax were far more dangerous than the tax itself. At that time Franklin believed that the safest and wisest choice for America was to remain in the strong, sheltering arms of the greatest military power on earth. The British viewed the colonies as a single entity, but Franklin knew from his experience working on his Albany Plan how zealously each colony protected its independence. Getting them to agree on even the smallest point took great effort; trying to convince them to fight together for a seemingly impossible goal seemed, well, impossible. The colonists reacted to Franklin's words as might be expected, accusing him of betraying them to gain favor with the king, pointing out among other rewards he'd received his son's royal appointment. The seeds for John Adams's questions about where his loyalties lay had taken root. As the homes of customs collectors were being sacked in Boston and other cities, some talked of destroying Franklin's Philadelphia home.

When Franklin realized the depth of this anger, he quickly changed course and began fighting the Stamp Act, using all of the diplomatic tools he had mastered. He wrote against the act in British newspapers and argued against it at social occasions, warning British merchants that the effects of the threatened colonial boycott could be devastating. Appearing before the House of Commons, he answered more than 170 questions, arguing repeatedly that Parliament did not have the power to tax or legislate the colonies. A month after his appearance, the Stamp Act was repealed. Whether or not he actually influenced that decision, he received credit for it.

While officially the colonies had no ambassador to England, he emerged as their spokes-

A French admirer commissioned Joseph Siffred Duplessis to paint the seventy-year-old Franklin upon his arrival in Paris in 1776. Franklin was never constrained by age, pointing out, "We do not stop playing because we grow old, we grow old because we stop playing!"

person in Europe. Georgia, New Jersey, and, most important, Massachusetts appointed him to represent their interests in court. The Stamp Act had forced him to finally declare his allegiance; after British troops had taken control of Boston in 1768 and the Boston Massacre occurred two years later, he set out to erase any doubt, believing, as he later wrote, "Even peace may be purchased at too high a price." He fought valiantly against the Townshend Acts, warning Parliament that these "acts of oppression" would "sour the American tempers and perhaps hasten their final revolt." When the 1773 Tea Act was passed, he published several provocative essays, among them, "Rules by Which a Great Empire May Be Reduced to a Small One." His purpose, he wrote to one of his sisters, was to hold up "a looking-glass in which some ministers may see their ugly faces, and the nation its injustice."

At the same time he tried to convince the colonists to have patience. New leaders, "Friends of liberty" as he described them, were soon to be in power. "The ministry are not all of a mind," he wrote, "nor determined what are the next steps proper to be taken with us."

Among his final attempts to preserve the uneasy alliance was his decision to secretly forward inflammatory letters written by Royal Governor Thomas Hutchinson.

Just before the American-born Hutchinson had assumed his position in Massachusetts in 1769, he and his brother-in-law and aide, Andrew Oliver, had written to Prime Minister George Grenville's private secretary, urging Grenville to take drastic action to crush the rising spirit of rebellion in the colonies. "There must be an abridgment of what are called English liberties," he wrote in one of the letters, suggesting that if necessary, force should be used against the colonists. In another he stated, "I have been begging for measures to maintain the supremacy of Parliament."

Hutchinson and Franklin had worked together creating the Albany Plan. But that was long ago. These were incredibly damning letters. It has never been discovered how Franklin got hold of them. He sent six of them to Thomas Cushing, the leader of the Boston Assembly, in an attempt to prove to Massachusetts leaders that Parliament's harsh attitude hadn't been initiated in London but rather by an American living in Boston, who had been feeding bad advice to leading British politicians. These letters, Franklin wrote, "laid the foundation of most if not all our grievances."

Franklin asked Cushing not to make these letters public, but after Samuel and John Adams got hold of them they were published in the *Boston Gazette*. Bostonians were outraged. Hutchinson fled to England as quickly as possible. The assembly immediately petitioned the king to remove Hutchinson and Oliver from their positions. The king turned to his advisers, the Privy Council, for a decision.

In England, the publication of the letters was the great scandal of the day. The London newspapers gleefully reported every rumor speculating on the identity of the person who leaked them. Two ranking government officials each claimed the other was the source, and the argument became so bitter that they fought a duel. One of them was injured slightly and they agreed to fight again when the wounded man was sufficiently healed. Franklin decided he could not allow innocent men to risk death and wrote an editorial for the *London Chronicle* confessing his role. "I think it is incumbent on me to declare for the prevention of further mischief that I alone am the person who obtained and transmitted to Boston the letters in question." These letters had been written "by public officers to persons in public stations, on public affairs," he wrote in his own defense, and the policy they suggested would "incense the Mother Country against her colonies, and, by the steps recommended, to widen the breach." By forwarding those letters that revealed the source of animosity to responsible people in Boston, he had hoped to reduce the existing tension between England and the colonies.

In 1774, Franklin was ordered to appear before the highest ranking members of the British government, where he admitted to leaking secret incendiary letters to the Boston Assembly, destroying his well-earned reputation in England.

Franklin was summoned to appear before the Privy Council, where he was accused of illegally disclosing private correspondence. While these hearings were taking place, news of the Boston Tea Party reached England and Franklin bore the brunt of growing British anger toward the colonies. On January 29, 1774, he stood before thirty-four of the highest-ranking British government officials, including Lord North, in an area of Whitehall known as "the Cockpit" because years earlier cockfights had taken place there. In a dramatic conclusion, he was vilified by the council, while the king's solicitor general, Alexander Wedderburn, defended Hutchinson, claiming that Franklin was using an honest man's words to incite rebellion. According to Wedderburn, Franklin was the "actor and secret spring by which all the Assembly's motives were directed," and his actions had caused a "whole province set in flame." By the time the hearing was done, Franklin's reputation in England had been shattered. To Franklin, who cared so deeply for England and reveled in the respect he had earned there, this attack on his character was a huge personal insult. The one man who might have been able to find some common ground between England and her American colonies had been completely alienated. Within days he was fired as postmaster general of the colonies. A harshly worded letter sent from the king's ministers to American postal authorities warned ominously, "Fleets and troops are talked of, to be sent to America."

Dismissed by England, distrusted by Americans, Franklin sailed home. And while he was at sea the first shots were fired at Lexington and Concord.

Upon landing in Philadelphia Franklin soon began taking steps to demonstrate his commitment to the colonies in the coming war. But that necessitated terminating one of the most important relationships in his life. His beloved son William had stood proudly by his father's side throughout much of his career, through all his European travels, his scientific experiments, and his political work. In return Benjamin Franklin had supported his son, financially, emotionally, and politically. They grew to become not just father and son but good friends and confidants. When William Franklin produced his own illegitimate son, his father helped raise that child. And when Ben Franklin departed for England in 1764, he gave responsibility for the welfare of his family and his estate to his son. At every opportunity Benjamin Franklin had used his power to secure his son's future and had been rewarded when William was appointed royal governor of New Jersey. He assumed that his son would resign his own position in support of his father after his harsh treatment. And he was dismayed when William refused to do so.

In fact, William seemed to dismiss the damage that had been done to his father's reputation, describing the public humiliation at the Cockpit as a minor incident. He apparently believed it was a good time for his father to retire and spend the remaining years of his life at home with his family.

Rather than simply responding to his father's wishes, William Franklin reached his own conclusion: whatever the consequences, he would remain steadfast in his loyalty, a loyalty he had been taught by his father. At some point every colonist had to decide if they were to remain loyal to the Crown or support the independence movement. For many that was a difficult decision. The answer was not so clear then as it has become in history. Many of those, like William Franklin, stayed loyal to the Crown, not necessarily because they supported the clearly abusive actions but rather because they sincerely believed that it was the best course for the colonies. As William said, "You can never place yourself in a happier situation than in your ancient constitutional dependency on Great Britain. No independent state ever was or ever can be as happy as we have been, and might still be, under that government."

Before Franklin could prove his patriotism in the colonies, a small force commanded by General Benedict Arnold and militia leader Ethan Allen took Fort Ticonderoga in upstate New York on May 10, 1775, without a single shot being fired.

Father and son remained on amicable terms until the war broke out. After that there was no healing the rift between them. As Benjamin Franklin admitted, "Nothing has ever hurt me so much and affected me with such keen sensations, as to find myself deserted in my old age by my only son; and not only deserted, but to find him taking up arms against me, in a cause wherein my good fame, fortune and life were all at stake."

When William was imprisoned for two years in Connecticut during the war, his father did nothing at all to help him. William did not say a single cross word about him, but Benjamin Franklin never forgave his son. After the war they saw each other only once, to clear up some financial matters. William refused to renounce his wartime stance, claiming he was

Patriot leader Dr. Joseph Warren died providing covering fire for retreating soldiers on Breed's Hill. He was among the most respected men in the colonies, and had he lived would have become an honored founding father.

doing his duty as he saw it. In the year before his death Benjamin Franklin disinherited him, explaining, "The part he acted against me in the late war, which is of public notoriety, will account for my leaving him no more of an estate he endeavored to deprive me of."

Ben Franklin actually had little opportunity to prove his loyalty to the colonists after arriving in Philadelphia. There had been only sporadic fighting after Lexington and Concord.

In early May, the leader of the Committee of Safety, the patriots' quasi government, Joseph Warren, had ordered Colonel Benedict Arnold to seize British arms and stores at Fort Ticonderoga. To accomplish this mission, Arnold joined Ethan Allen and his Green Mountain Boys, a Vermont militia, to attack the British garrison at Fort Ticonderoga. In fact, Ticonderoga was lightly defended and in great disrepair, but inside its crumbling walls the British stored valuable cannons, mortars, howitzers, and ammunition. A surprise attack was launched at dawn on May 10. The only sentry on duty raised his musket, but when it misfired, he turned around and started running. The Green Mountain Boys poured into the fort, waking up its defenders by sticking guns in their faces. The commander surrendered his sword and no one was injured. This was the first colonial victory of the war, and the captured artillery would later prove vital.

Even after that there remained a slim hope that a war could be avoided, but that was extinguished on a small hill overlooking Boston on the night of June 16, 1775. The geography of Boston was different at that time from what it is today. It was a peninsula, connected to land by the narrow Roxbury Neck. While the city remained firmly in British control, Roxbury Neck, the only overland path out of the city, remained under the firm control of colonial general Artemas Ward. For more than a month militiamen had been arriving on horseback, by wagon, and on foot, ready to make a fight for the city. By mid-June Boston was surrounded by more than fifteen thousand men, while Royal Navy warships maintained control of the harbor and the sea. It was a classic stalemate.

Even after the colonial success at Lexington and Concord, the British generals too easily dismissed the colonists' military capability. They simply could not believe that this untrained, under-equipped, undisciplined army was a match for the well-supplied, superbly trained, and highly disciplined British regulars.

In early June, after reinforcements landed by the navy had brought his army to six thousand men, General Thomas Gage, the commander of all British forces in North America, and

This oil of the Honorable General Thomas Gage, Commander of the British Forces in North America, was painted at about the same time the war began in 1775. It was his decision to seize patriot munitions in April 1775 that led to the fighting at Lexington and Concord. He was replaced after the disastrous "victory" at Bunker Hill.

his staff began planning to break out of the city in order to open a vital overland supply line. They intended to smash the upstart army and put a quick end to this rebellion. But a colonial spy in the city reportedly overheard British commanders discussing the plan and alerted the Massachusetts Committee of Safety. General Ward ordered General Israel Putnam to organize a defense against the British, specifically telling him to fortify the tallest ground in the area, 110-foot-tall Bunker Hill. Putnam marched about twelve hundred men from Cambridge, but instead of making a stand as ordered on Bunker Hill, his men began setting up a defense on the smaller Breed's Hill. No one truly knows why this happened; it might well have been a simple mistake made in the dark of night. An eyewitness narrative prepared two weeks after the battle explained, "About 9 o'clock in the evening the detachment marched upon the design to Breed's Hill situated on the further part of the peninsula next to Boston, for by a mistake of orders this hill was marked out for the entrenchment instead of the other." However, some historians believe this was the intent, as Breed's Hill was thought to be more easily defensible and brought the city within range of the few cannons they had.

Under the command of Colonel William Prescott, the troops built a square redoubt, with six-foot-high dirt walls topped with fence rails, wheat, and stones with a raised platform inside enabling the soldiers to shoot over it. It was supported by a well-defended rail fence extending from one side down to the shore. Their presence was quickly detected and long before dawn the 128 guns aboard the three warships anchored in the harbor as well as additional cannons on land began bombarding the position. The barrage decapitated one man, causing several others to desert, but otherwise did little damage.

At first light in the morning, General Gage decided to launch an attack before the colonists could complete their preparations. While some of his officers suggested flanking the position, thus cutting the troops off from supplies and eventually starving them into surrender, General William Howe, who would lead the attack, argued for a frontal assault, explaining that the hill was "open and easy of ascent and in short . . . would be easily carried." Howe launched the attack on the flank, which was stopped on the beach, then launched his frontal assault on the rail fence.

Among the reinforcements who rushed to Breed's Hill that morning was Dr. Joseph Warren. Although he had been commissioned a major general by Washington two days earlier, he insisted on joining the infantry in the front lines. "Don't think I came to seek a place of safety," he supposedly told General Putnam, "but tell me where the onset will be the most furious." Warren, who had dispatched Paul Revere on his midnight ride, was a greatly admired local figure and was known for having told his mother after being grazed by a musket ball in the midst of the fighting at Concord, "Where danger is, dear mother, there must your

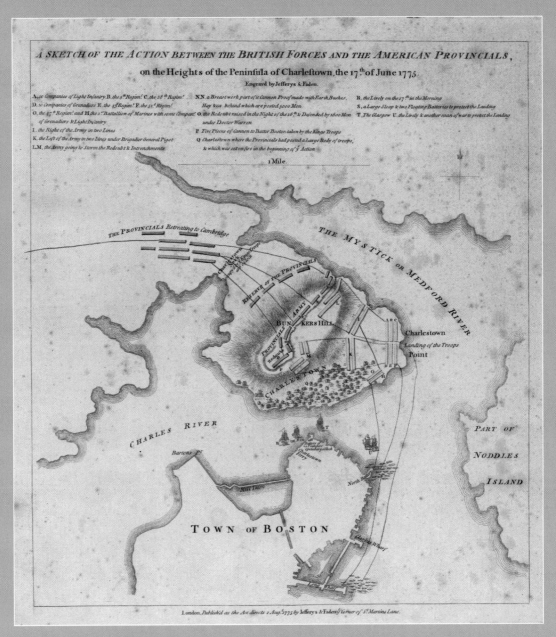

When war began, Charlestown was a peninsula with only a narrow bridge to land. This sketch, published in London, illustrates the course of the Battle of Bunker Hill.

son be. Now is no time for any of America's children to shrink from any hazard. I will set her free or die."

It was afternoon before the attack could be mounted. The British rowed to Moreton's Point, where they came under relentless sniper fire from Charlestown. In response, the big guns from the warships in the harbor began bombarding the city, setting it on fire. Soon afterward, according to the narrative, "flames and smoke were seen to arise in large clouds from the town of Charlestown which had been set on fire by a carcase fired from one some of the enemy's batteries with a design to favor their attack upon our lines by the smoke which as they imagined would have been blown directly [upon them] their way and covered them in their attack but the wind changing at this instant it was carried [beyond them] another way."

As townspeople in Boston watched from high points, church steeples, and rooftops, among them Abigail Adams and her son, John Quincy, and British general "Gentleman Johnny" Burgoyne, the battle began. Snipers fired down on the redcoats as they gathered in Charlestown. Then the British began the assault, marching across an open field in two long lines, each two men deep, with a separation between them, then up the hill in a ragged formation. Their march was slowed as they had to maneuver around fences, brick kilns, and other obstructions. It is said that one officer, so confident of victory, marched with a servant at his side, carrying a celebratory bottle of wine.

The colonists waited patiently, having been ordered to conserve ammunition and fire low. In legend, General Putnam gave the command, "Men, you are all marksmen; don't one of you fire until you see the white of their eyes," although in actuality there is no evidence he—or anyone else—said that. But it was hardly an original thought, as variations of that order had been reported through much of military history.

The colonials waited, they waited, they waited—and then the slaughter began. As the contemporary narrative reported, "The provincials in the redoubt and the lines reserved their fire till the enemy had come within about 10 or 12 yards and then discharged at once upon them. The fire threw their body into very great confusion, and all of them after having kept a fire for some time retreated in very great disorder." The colonists, many of them expert shots, aimed first at the officers, who were easily identified by their uniforms. After the officers fell, their dazed troops attacked without direction, sometimes bunching up to make even easier targets. At the conclusion of that initial attack, a colonial officer wrote, "The dead lay as thick as sheep in a fold."

At the bottom of the hill the British re-formed their lines, although some officers were seen "to push forward the men with their swords." This second attack had the same result;

Breed's Hill was littered with the bodies of the dead and wounded. The British retreated again.

By this time, though, the militia had expended much of its ammunition. There was little chance they could repulse a third attack, but rather than retreating, many of the men stayed in the redoubt to give others cover. Among them was Warren. Then the British began mounting an all-out attack. They were reinforced by troops who were rushed into the battle from Boston, and as many as two hundred wounded men rejoined the fight. The warships opened up on the hill with all their cannons. General Howe changed tactics, forming his men into carefully spaced columns rather than a single long line and attacked the redoubt opposite the rail fence.

The colonists fired the last of their ammunition. As Colonel Prescott recalled, their firing became sporadic, then "went out like a candle." When their guns were empty, they began throwing rocks, then fought hand to hand with the butts of their muskets as British troops came over the wall in waves and began bayoneting the defenders. The battle had become a deadly melee; British troops who had broken the line took their revenge. As British marine lieutenant John Waller described the scene, "I was with those two companies, who drove their bayonets into all that opposed them. Nothing could be more shocking than the carnage that followed the storming [of] this work. We tumbled over the dead to get at the living, who were crowding out of the gorge of the redoubt . . . the soldiers stabbing some and dashing out the brains of others." In fact, the greatest number of patriot casualties were suffered during this retreat, and it could have been much worse if brave men had not set up a line behind a fence and provided as much cover as possible to hold back British pursuit.

Among those who died in those last moments was Joseph Warren; he was swinging his musket like a club as he tried to fight his way out of the redoubt. He had successfully gotten out and was about sixty yards away when he was recognized by a British officer, who shot and killed him.

The battle lasted less than two hours. A total of 260 British soldiers were killed and another 828 wounded, a disproportionate number of them officers; the colonists lost about 140 men with an estimated 300 more wounded. But most devastating was the loss of Warren. As Abigail Adams said, "Not all the havoc and devastation they have made has wounded me like the death of Warren. We want him in the Senate; we want him in his profession; we want him in the field. We mourn for the citizen, the senator, the physician, and the warrior." His death was a terrible blow to the colonial army; British general Howe declared that Warren's life was worth the lives of five hundred other men.

Several historians claim that Warren's body was mutilated by the enraged British until it was no longer recognizable, and a day later his corpse was dug up and beheaded. What

The death of thirty-four-year-old Joseph Warren in battle was a terrible blow to the colonists. But they remembered his words, "Our streets are filled with armed men; our harbor is crowded with ships of war; but these cannot intimidate us; our liberty must be preserved, it is far dearer than life."

THE DEATH OF WARREN

is known for certain is that about ten months after the battle, his body was unearthed and positively identified by Paul Revere, who found a false tooth he had fashioned and implanted. While we can only speculate what great deeds Warren might have accomplished had he lived, it is clear he would have been among the leaders of the new country, a signer of the Declaration of Independence, and a man whose name would be celebrated by all Americans.

The Battle of Bunker Hill proved to be the bloodiest battle of the entire war. About half of the British soldiers who marched so proudly into battle became casualties. While General Burgoyne wrote, "The day ended with glory," the night in Boston was grim, as the dead and wounded were taken off the boats that ferried them back to the city. As a local man named Peter Oliver described the scene, "It was truly a shocking sight and sound, to see the carts loaded with those unfortunate men and to hear the piercing groans of the dying and those whose painful wounds extorted the sigh from the firmest mind." Among the British officers killed was John Pitcairn, the highly respected major whose loss greatly damaged British morale.

While Bunker Hill was considered a British victory, in reality the conduct and skill of the patriots shook British resolve. The path to victory had not been nearly as easy as they had anticipated. While publicly General Gage reported, "This action shows the superiority of the King's troops," in a private correspondence he admitted, "The trials we have had, show that the rebels are not the despicable rabble too many have supposed them to be. . . . In all their wars against the French, they never showed so much conduct, attention and perseverance as they do now." And in another letter pleading for more soldiers he confessed, "The loss we have sustained is greater than we can bear."

Other British officers remarked about the "ungentlemanly" tactics employed by the patriots. Just as they had at Concord, the colonists fought from behind barriers; they fired their weapons and were gone before feeling a response. These new Indian-like tactics concerned British commanders. As a result of this battle, General Gage was relieved of his command and ordered to return to England, and General Howe was given command.

News of the bloody battle shook the representatives' meeting in Philadelphia. They were especially infuriated by the burning of Charlestown, an unnecessarily brutal act. Ben Franklin, who sensed that he still had not gained the trust of John Adams or other leaders, saw his chance to prove his loyalty to the patriot cause. He wrote a letter to a friend in London, William Strahan, that apparently was left for Adams to find and read. "Mr. Strahan," it began, "You are a Member of Parliament, and one of that majority that has doomed my country to destruction. You have begun to burn our towns and murder our people. Look upon your hands, they are stained with the blood of your relations! You and I were long friends; you are now my enemy, and I am yours. B. Franklin."

That letter may simply have been a clever ploy; it was never mailed and Strahan never saw it. In fact, while Franklin and Strahan found themselves on opposite sides they somehow managed to maintain a friendship. A decade after the war ended and after America had won its independence, Franklin still signed his letters to Strahan, "I am ever, my dear friend, yours most affectionately."

However, the letter accurately stated Franklin's sentiment and convinced Adams and others that Franklin was an ally. In another letter, one that was mailed to the scientist Joseph Priestley, Franklin wrote, "America is determined and unanimous. . . . Britain, at the expense of three millions, has killed one hundred and fifty Yankees this campaign, which is about twenty thousand pounds a head; and at Bunker's Hill she gained a mile of ground. . . . During the same time sixty thousand children have been born in America. From these data his mathematical head [respected theologian and economist Dr. Richard Price] will easily calculate the time and expense necessary to kill us all, and conquer our whole territory."

As the Second Continental Congress set to work, Franklin was appointed to several committees. But his first official appointment for this new government was the first postmaster general of the United Colonies. Perhaps it was another jab at the British, who had fired him from that post, but he also was by far the best qualified.

History proves that the congress did do a fine job appointing the right people to vitally important posts, but none was more important than giving control of the army to George Washington. About two weeks after Bunker Hill, General Washington arrived in Cambridge to take command of this makeshift army. News of the fight had reached him along the way, and he was reportedly cheered by the bravery displayed by the patriots.

Washington's own bravery had been proved in 1755 during the Battle of Monongahela in the French and Indian War, when General Edward Braddock took twenty-six hundred troops to try to capture Fort Duquesne from the French. About ten miles from the fort, a smaller number of French and Indians ambushed a segment of Braddock's force. As the battle raged, most of the officers were killed—including General Braddock. The leaderless British troops were being decimated when George Washington, who had been serving as an aide-de-camp to Braddock, rode into the battle and took command. His display of courage caused the army to rally around him. During the bitter fighting two horses were shot from under him and four musket balls ripped through his coat. But he never wavered. His cool, efficient leadership enabled many soldiers to escape with their lives. While the British were defeated in that battle, Washington received a promotion to colonel, and several years later Washington successfully captured that fort.

Washington served under several British generals during the French and Indian War and learned lessons in military leadership from all of them. By the end of the war he had gained experience in commanding troops, delegating authority to subordinates, organizing equipment and supply lines, maintaining discipline and order in the ranks, and constructing forts and defensive positions—and obviously each of these skills would prove vital during the war he was about to fight.

The encampment in Cambridge could hardly be described as an army. While in sheer numbers, the estimated fifteen thousand volunteers actually outnumbered the ten thousand British troops occupying Boston, it was a motley assortment of poorly trained and ill-equipped militias from all thirteen colonies. There was little cohesion. The soldiers wore no standard uniforms; they carried the arms they brought with them; they were undernourished and poorly clothed. They were supposed to be paid by their local government, but those payments rarely arrived as scheduled. Morale was terrible. The pride and loyalty of each of these men was to the colony from which they'd come rather than to some abstract concept of a single united nation. What many of them were actually fighting for was relief from unjust taxation and harsh British regulation and the freedom to be left alone, rather than the dream of some new country.

Most of these militiamen knew about George Washington, though. These were hardened men—many of them depended on their hunting skills for survival—and they admired the general's mettle. Washington had proved himself in battle; he was the kind of man they didn't mind taking orders from. When he rode into the camp he made an impressive sight. At six-foot-two, he was almost seven inches taller than the average man of that time. As Dr. James Thacher reported, "His excellency was on horseback, in company with several military gentlemen. It was not difficult to distinguish him from all others. His personal appearance is truly noble and majestic, being tall and well proportioned. His dress is a blue coat with buff-colored facings, a rich epaulette on each shoulder, buff under-dress, and an elegant small sword; a black cockade in his hat. . . . He has been received here with every mark of respect, and addressed by our Provincial Congress in the most affectionate and respectful manner. All ranks appear to repose full confidence in him as commander-in-chief."

After reviewing his new command, Washington summed up this army with candor, "The abuses [problems] in this army, I fear, are considerable, and the new modeling of it [reorganization], in the face of an enemy, from whom we every hour expect an attack, is exceedingly difficult and dangerous."

Washington went to work immediately. On July 4, 1775, he issued one of his first General Orders, an attempt to turn the many disparate units into an army and to eliminate the suspicion and competition among them. "The Continental Congress having now taken all the troops of the several colonies which have been raised or which may be hereafter raised for the support and defense of the liberties of America into their pay and service, they are now the troops of the United Provinces of North America; and it is hoped that all distinctions of colonies will be laid aside, so that one and the same spirit may animate the whole, and the only contest be, who shall render, on this great and trying occasion, the most essential service to the great and common cause in which we are all engaged."

Among those men who soon visited Washington at Cambridge was none other than Benjamin Franklin, who wanted to know what supplies were most urgently needed. Everything,

This hand-painted Currier & Ives litho
portrays General George Washington
assuming command of the American
army in Cambridge, on July 3, 1775.

Washington apparently told him. But as important as provisions were weapons. The inventor Franklin urged that soldiers be armed with bows and arrows, pointing out that they were less expensive and easier to supply than muskets; four arrows could be fired in the time it took to fire and reload a musket, and a soldier struck by an arrow was out of combat until the arrow was removed. Both Washington and Franklin also wanted to equip their troops with fourteen-foot-long pikes and spears, which would be especially effective against cavalry, Washington noted, if they had "a spike in the butt end to fix them in the ground."

The patriot army was being created as the war began, and, looking at it realistically, even Washington and Franklin must have held doubts about the possibility of success.

The Liberty Bells

On the afternoon of July 4, 1776, the mammoth Liberty Bell in the tower belfry of Philadelphia's Independence Hall began ringing out loud and clear the long-awaited and glorious news throughout the city and countryside: independence had been declared! On that momentous day, a huge crowd, summoned by the rhythmic and resonant tolling of the one-ton bell, gathered in front of the Pennsylvania State House to hear Colonel John Nixon read the Declaration of Independence aloud for the first time.

It is a wonderful story, even if almost none of it is true. The Liberty Bell is among the most cherished symbols of freedom. Every schoolchild learns about the famous crack in the bell. The bell, its crack visible, has appeared on the reverse side of several half-dollar and silver dollar coins. America's Mercury astronauts named one of their capsules after it. Legendary frontiersman Davy Crockett was said to have gone to Washington and "patched up the crack in the Liberty Bell."

The State House Bell, as it was known until the late 1830s, certainly was not rung on July 4, and probably was not the bell that was rung four days later, the actual day the Declaration of Independence was read publicly. The wooden steeple in which it hung had been long neglected and was in such poor condition that it was feared it would topple if the bell was rung, so in all probability a considerably smaller backup bell enclosed in a second belfry "rang all day, and almost all night," according to John Adams.

The bell itself had been ordered by the Pennsylvania Provincial Assembly from London's famed Whitechapel Bell Foundry in 1751—the same company that made Big Ben a century later—to celebrate the fiftieth anniversary of William Penn's 1701 Charter of Privileges. It was finally delivered in September 1752; the copper and tin bell weighed almost a ton, was about twelve feet in circumference around the bottom and seven and a half feet at the crown, and cost £100. It was inscribed with a phrase from Leviticus 25:10, "Proclaim Liberty throughout all the land unto all the inhabitants thereof." It took six months to hang it; unfortunately, as a bell ringer named Isaac Norris wrote, "I had the mortification to hear that it was cracked by a stroke of the clapper without any other viollence [*sic*] as it was hung up to try the sound." It had cracked on the very first test stroke. Whitechapel later placed the blame on Pennsylvania, pointing out, "They did not appreciate that bell metal is brittle, and relies on this to a great extent for its freedom of tone."

Two experienced workers in a Philadelphia foundry, John Pass and John Stow, recast the bell for a fee of £36, adding copper to strengthen it and silver to sweeten its clanging tone. When it was hung for the second time and tested, the sound was so jarring that it was taken down and recast again by Pass and Stow. When the result proved no more agreeable, a second bell was ordered from Whitechapel Bell. That second bell was no more pleasing, so the original bell was left in the tower of the state house building—which years later was to become known as Independence Hall. It was hung in the attic and rung hourly to mark the time.

After the Pass and Stow bell was lowered into the brick portion of the belfry, it was used to call the Pennsylvania State Assembly together and alert citizens to special occasions and events. It announced the ascension to the throne of King George III in 1761, it summoned people for a debate about the Stamp Act—and later its repeal, it alerted them to the Battle at Lexington and Concord, and several years later was rung to mark the signing of the Constitution, George Washington's birthday, and the deaths, in turn, of founding fathers Franklin, Washington, Hamilton, and Jefferson.

During the Revolution, the bell was taken down and hidden in the floorboards of Zion's Reformed Church in Allentown, Pennsylvania. According to legend, this was done out of fear that the British would melt it down and turn it into cannons—which was highly unlikely as England's arms manufacturers were among the best in the world.

In fact, it wasn't until 1837 that it became known as the Liberty Bell, when it became a symbol for the abolitionist movement. The story that it rang out the news of independence was created by author George Lippard in an 1847 issue of the *Saturday Courier*. According to Lippard, an elderly bell ringer waiting anxiously in the steeple had begun to lose faith in the founding fathers when his grandson, who had pressed an ear to the door against the closed doors of Congress, shouted gleefully to him, "Ring, Grandfather, ring." And so the news was announced.

The news that the Declaration of Independence had been signed was actually spread by newspapers, being announced first on July 6 by the

"LIBERTY BELL."—[SKETCHED BY THEO. R. DAVIS.]

By 1869, when this image was published in *Harper's Weekly*, the Pennsylvania State House bell had been cracked and recast and taken its place in American history as the Liberty Bell.

Pennsylvania Evening Post. It took more than a month for the news to reach England, as the *London Gazette* reported on August 10, "I am informed that the Continental Congress have declared the United Colonies free and independent states."

Incredibly, no one knows exactly when the crack in the Liberty Bell first appeared. Among the many stories was that it first cracked when celebrating the 1824 visit of Revolutionary War hero the Marquis de Lafayette to Philadelphia. Other stories claim it was damaged in 1835 during the funeral of Chief Justice John Marshall or in 1846 when it was rung to commemorate Washington's birthday. The original thin crack was intentionally widened to the expanse it is today during a repair effort that failed. It was silenced in 1846, as the *Philadelphia Public Ledger* reported, "The old Independence Bell rang its last clear note on Monday last in honor of the birthday of Washington and now hangs in the great city steeple irreparably cracked and dumb. . . . It gave out clear notes and loud, and appeared to be in excellent condition until noon, when it received a sort of compound fracture in a zig-zag direction through one of its sides which put it completely out of tune and left it a mere wreck of what it was."

The bell was put on display in 1852 and became a popular tourist attraction. In the 1880s it was brought to cities across the country to "proclaim liberty" and inspire patriotism. In 1915 it was displayed at San Francisco's Panama-Pacific International Exposition. While it never rang again, on very special occasions it is tapped. On D-day, June 6, 1944, for example, the dull sound of the bell being struck was broadcast on the radio to announce the Normandy invasion. And to commemorate its importance to the antislavery movement, each year it receives a gentle tap on Martin Luther King's birthday.

CHAPTER 4

GENERAL GEORGE WASHINGTON

Commanding Revolution

The situation was far worse than Washington had believed. Within months of taking command of the army he wrote, "Could I have foreseen what I have experienced and am likely to experience, no consideration upon earth should have induced me to accept this command." While these soldiers had courage and energy in abundance, they lacked discipline and the willingness to make sacrifices. Enlistments were brief, and many of the men in Cambridge would be done with it by the end of the year.

Washington immediately began trying to transform the scattershot militias into something resembling an army. As his General Orders issued on July 4 set forth:

> It is required and expected that exact discipline be observed, and due subordination prevail thro' the whole army, as a failure in these most essential points must necessarily produce extreme hazard, disorder and confusion; and end in shameful disappointment and disgrace.

General George Washington at Valley Forge in the winter of 1777, as engraved by Nathaniel Currier.

The general most earnestly requires, and expects, a due observance of those articles of war, established for the government of the army, which forbid profane cursing, swearing and drunkenness; and in like manner requires and expects, of all officers, and soldiers, not engaged on actual duty, a punctual attendance on divine service, to implore the blessings of heaven upon the means used for our safety and defense.

All officers are required and expected to pay diligent attention to keep their men neat and clean; to visit them often at their quarters, and inculcate upon them the necessity of cleanliness, as essential to their health and service. They are particularly to see, that they have straw to lay on, if to be had, and to make it known if they are destitute of this article. . . .

It is strictly required and commanded that there be no firing of cannon or small arms from any of the lines, or elsewhere, except in case of necessary, immediate defense, or special order given for that purpose.

This army was desperate for the benefits of prayer, as they had little else. Among Washington's first directions was to make sure each man had at least one blanket. Feeding the army was to be a continuous problem that would get progressively worse. More immediately dangerous was the reality that the army was almost out of ammunition, possessing only thirty-six barrels of gunpowder. If the British attacked, it would be difficult to sustain a proper resistance. At one point, in fact, the commanding officer of each regiment was ordered to issue spears to thirty men who were "active, bold and resolute . . . in the defense of the line instead of guns."

Fortunately for Washington, the British were busy tending to their own needs. While the army General Howe took over was better trained and equipped than the rebels' army, it also was smaller and lacked sufficient food, as well as wood to keep its fires burning through the winter. Many of Howe's men were recovering from wounds or suffering from scurvy and smallpox. And although they had been victorious at Bunker Hill, the ferocity of the defense had been a great surprise. Gage's troops had expected to face a disorganized mob that would flee upon encounter; instead they had faced brave men who gave no quarter. This newfound respect for the rebels gave Howe pause. His army, he knew, was in no condition to launch an attack.

While few people questioned Washington's leadership, they did speculate about his tactical skill. In late August, he outlined a plan to launch a daring attack on Boston. He feared that a cold winter would make it difficult for his troops to maintain the siege. It certainly was something Howe would not expect. The element of surprise, he figured, might make up for the lack of supplies. In any case, supplies were shrinking, and if he let this time pass he might never again be sufficiently equipped to make such an attack. Washington argued for this plan passionately. His staff dissuaded him, pointing out that the British could still receive resupplies and reinforcements by sea; they suggested that he instead wait until the hardest part of the winter when the harbor would freeze. Washington agreed. But several months later, in preparation for this frontal assault, he was forced to send Henry Knox to Fort Ticonderoga to bring back the cannons, powder, and shells that had been left there after Ethan Allen and his Green Mountain Boys, along with Benedict Arnold, had captured the weapons and ammunition.

Meanwhile, Washington had to build his army, and to accomplish that, he knew, discipline was essential. Troops had to be taught to respect authority and respond to orders

In January 2005, this painting, Charles Willson Peale's *Washington at Princeton*, sold for $21.3 million, making it the most valuable Washington portrait in history. Peale produced eight copies, completing the first in 1779.

without question or complaint. "Discipline is the soul of an army," he wrote. "It makes small numbers formidable; procures success to the weak and esteem to all." He had significant work to do in order to build this discipline in his army. George Washington, the benevolent "Father of Our Country," the boy who was so honorable he would not lie about cutting down a cherry tree, was, by necessity, also a brutal disciplinarian who understood the value of fear. When appointed commander of the Virginia Regiment, the state militia, in 1755, he had imposed strict penalties: for swearing or uttering an oath of excretion a man received twenty-five lashes on the spot; for dereliction of duty or visiting an off-limits "tippling house or gin shop" he got fifty lashes. At one point, when soldiers were deserting, he erected a forty-foot-high gallows and sentenced fourteen men to hang. He chose that method of execution rather than a firing squad, he said, because "it conveyed much more terror to others." Eventually he relented and hanged only two men.

Maintaining order among as many as seventeen thousand poorly supplied, underfed men living in fetid conditions was almost impossible. Fights broke out almost daily. The oppression of the summer heat eventually gave way to the bitter cold of early winter snows. In November a company of fewer than a hundred riflemen arrived from the Virginia mountains and, according to a soldier named Israel Trask, their strange uniforms attracted attention: "Their white linen frocks, ruffled and fringed, excited the curiosity of the whole army, particularly the Marblehead [Massachusetts] regiment, who were always full of fun and mischief." Some pointed comments led to a snowball fight, which turned into a real fight "with biting and gouging on the one part, and knockdown on the other part . . . in less than five minutes more than a thousand combatants were on the field." Into the midst of the brawl, wrote Trask, "George Washington made his appearance, whether by accident or design I never knew. . . . With the spring of a deer, he leaped from his saddle . . . and rushed into the thickest of the melee, with an iron grip seized two tall, brawny, athletic, savage-looking riflemen by the throat, keeping them at arm's length, alternately shaking and talking to them. . . the belligerents caught sight of the general. Its effect on them was instantaneous flight at the top of their speed."

Washington moved into a grand mansion in Cambridge that had been abandoned by a Loyalist. He had brought with him from Virginia a considerable staff, including two cooks, his tailor, and several slaves, among them his aide, Billy Lee. Unlike many commanders, Washington believed in leading from the front and was often seen on the lines, and the troops got accustomed to seeing Washington and Billy Lee riding together.

After Washington's appointment as commander of the army, letters of congratulations from both the New York and Massachusetts legislatures addressed him formally as "Your

Excellency." While the title had royal connotations, he apparently accepted it, as he was addressed this way by his officers and men, and in official correspondence with Congress, for the rest of the war; and there is absolutely no evidence that he ever attempted to correct it.

Throughout the summer and into the fall the two sides skirmished. In late July the redcoats burned several houses in Roxbury. On August 2 an American rifleman was killed—his body was left hanging for the patriots to see. American sharpshooters spent the remainder of the day picking off British troops while losing only one additional man. On July 30, the British attempted to break out of the siege from the Boston Neck, but they were repulsed and ended up retreating, burning the popular George Tavern as they did. The following night, three hundred patriots rowed to Little Brewster Island and burned the lighthouse there while killing several troops and capturing twenty-three. Passage in and out of the city was possible with great care, so spies for both sides worked efficiently. Washington learned in late August from "various people who had just left Boston," that they [Howe's army] were preparing to "come out" through Charlestown. He sent one thousand men to prepare entrenchments and another fifteen hundred to protect them in case the British attacked. They dug through the night despite a continuous bombardment. Four men were killed, as Washington reported to Virginia's Richard Henry Lee; there was little to be done to prevent it, "not daring to make use of artillery on account of the consumption of powder, except with one nine-pounder placed on a point, with which we silenced, and indeed sunk, one of their floating batteries."

The British also had their spies, none more infamous than the supposed patriot Dr. Benjamin Church. Spy craft at the time was quite rudimentary, consisting of ciphers and simple codes, invisible inks—or "sympathetic stains"—other substances that could be materialized by exposure to heat, and masked letters in which the secret message could be read when a precut cover page was placed over the original letter. Documents were hidden in ordinary yet ingenious places; in addition to being sewn into clothing, messages might be slipped into the hollowed-out quill of a large feather or hidden in buttons. Benjamin Church was a respected patriot leader, a member of the Sons of Liberty, the Committees of Correspondence and Safety, a delegate to the Massachusetts Congress, and a liaison to the Continental Congress. Washington named him chief physician of the Continental army, essentially the surgeon general. While serving in those positions, Church was trusted with important information—which he apparently had been sharing with the British for several years. It is believed that he supplied at least some of the intelligence to General Gage regarding the captured cannons that were being kept in Concord, which prompted the British march that ended with the

While the traitorous act of Benedict Arnold is well known, the treachery of Benjamin Church might well have caused far more damage. One of Washington's most trusted aides, Church supplied vital intelligence to the British until he was caught—and served less than a year in prison before being pardoned.

shots heard round the world. But as has been the fate of spies through history, Benjamin Church was undone by a woman.

Church's career began unraveling in August 1775, when a former mistress of Godfrey Wainwood—a Newport, Rhode Island, baker—traveled from Cambridge to ask Wainwood for his assistance in delivering a letter to a British official aboard a ship docked in the harbor. Wainwood was not told the contents of the letter, nor that the official was to hand it to a Major Cane when this ship arrived in Boston. Wainwood's suspicion was raised by this strange request and he eventually opened the letter—it was totally unintelligible, consisting of cryptic Greek characters, numbers, letters, and symbols. Obviously it was a secret message. Wainwood held on to it for another month or so, but when the young woman complained that it hadn't been sent, he decided to take it to Washington's headquarters.

Henry Ward, a member of Rhode Island's assembly, wrote to Washington and warned him that there was a spy in his inner circle and suggested he "take up the woman in so private a way as to arouse no suspicion, and it is probable that rewards and punishments properly placed before her will induce her to give up the author."

Washington heeded Ward's advice. "For a long time," Washington wrote to Congress, "she was proof against every threat and persuasion to discover the author. However, at length she was brought to a confession, and named Doctor Church." As it turned out, the woman had been "kept" by Church. Church was immediately taken into custody. He admitted having written the letter but denied it contained important information, instead claiming that it was a note to his brother-in-law. But he steadfastly refused to decipher it. Within a few days two teams of men were able to break the code. The letter contained vital intelligence concerning the location of cannons in New York, troop strength in Philadelphia, details of a proposed attack on Canada, and, most important to Washington, an estimate of his ammunition stores.

Church claimed that he had intentionally exaggerated the army's situation in this letter, hoping to convince the British to make peace even at that late date. Although this was the only letter found, Washington surmised that Church might have passed other information that had caused unexpected failures in his strategy. In fact, the full extent of Church's betrayal wouldn't be discovered for decades. Oddly, there was no official mechanism in place for dealing with a spy. Church was sent to prison in Norwich, Connecticut, and forbidden to have pen, ink, or paper or speak with anyone at any time except the magistrate. He served less than a year, then was pardoned, supposedly because he was in poor health. He returned to Massachusetts and eventually received permission to travel to the West Indies; during that passage in 1780 his ship was lost and presumably he went down with it.

Fortunately, Church's deception was uncovered only months after Washington had assumed command of the army and long before his espionage could cause permanent damage.

The siege of Boston continued through the winter of 1776. While the winter at Valley Forge has become an important symbol of American courage, in this first winter of the war both armies suffered greatly. For the British army blockaded on the Boston Peninsula as well as Washington's troops, survival depended on the availability of wood, livestock, and plants—all of them in short supply. By November, Washington complained, "Different regiments were upon the point of cutting each other's throats for a few standing locusts near their encampments to dress their victuals with." In Boston, fences, houses, and even the Old North Meeting House were knocked down and used to fuel ovens and hearths—the famed Liberty Tree was cut down and provided fourteen cords of firewood. British soldiers joked openly about joining whatever army could provide fresh meat. One Boston fisherman wrote, "No language can paint the distress of the inhabitants, most of them destitute of wood and of provisions of every kind. . . . The soldiers . . . are uneasy to a great degree, many of them declaring they will not continue much longer in such a state, but at all hazards will escape." In fact, much of the fighting that took place in the winter months was a by-product of either getting supplies or keeping them from the enemy.

As winter settled in, Washington wrote to his wife, Martha Custis Washington, at their

This 1865 engraving depicts George and Martha Washington with their grandchildren, George Washington Parke Custis and Nelly Custis, looking at plans for the new American capitol named Washington, D.C. The servant at right may well be the renowned William Lee.

home in Mount Vernon, asking her to join him in Cambridge. While certainly he was concerned that the general's wife might be in jeopardy should there be fighting in Virginia, it's probably more accurate that he simply missed her. Martha was barely five feet tall, but she was a strong, smart woman, and the two of them formed an imposing pair. Apparently she had never before traveled outside Virginia, but after receiving his invitation she agreed to be inoculated for smallpox and then travel north. She brought with her on the three-week trip their two children and four slaves. As her coach passed through each town on her journey, people would turn out to cheer her, and an honor guard of Continental troops would escort her to the next town.

When she arrived in December, she apparently was shocked at the situation; a child of affluence, it is probable she had never been exposed to such harsh conditions. Supposedly she was stunned to see the circumstances under which the Continental army was living—many of the soldiers lacked sufficient clothing, and some didn't even have socks. Apparently she immediately went to work: She organized the women of the encampment into a sewing and knitting circle. She made socks and shirts, mended clothing for bachelor soldiers, visited the wounded in hospitals, changed bandages, and distributed food. The grateful troops began referring to her as Lady Washington. Most often she could be found sitting in the parlor, wearing a work apron and knitting. But she never forgot that she was in the middle of a war. As the cannons boomed around her she wrote, "To me that has never seen anything of war, the preparations are very terrible indeed, but I endeavor to keep my fears to myself as well as I can."

These winter hardships decimated Washington's army. The enlistment for thousands of his troops expired at the end of the year, and, rather than reenlisting, many of them were ready to go home, the lack of all supplies and necessities having, as Washington predicted, "an unhappy influence upon their enlisting." By the beginning of 1776 Washington found himself "weaker than I had any idea of," and warned Congress, "This army, if there comes a spell of rain or cold weather, must inevitably disperse." While his army still numbered ten thousand troops, in fact probably only half that number was fit for duty, and it wasn't clear that they had sufficient weapons even for those troops. As he wrote to a friend, "If I shall be able to rise superior to these and many other difficulties . . . I shall most religiously believe that the

Charles Willson Peale painted this portrait of sixty-four-year-old Martha Washington in 1795. George Washington told the artist his wife would be happy to pose for him, as "the temptation of looking well was too strong to be resisted."

finger of Providence is in it, to blind the eyes of our enemies; for surely if we get well through this month, it must be for want of their knowing the disadvantages which we labor under."

But the British government had made several significant mistakes. Among them was ordering the Royal Navy to burn patriot ships and seaports in retaliation for colonial attacks on British supply vessels. They had completely misjudged the consequences of that policy. Even after the first shots were fired at Lexington and Concord, considerable debate continued throughout the colonies about making a clean break with England; many people saw the fighting as Massachusetts's problem. In many cities, citizens' complaints focused on local enforcement of the laws and collection of the taxes, problems that might be resolved. But in October a British fleet commanded by Captain Henry Mowat anchored in the harbor of Falmouth (now Portland), Maine, as part of the plan to burn colonial ships and seaports. Falmouth certainly was not a hotbed of rebellion; in fact, there may have been as many Loyalists living there as patriots. Mowat gave the residents two hours to pack and evacuate, informing them that he had orders "to fire the town." Desperate town leaders tried to negotiate with him, but according to the newspapers he told them that "his orders were to set on fire all the seaport towns between Boston and Halifax, and then he expected New York was then burnt to ashes."

Ignoring the pleas, "in the morning he began to fire from the four armed vessels. . . . He continued firing till after dark that same day, which destroyed the large part of the town." Mowat also sent a raiding party ashore to set fire to those places the ships' guns couldn't reach. More than four hundred buildings and houses, as well as eleven ships, were destroyed. More than a thousand people were left homeless at the beginning of winter. The job done, the fleet then sailed for the next town.

The wanton attack and burning of the city was reported in newspapers in every colony. George Washington called the attack "an outrage exceeding in barbarity and cruelty every hostile act practiced among civilized nations." For many colonists this was the turning point. "Good God! What savage barbarity!" exclaimed Josiah Quincy, who had assisted John Adams in the Boston Massacre trials. "Let us no longer call ourselves Englishmen but free born Americans." Many other towns that were far from the fighting and had been protective of their independence and reluctant to become involved now opted to join the fight.

But even this renewed and expanding spirit could not substitute for a lack of supplies. Washington knew he could not maintain the blockade forever, but without sufficient guns and powder he couldn't risk an attack. The solution came through a remarkable display of courage and fortitude. On January 27, 1776, Henry Knox returned.

Henry Knox was a bookstore clerk when he witnessed the Boston Massacre. It is said that he had tried to intervene, beseeching the British soldiers to return to their barracks. Later, he testified at their trials. Knox had left school at the age of twelve and was apprenticed to a bookseller, where he developed an interest in engineering and the military. In 1771 he opened his own shop in Boston, the London Book Store. At the start of the rebellion, he aligned with the Sons of Liberty and might well have been one of the many unidentified colonists who participated in the Boston Tea Party. After war broke out, Knox and his wife of less than a year, Lucy, fled Boston. He joined the militia, helped erect fortifications, and even directed cannons during Bunker Hill. Although Knox had not yet received a commission, Washington quickly came to respect his talents—and perhaps his size. Knox was one of the few men taller than Washington—by an inch—and his weight was estimated at 280 pounds. When Knox suggested a mission to retrieve the cannons abandoned at Fort Ticonderoga in upstate New York, after the fort had been captured by General Benedict Arnold and Ethan Allen, Washington placed him in charge of the effort. "No trouble or expense must be spared to obtain them," he wrote, and authorized Knox to spend as much as £1,000—a substantial sum—if necessary. It turned out to be an epic journey.

Knox arrived at Fort Ticonderoga on December 5 with mild expectations. While at one time the fort had been well defended, Knox had no idea what he would find there now. Even if the artillery was still there, it had lain exposed without proper care for months. But Knox must have been stunned when he walked into the remains of the fort and discovered a treasure of British artillery. He eventually selected fifty-nine guns from the fort and the nearby bastion at Crown Point, consisting of forty-three brass and iron cannons, eight full-size mortars and six smaller coehorn mortars, and two howitzers—plus twenty-four boxes of ammunition and flint. He'd found more than sixty tons of weaponry, ranging in size from twenty-six iron guns weighing five thousand pounds each and capable of firing twenty-four pound cannon balls to portable coehorn mortars. And all he had to do was transport all of it three hundred miles through forests and narrow paths, across lakes, rivers, vast flatlands, and snow-covered mountains.

The incredible story of his struggle to get the cannons to Washington is equal to any tale of the Revolution. Knox's "noble train of artillery," as it became known, began by hauling the armament overland more than fifty miles until they reached Lake George. There the cannons were transferred onto large gundalows, flat-bottomed cargo transport ships built for use on shallow rivers, and the journey across the lake began. On the second day one of the boats hit a submerged rock, foundered, and sank. Knox feared its cargo was lost, but his brother, in command of the boat, managed to refloat it and land it at Fort George. There, Knox ordered built "42 exceeding strong sleds" and secured 160 oxen and horses "to drag them [over snow-covered ground] as far as Springfield [Massachusetts]." In slightly longer than two weeks, he wrote Washington quite optimistically, he hoped "to be able to present your Excellency a noble train of artillery."

Unfortunately, the ground was dry, making the sleds temporarily useless. Knox and his men and the hungry animals sat waiting for a week, until more than two feet of snow fell on Christmas Day. Then the deep and drifting snow made the roads impassable. The horses quit and the men had to leave the sleds "to undertake a very fatiguing march of about two miles in snow three feet deep, through the woods, there being no beaten path." When they finally reached Albany, General Philip Schuyler provided additional men, horses, oxen, and sleds, enabling them to slide on.

The quickest route to Cambridge required crossing the Hudson River four times. The first two passages over the frozen river were completed without difficulty. But when "the train" finally reached Albany, the weather turned and a "cruel thaw" made the ice too thin. Knox and his men, and probably some townspeople, cut holes in the ice and poured water into those holes to thicken and strengthen it; when the water froze, the ice in those places was strong enough to support the sleds. Most of them made it across successfully, but one sled fell through the ice at a place called Half Moon, a small outpost south of Saratoga. Again, Knox had chosen that spot because the river there was not especially deep, and his men were able to retrieve the cannons without too much difficulty. As Knox recorded in his diary on January 7: "Went on the ice about 8 o'clock in the morning & proceeded so carefully that before night we got over 23 sleds & were so lucky as to get the cannon out of the river, owing to the assistance the good people of the city of Albany gave. In return for which we christened her, the Albany."

This "train" climbed over the Berkshires, which he described as "mountains from which we might almost have seen all the kingdoms of the earth." When he reached Blandford, Massachusetts, his lead crew had had enough. The lack of snow and the steep descent to the Connecticut River were just too much. Knox hired more oxen and convinced his crew to persevere. By then news of this journey had reached townspeople along his route and they turned out to cheer and urge him onward. In the town of Westfield scores of people, most of whom had never seen large cannons up close, turned out to touch the guns. Knox gave them a treat; he loaded one of the large cannons and fired it.

It seemed like every day Knox was forced to deal with a new crisis. When he reached Springfield he was stalled by a second thaw. As the guns sat in the mud by the side of a road, several members of his crew from New York decided to return home, forcing him to find replacements. On the twenty-fifth, John Adams rode to Framingham to view the now celebrated train. Two days later, after fifty days of dragging, pushing, floating, and sliding, Knox arrived in Cambridge. The journey had cost exactly £520, 15 shillings, 8¾-pence, not an especially large sum in that day. But his arrival may have changed the outcome of the war. In addition to pikes and spears, Franklin's bows and arrows, and the dwindling supply of powder, General Washington had big guns.

In late January, when the waters between Roxbury and Boston had frozen, Washington considered launching a direct assault across the ice. His staff convinced him it would be disastrous. But the presence of the cannons offered another, more enticing plan.

Since the beginning of the siege, Washington had his eye on Dorchester Heights, an area overlooking Boston. General Howe, although certainly aware of its strategic value, had chosen not to occupy it. It had remained an intriguing no-man's-land through the New Year. Washington

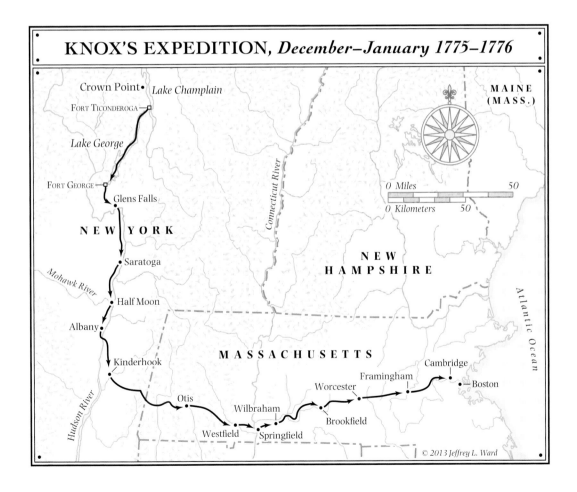

KNOX'S EXPEDITION, *December–January 1775–1776*

© 2013 Jeffrey L. Ward

KNOX ENTERING CAMP WITH ARTILLERY.

This 1855 litho depicts Henry Knox (on horseback) arriving in Cambridge with fifty-nine cannons, mortars, and howitzers after an incredible three-hundred-mile journey from Fort Ticonderoga across seemingly impassable terrain.

decided it was the perfect place from which his new artillery could rain down hell upon occupied Boston. His problem was that the frozen ground made it impossible to construct defensive earthworks, the absence of which would leave his soldiers unacceptably vulnerable. One of his soldiers suggested a relatively simple solution: construct a barrier of logs, hay bales, sticks, and rocks to offer protection from musket fire and grapeshot. Washington approved of the idea, but getting it built within range of that British musket fire and grapeshot would be more difficult. Undoubtedly Howe had learned the lesson of Breed's Hill, and as soon as he heard the sounds of building work in the night, he would organize an offensive. Washington, who of necessity rapidly was becoming a master of military improvisation, devised a plan to prevent that from happening.

Meanwhile, despite the hardships of the occupation, Howe seemed content to keep his army safely in Boston through the winter. As he wrote to Lord Dartmouth, "We are not under the least apprehension of an attack upon this place from the rebels, by surprise or otherwise." In fact, he boasted that he wished Washington would attack "and quit those strong entrenchments to which they may attribute their present safety." Apparently Howe planned to evacuate Boston in favor of New York, with its larger harbor and its proximity to the other colonies, but had decided to wait until more ships were available for transport and the weather was favorable. While the troops struggled in their barracks, the officers fared quite well. They passed the early days of 1776, wrote one officer, as agreeably as possible. "We had a theatre, we had balls, there is actually a subscription on foot for a masquerade."

Washington actually had similar thoughts as his adversary and completely understood Howe's intention, but he wanted to force Howe to fight. As he informed the council, "I am preparing to take post on Dorchester Heights, to try if the enemy will be so kind as to come out to us." Then he told Congress, "I should think, if anything will induce them to hazard an engagement, it will be our attempt to fortify these heights, as on that event taking place, we shall be able to command a great part of that town, and almost the whole harbor, and to make them rather disagreeable than otherwise."

In late February Washington received a shipment of three thousand pounds of desperately needed gunpowder from Rhode Island. While not as much as he had been hoping for, it was sufficient to allow him to put his plan into action. On February 27 he alerted his troops that the campaign was finally about to begin: "As the season is now fast approaching when every man must expect to be drawn into the field of action, it is highly necessary that he should prepare his mind." And he warned that any soldier who shirked his duty "will be instantly shot down as an example of cowardice."

Washington's message was clear: the gravity of the situation could not be overestimated.

As one of his officers noted in his diary, Washington "told the soldiery that on our present conduct depends the salvation of America." Washington had his troops prepare as much of the materials they would need as possible; wooden barricades, gunpowder, and cannons, as well as barrels filled with dirt and stones, were quietly moved into position below the heights. The barrels would be rolled down the hill if the British attacked to disrupt their formation. During the first days of March, Washington moved some of Knox's cannons into position on Lechmere's Point and Cobble Hill in Cambridge and Lamb's Den in Roxbury. On the night of March 2 these emplacements began firing on Boston, although they were too far from the city to cause much harm. The British returned fire, also to little effect. The following night Washington again began bombarding the city and again Howe returned fire. On the night of March 4, the cannons opened fire once more, and again Howe responded. But what Howe did not grasp was that this seemingly useless exchange actually was a means of providing cover while Washington's troops occupied Dorchester Heights.

Two thousand patriot troops under the command of General John Thomas marched up

The city of Boston in peacetime, 1793, as seen from the Dorchester Heights

the hill and began putting in place their previously built protective shield—with every sound drowned by the artillery battle in progress around them. While the British were "amused," or misled by the shelling, the patriots worked at a fever pitch through the night. They were hidden from view by a fog that covered the hilltop as well as smoke from the bombardment, but they could see by the light of a bright moon. General Howe's attention reportedly was distracted not just by the shelling but by a game of faro or, in some reports, the charms of a woman named Elizabeth Loring. By the time the sun rose the following morning, Washington's troops had put up a wall of timber and several levels of barriers in front of it, then fixed forty-three cannons and fourteen mortars in position.

Howe was stunned—and incredulous—when he woke in the morning and saw what had happened while his own guns were engaging the enemy. He was also surprised that Washington, who had not previously shown such impressive tactical ability, had somehow managed to pull off this feat. "The rebels have done more in one night," he supposedly commented, "than my whole army would have done in one month."

Howe's troops were equally astonished. One of his officers wrote that putting these cannons and entrenchments in place in one night was possible only "with an expedition equal to that of the genii belonging to Aladdin's wonderful lamp."

The success of the operation put the redcoats' continued presence in Boston in great jeopardy. The commander of the fleet informed Howe that his ships could not safely remain in the harbor. Howe ordered his own artillery to engage the guns on the heights. His cannons opened fire, but he watched helplessly as the shells fell well short of the top. They tried to elevate the guns by burying their rear wheels in the ground, but they still lacked sufficient range to reach Washington's entrenched and protected guns. Howe knew he could not remain in Boston with those guns towering above him. He had only two options: attack Washington's position in force and drive the rebels off the heights or abandon the city. The thought of giving up the town in which the rebellion had started to such an inferior force, to give them such a meaningful victory, was more than he was willing to accept. Leaving Boston for New York on his own terms and by his own timetable was an acceptable military maneuver; being forced from the city had very different ramifications. He decided to attack, and in such force that he would drive them off the hill and cause the patriot army to scatter. He gave orders for twenty-four hundred men to prepare to assault the American position that night.

Howe had taken the bait. Once again he had underestimated Washington. The rebel commander had never given up his plans to take back the city. He had about four thousand men and several floating batteries waiting on the banks of the Charles River for his signal to cross Back Bay and attack the town from three different places. When the British began their frontal assault on his positions on Dorchester Heights, he would surprise them by attacking from the rear. It was an audacious and risky maneuver, and failure could have broken his army. Once his troops landed there could be no retreat. This battle would be bigger, and bloodier, than Bunker Hill.

At the same time Washington sent additional troops to fortify the line on the heights. His troops there waited anxiously. When the assault began, they would continue to wait, until the British formation began marching up the hill. Then they would roll their dirt- and stone-filled barrels down the hill, completely disrupting the redcoats' order—and then they would let loose whatever powder they had left. There was a chance that the fate of the entire colonial uprising would be determined by Washington's bold gamble.

And then the winds began blowing.

Accurate weather forecasting did not exist at that time; predictions were as reliable as Franklin's Poor Richard could make them a year in advance. As the two armies prepared for battle, dark, ominous clouds blanketed the sky. By late afternoon the waters were so treacherous

As General Henry Lee said upon George Washington's death, he was "First in war, first in peace, and first in the hearts of his countrymen." This romanticized portrait shows him on Dorchester Heights, perhaps with the cannons carried by Knox behind him.

that no attack from the sea was possible. Howe's boats would be smashed on Dorchester's shore, while Washington's troops might be swept away. The winds continued increasing in strength; then it began raining. The "hurricane" raged into the night, forcing Howe to postpone his offensive. On the heights, Washington continued to reinforce and strengthen his barricades. The storm continued into the second day. There was nothing Howe could do but wait—and reconsider his strategy. In Boston the Reverend William Gordon had watched as the army prepared to attack. And then he wrote, "When I heard in the night how amazingly strong the wind blew (for it was such a storm as scarce any one remembered to have heard) and how it rained towards morning, I concluded that the ships could not stir, and pleased myself with the reflection that the Lord might be working deliverance for us and preventing the effusion of human blood."

By the time the storm finally ended, Howe had changed his mind. Rather than risking his army on a daring but dangerous attack, he decided to withdraw. Instead of sailing directly

General William Howe, 5th Viscount Howe, served as Commander of the British forces in North America from 1775 to 1778. Although Howe disagreed publicly with Parliament's policy concerning the colonies, he accepted the command, explaining "he was ordered, and could not refuse."

to New York, his army went north to Halifax, Nova Scotia, where a massive thirty-two-thousand-man force was being assembled. When he attacked again, it would be with an overwhelming number of troops. Munitions and property would be left behind but could be replaced. The patriots occupied a superior position that was exceedingly dangerous to his army and the ships in the harbor. It was better to withdraw to fight on better terms than to lose an army in a futile effort.

On March 8, a signed letter from several Boston residents was delivered to Washington's headquarters informing him that the British intended to make an orderly withdrawal from the city by sea. "General Howe . . . has no intention of destroying the town, unless the troops under his command are molested during their embarkation or at their departure. . . . If such an opposition should take place, we have the greatest reason to expect the town will be exposed to entire destruction." The threat was clear: if Washington interfered with the British withdrawal Howe would burn the city. To emphasize that point, Royal Navy ships moved into position. Washington did not respond to these terms, as the letter did not come from the British and it was not addressed to him by name or rank. But he understood its meaning.

The British army made preparations to abandon the city. This was not simply moving some troops to another post; this was a complete departure from what was essentially a military fortress. In addition to all of the troops and as much equipment as could be packed and carried to Halifax, those public officials and people who had remained loyal to the Crown throughout the occupation, and surely would suffer the consequences of that choice when the patriots returned, were offered passage with the army.

Taking no chances, Washington decided to move his troops closer. On the night of March 9 they occupied Nook's Hill, putting them in position even closer to the city. British artillery detected the movement and began a relentless shelling, but it had little effect. The following day colonists picked up more than seven hundred cannonballs.

The British spent the next few days packing the ships and destroying anything that had to be left that might benefit the enemy. The fort on Castle Island was set on fire and allowed to burn to embers. On March 10 Howe ordered all residents of Boston to hand over all the linen and woolen goods they possessed, warning that anyone who "secrets or keeps in his possession such articles, he will be treated as a favorer of the rebels"—in other words, a traitor. The cannons that could not be carried on board were spiked, their transport was smashed, and a large amount of ammunition was thrown into the harbor. Officers who had purchased goods anticipating a long stay destroyed and burned as much as they could. Loyalist looters, enraged at having to leave their homes, broke into shops and took what they wanted. As Reverend Gordon wrote, they went through the city, "carrying destruction wherever they went; what they could not carry away they destroyed." Howe did not condone this activity and, in fact, when he was informed that his troops were breaking into houses, he warned, "The first soldier who is caught plundering will be hanged on the spot." He also warned patriots that anyone found to be destroying or defacing pictures of the king or queen would be fined £50, for many people nearly a year's salary.

Days passed as British preparations progressed. The winds refused to assist a rapid departure. Meanwhile at sea, colonial privateers began intercepting inbound British merchants carrying military supplies and provisions—ships that had not been made aware of Howe's decision—and diverted them to ports under patriot control.

A wary Washington carefully watched this activity, ready to pounce should there be any signs that Howe had changed his mind. On March 16 Boston residents were warned to stay indoors to prevent harassment of the troops as they boarded their ships. But once again the winds shifted, preventing them from leaving, and they returned to their barracks. Washington was beginning to have his doubts about Howe's real intent. But on Sunday the seventeenth almost nine thousand troops, an additional thousand wives and children, and twelve hundred

Washington's success in fortifying Dorchester Heights with cannons brought from Fort Ticonderoga left Howe no choice but to withdraw from Boston. On March 17, 1776, more than eleven thousand troops sailed for Nova Scotia, a day still celebrated in Boston as Evacuation Day.

Loyalists—including Mrs. Loring—boarded more than 120 ships and sailed out of the harbor.

The evacuation of Boston was roundly criticized in England, and Howe's career was in jeopardy. It was a tremendous victory for George Washington, who had proved he was the strategic equal and perhaps even better than one of Great Britain's respected generals. Through a difficult winter he had transformed the assembly of colonial militias into an American army. His men had gained great confidence in his leadership abilities, which would prove vital as the war continued. Desperate to save his honor, Howe painted a very different picture: "The troops had evacuated Boston after having made every possible use of the town; they had left it voluntarily, and without any conversation between the king's and the rebel general. They were now gone to effect a matter of great consequence, to put Halifax in a state of safety." But that claim was intended to mask the enormity of this action.

As Washington's army watched the British fleet sail, they noticed that some sentries seemed to have been left behind on Bunker Hill to keep watch. Two scouts carefully moved forward, only to discover that the British had left wooden dummies dressed in uniforms. The colonial army went ahead and took possession of the once-bloodied battlefield. An advance force of about five hundred men commanded by General Putnam marched into Boston and claimed it, reported the *New England Journal*, "in the name of the thirteen United Colonies of North America . . . which the flower of the British army, headed by an experienced general, and supported by a formidable fleet of men-of-war, had but an hour before evacuated in the most precipitous and cowardly manner."

Not satisfied by seeing the British depart, Washington ordered his ships to harass the fleet. Among several ships captured by the patriots was one of the two carrying a vast amount of goods—including linen and woolens—stolen from the city.

Because there was an outbreak of smallpox in the city, Washington initially limited occupying troops to those who had suffered from it and therefore now had immunity. But days later his army marched in. And when they did, wrote a citizen, "the inhabitants appeared at their doors and windows . . . [and] manifested a lively joy at being liberated from their long confinement."

The end of the siege of Boston marked the beginning of a new and stronger relationship among the colonies. As historian Richard Frothingham wrote in 1850:

> The patriots now felt their strength. . . . When the siege of Boston commenced, the colonies were hesitating on the great measure of war, were separated by local interests, were jealous of each other's plans, and appeared on the field, each with its independent army under local colors: when the siege of Boston ended, the colonies had drawn the sword and nearly cast away the scabbard; . . . they had united in a political association; and the union flag of the thirteen stripes waved over a continental army. When the siege of Boston commenced, the great object and the general desire were for a work of restoration, for a return to the halcyon days of a constitutional connection to the mother country: when the siege of Boston ended, a majority of the patriots had irrevocably decided, that the only just and solid foundation for security and liberty was the creation of an independent American empire.

The Voyage
of the Turtle

When the Revolutionary War began in 1775, the vaunted Royal Navy had 131 ships of the line, although only 39 of them were considered battle ready. The colonists had no navy, although small sloops were used to harass British merchant vessels and privately owned schooners were granted letters of marque, essentially legal permission to engage and capture enemy ships. But the heavily outgunned colonists also utilized a remarkable device in an attempt to even the odds—history's first combat submarine.

The *Turtle*, as it was named by its inventor, David Bushnell, because it resembled "two upper tortoise shells of equal size," bound together side by side by iron hoops, was made of oak beams and hand "powered" by its single occupant. Bushnell, a Yale graduate, had previously invented the torpedo by proving that gunpowder could be detonated underwater. His plan was to attach this bomb to the hull of an enemy ship, but he lacked a reliable delivery system. The *Turtle* was his ingenious solution to that problem.

It was a fittingly revolutionary device. The *Turtle* was reportedly six feet in length and was the first submersible to contain its own breathing system, employ water as ballast for submerging or rising, and use a screw propeller—although it was maneuvered with a single oar. It was equipped with an extraordinary biological "lighting" system to enable the pilot to read his dials; called "foxfire," it was a luminescent blue-green fungus often found in decaying wood.

In a desperate attempt to break the British blockade of New York, the *Turtle* set out to attack Admiral Richard Howe's sixty-four-gun flagship, HMS *Eagle*, very early in the morning of September 7, 1776. Piloted by

Sergeant Ezra Lee, the craft carried one watertight wooden keg packed with gunpowder, a fuse, and a timing device attached near its top. Under the cover of darkness, Lee successfully maneuvered his craft beneath the *Eagle*'s keel without being spotted. He actually brushed against its stern and touched it before descending. As Lee began attempting to affix his time bomb to the *Eagle*, he could see British sailors on deck, completely oblivious of what was taking place just below their feet. According to the journal of Dr. James Thacher, he "struck, as he supposes, a bar of iron which passes from the rudder hinge. . . . Had he moved a few inches, which he might have done without rowing, there is no doubt he would have found wood where he might have fixed the screw. . . . But not being well skilled in the management of the vessel, in attempting to move to another place, he lost the ship." The iron sheathing had saved Howe's flagship.

This replica of the wooden *Turtle*, with barely enough room for its one-man crew, is in the Royal Navy Submarine Museum in Portsmouth, England.

Lee had no choice. He rowed away from the *Eagle* and after several minutes surfaced—into the first rays of the sunrise. There was no way to make a second attempt without being spotted. He aborted his mission and began moving as rapidly as possible toward shore. "As he passed near Governor's Island," Thacher continued, he "thought he was discovered by the enemy on the island. Being in haste, to avoid the danger he feared, he cast off the magazine, as he imagined it retarded him in the swell. . . . After the magazine had been cast off an hour, the time the internal apparatus was set to run, it blew up with great violence, throwing a vast column of water to an amazing height in the air, and leaving the enemy to conjecture whether the stupendous noise was produced by a bomb, a meteor, a water-spout, or an earthquake."

During the following week several additional attempts failed, as Lee had difficulty maneuvering in the harbor's swirling currents. The *Turtle* eventually was lost when the sloop transporting it was spotted and sunk

This nineteenth-century woodcut illustrates how inventor David Bushnell's submarine was hand-propelled and steered.

during the Battle of Fort Lee. The submersible did achieve a minor success when the unexplained explosion caused Admiral Howe to move his fleet to a less vulnerable position.

Bushnell made several additional—and unsuccessful—attempts to sink the British navy. In August 1778 one of his floating mines nearly sank the HMS *Cerberus* in Connecticut's Black Point Bay—but instead struck a small tender, killing four men and wounding several others. British troops, alerted to the threat, were ordered onshore and told to shoot at any floating pieces of wood. Several months later Bushnell launched several mines down the Delaware River in what became known as the Battle of the Kegs. These barrels of gunpowder failed to hit any ships, but one of them unfortunately exploded and killed two curious boys.

Washington recognized Bushnell's talents, referring to him in a letter to Jefferson as "a man of great mechanical powers, fertile in invention and a master of execution." In 1779 Washington appointed him commander of the Corps of Sappers and Miners, a predecessor of the Corps of Engineers. After the war, the father of submarine warfare spent time in France, perhaps working there with Robert Fulton, eventually returning and settling in Georgia where he worked as a physician.

❧❧

CHAPTER 5

THOMAS JEFFERSON

INDEPENDENCE DECLARED

Early in the morning of August 27, 1776, William Howard Jr. was asleep in his bedroom above his father's tavern, the Halfway House, in the city of Brooklyn. He was brusquely shaken awake and opened his eyes to see a British soldier holding a musket and bayonet inches from his head. The soldier led him downstairs, into the barroom. General William Howe, his uniform covered by a cloak, was standing by the bar, a drink in his hand. As young William would later remember, "I saw my father standing in one corner with three British soldiers before him with muskets and bayonets fixed. The army was then lying in the field in front of the house."

Howe engaged the tavern owner in calm conversation but eventually told him, "I must have some one of you to show me over the Rockaway Path." William Jr. immediately understood the gravity of the situation. There were three main roads to Brooklyn Heights where Washington's Continental army was entrenched; the passes at Gowanus, Bedford, and

☙ A detail from John Trumbull's historically inaccurate *Declaration of Independence*. The men in this painting were never together in the same room. It was hung in the Capitol rotunda in 1826.

Flatbush were all strongly guarded. But there was one additional route, through Jamaica Pass, an old Indian trail that was little more than a narrow footpath. It was guarded by only five mounted troops. While a smaller force coming through the Gowanus Pass made a frontal assault on Washington's defenses, Howe intended to march ten thousand men through this little-used pass to launch a surprise attack on the flank.

The older Howard bravely stood his ground, saying defiantly, "We belong to the other side, General, and can't serve you against our duty."

"That is all right," the young man later recalled the general responding, "stick to your country or stick to your principles, but Howard, you are my prisoner and must guide my men over the hill." The tavern owner refused again, and Howe let him speak. But when he paused the general said coldly, "You have no alternative. If you refuse I shall shoot you through the head."

William Howard understood that he had no choice. He nodded acceptance. The Battle of Brooklyn was about to begin.

After the British evacuation of Boston, Washington had taken little time to savor his victory. He guessed that Howe would next mount a campaign to capture the much larger port city of New York, "a post of infinite importance" that was not nearly as committed to the patriot cause as Boston. While the British were boarding their ships in the harbor, Washington ordered troops under the command of Brigadier General James Sullivan to rush to New York to fortify the city's defenses before Howe could get there.

Washington didn't know that Howe had no intention of proceeding directly to New York and was instead sailing to Halifax, Nova Scotia. Howe knew he had underestimated the grit, daring, and courage of the colonists' citizen army—and its commander. That was not an error he would repeat; the next time he met Washington, Howe intended to show him the might of the British army. So he would pause in Halifax to wait for thousands of reinforcements that had set sail from Europe to join his army. Washington was right: they would fight in New York, but Howe would bring with him an overwhelming force and, he hoped, once and for all end this rebellion.

On April 4 Washington wrote to Richard Henry Lee that the British withdrawal was done—"The coast is now clear of them"—and began his journey to New York. Among those who marched with his army was the recently formed Commander-in-Chief's Guards, the "Life Guards," which were charged with protecting Washington, his official papers, and considerable cash.

The army faced an uncertain welcome in New York. While the royal governor, William Tryon, had fled and was living safely aboard the seventy-four-gun HMS *Duchess of Gordon*

In one of the greatest acts of courage in American military history, at the Battle of Long Island in August 1776, troops from Maryland and Delaware militias successfully covered the retreat of Washington's army, suffering grievous casualties before withdrawing under direct British fire, as pictured here.

docked in the harbor, many Loyalists still resided in the city. The war was devastating their business. In fact, tradesmen and merchants of the city had continued to supply the British ships anchored in the harbor. One of the first things Washington did upon arriving in New York on April 14 was send a note to the city's Committee of Safety, the ruling body, pointing out, "We are to consider ourselves either in a state of peace or war with Great Britain. If the former, why are our ports shut up, our trade destroyed, our property seized, our towns burnt, and our worthy and valuable citizens led into captivity and suffering the most cruel hardships? If the latter, my imagination is not fertile enough to suggest a reason in support of the intercourse." While such trade may well have been understandable in the past, he continued, it now constituted a real danger as "it also opens a regular channel of intelligence, by which they are from time to time made acquainted with the number and extent of our works, our strength, and all our movements; by which they are enabled to regulate their own plans to our great disadvantage and injury." But he was to soon learn that at that moment it was not the British whom he had to fear.

While Washington was settling on the southern part of Manhattan Island and preparing to reinforce his defenses, the representatives of the thirteen colonies were gathering in Philadelphia to make important political decisions. Among them was the tall and elegant thirty-three-year-old scholar from Virginia, Thomas Jefferson. Unlike the firebrands from Boston, Jefferson was the epitome of quiet reason. The word "gentleman" fit no one better than him. His father had been a planter and surveyor who had married into one of the wealthiest and most prominent Virginia families, and upon the death of his parents he had inherited a vast plantation and as many as two hundred slaves. A graduate of William and Mary College, where he had read the works of the great British philosophers, he had pursued law as a career before entering public life as a magistrate and then as a member of the House of Burgesses. While serving there he had been inspired by the stirring words of another delegate, Patrick Henry, who had responded, when accused of committing treason for comparing King George III to other tyrants, "If this be treason, make the most of it." Jefferson had laid out his own belief that Great Britain had no right to govern the colonies in his radical pamphlet, "A Summary View of the Rights of British America," which had been widely circulated and established him as a leader of the liberty movement.

When Jefferson arrived in Philadelphia, he immediately joined the debate about the future of the colonies. While many delegates wanted the congress to finally declare independence, others still held hope that they might find some way of reaching a peaceful resolution. Jefferson pointed out that it was the king who had insisted the colonies bow down to him; in fact Parliament had practically declared war by passing the Prohibitory Act of 1775, which

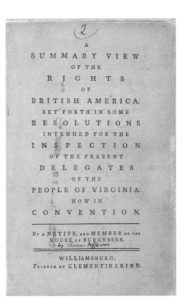

Virginia's Thomas Jefferson set down for posterity—but especially for that state's House of Burgesses—the British abuses that left colonists little choice but armed rebellion.

outlawed "all manner of trade and commerce" with the colonies and was now pressuring England's European allies to do the same.

Washington left debate to the politicians; if he was going to protect New York he needed more soldiers and equipment. His plan to defend the city required constructing earthwork fortifications in Manhattan, Brooklyn, and the Battery, the southern tip of Manhattan. At the north end of the island he reinforced Fort Washington. While these positions were strong, arming them had forced him to spread his army too thin. He stationed more than four thousand of his best men on the Brooklyn Heights, which left him woefully light in other places. Although he supposedly had twenty thousand troops, thousands of them were poorly trained, poorly equipped, or suffering from a camp illness.

In May he rode to Philadelphia, escorted by his Life Guards, to ask Congress for more troops and arms. By this point he had heard rumors that Howe was gathering a massive army in Halifax and that his brother, Admiral Howe, would join him for the attack. In fact, the king, furious after the defeat in Boston, had begun hiring seventeen thousand professional German soldiers, Hessians, to support the British army. Washington beseeched Congress: "We have not one-half the men absolutely required to hold this position; and what we have are poorly clad and equipped, and not half fed. Then we have reason to expect that the enemy will come with greater inhumanity to man, and that fire and sword will do a more fearful work than ever."

Congress eventually agreed to add twenty-three thousand men to his army. It was soon after Washington's return to New York that he discovered that he had been betrayed; Governor Tryon had somehow managed to infiltrate his closest circle, and there was a plot in progress to kill or kidnap him and his top commanders, then set fire to the city. It was, wrote future Massachusetts governor William Eustis, "the greatest and vilest attempt ever made against our country."

The Loyalists in New York had secretly remained quite active. Throughout May numerous Tories were arrested for assisting the enemy, many of them offering information to the British, but none of them had reached this level of infiltration. Governor Tryon had hatched and financed an incredibly audacious plot that, if carried out, might have ended the war. No one knows for sure how it was uncovered. In one story a woman approached Washington in mid-June and asked him for a private meeting, during which she confided in him that his life was in danger.

In another version, the daughter of tavern keeper Samuel Fraunces was working as Washing-

Long before we had a national flag, military units had their own banners. This one was created for Washington's Life Guards, the forerunner of the Secret Service, charged with protecting him.

Because the British army was fighting European enemies, Parliament hired thirty thousand German mercenaries, who fought under their own flags, commanded by their own officers. In this drawing, soldiers are departing from Hesse in 1776.

ton's housekeeper when she learned of a plan to poison his green peas with arsenic and confided in her father. Fraunces then exposed the plot to authorities. In 1785 Congress agreed that Fraunces was "instrumental in discovering and defeating" the plot and paid him a substantial sum.

What is certain is that a member of Washington's Life Guards, Thomas Hickey, was deeply involved. According to legend, Hickey was a British army deserter who had been selected to become part of this elite group in March. But after arriving in New York he had become less confident of an eventual patriot victory. At some point he had taken on a major role in this conspiracy; he was to be the assassin or the kidnapper, and after killing Washington or delivering him to Howe, he was to join others in spiking cannons in strategic locations and destroying ammunition stores.

Fortunately for Washington, on June 15 Hickey and one other member of the Guards were arrested for trying to pass counterfeit bills of credit and they were locked in custody. While awaiting trial, Hickey attempted to recruit another member of the Guards. He revealed the plot to a prisoner named Isaac Ketchum. Ketchum, who also had been caught passing counterfeit bills, reported this news to officers in an attempt to get a better deal for himself. In the following few days a small group of men loyal to Washington conducted a series of late-night raids in which more than forty people were placed under arrest, among them the mayor of New York, David Mathews, Washington's housekeeper, and an additional five or six members of his security guard. Washington himself led one of the raids. Apparently during questioning it was revealed that a woman General Washington was "especially fond of" and "maintained her genteelly" was also part of the conspiracy.

WASHINGTON AND THE GREEN PEAS.

In this 1877 wood engraving, housekeeper Phoebe Fraunces serves supposedly poisoned green peas to Washington, whom she had warned about the plot, while one of the would be assassins watches surreptitiously.

Less than two weeks later, Hickey was court-martialed, charged with "joining in a mutiny and sedition . . . and receiving pay from the enemies." He didn't deny his involvement but claimed he was only trying to make some money and ensure that if the British army were victorious, he would be safe. He was immediately declared guilty and was sentenced to be hanged. On June 28 an estimated twenty thousand people turned out to watch his execution. Intending "to make this a warning," Washington ordered every soldier not on duty to be there. At eleven a.m. Hickey was hanged, the first "American" soldier to be executed for treason.

The poisoned green peas story has been repeated for centuries, but there isn't much evidence that it's true. In the most popular versions, Phoebe Fraunces either grabbed the peas away from Washington at the very last second and threw them out the window, or warned him about them and he threw them out the window: in both, chickens ate the peas and died, proving the plot was real, and deadly.

While Washington was distracted by the conspiracy, events were taking place that would shape history. On June 8 the British fleet under the command of Admiral Lord Richard Howe had quietly slipped anchor at Halifax and sailed for New York. On the same day Hickey was hanged, the first four warships arrived off Staten Island. A lantern signal informed Washington that the British fleet had been spotted. By the next morning forty ships had assembled, and for the next several days they continued to arrive, until more than four hundred ships and transports carrying an estimated forty thousand soldiers—the largest expeditionary force in England's history—were ready to land their men and munitions. It would be more than 150 years, until World War II, that a larger naval invasion force was assembled. An American soldier wrote, "The whole bay was full of shipping as it ever could be . . . I thought all of London was afloat." On July 2 the British army landed unopposed on Staten Island. Washington had his men in place. There was nothing for him to do but wait for General Howe to attack.

Meanwhile, in the Second Continental Congress, the months of debate had finally narrowed down to one question: Would the colonies declare independence? The answer would not be reached easily. The representatives all understood that by taking this step, they would be committing high treason against the king, which had a clearly established penalty: A traitor was to be hanged by the neck but cut down while still alive, and his bowels were to be cut out and burned. Only then was his head to be cut off and his body cut into four pieces. Additionally, all of his property was to be forfeited and his family and immediate heirs were prohibited from owning property or conducting business.

On May 15 the Virginia Convention had committed itself to the path of independence, instructing its delegates "to propose to [the Congress] to declare the United Colonies free and independent States, absolved from all allegiance to, or dependence upon, the Crown or Parliament of Great Britain." On June 7 Richard Henry Lee stood up in Congress and offered the Lee Resolution, the official act of declaring independence. The following day debate began. As Jefferson wrote in his diary, some of the delegates had not yet received instructions from their legislatures and therefore could not vote. "That tho' they were friends to the measures themselves," he wrote, "and saw the impossibility that we should ever again be united with Gr. Britain, yet they were against adopting them at this time. . . . That the people of the middle colonies (Maryland, Delaware, Pennsylvania, the Jerseys and New York) were not yet ripe for bidding adieu to British connection but that they were fast ripening and in a short time would join in the general voice of America."

Other delegates, led by John Adams and Richard Lee, argued for an immediate declaration, pointing out, as Jefferson recorded, "that the question was not whether, by a declaration of independence, we should make ourselves what we are not; but whether we should declare a fact which already exists."

The opposition, led by the greatly respected John Dickinson of Pennsylvania, urged moderation, still believing that reconciliation was possible without bloodshed. A vote on Lee's resolution was postponed for three weeks to allow the delegates to receive instructions. But in anticipation of eventual approval, a Committee of Five—consisting of John Adams, Benjamin Franklin, Thomas Jefferson, Robert R. Livingston of New York, and Roger Sherman of Connecticut—was appointed to prepare a written declaration of independence. Initially they turned to John Adams, who refused, instead suggesting Jefferson. As Adams related in a letter, "Jefferson proposed to me to make the draft. I said, 'I will not,' 'You should do it. . . . Reason first, you are a Virginian, and a Virginian ought to appear at the head of this business. Reason second, I am obnoxious, suspected, and unpopular. You are very much otherwise. Reason third, you can write ten times better than I can.' 'Well,' said Jefferson, 'if you are decided, I will do as well as I can.' 'Very well. When you have drawn it up, we will have a meeting.'"

Jefferson drew up his document in only two or three days, but then spent another two weeks perfecting it, meeting occasionally and separately with "Doctor Franklin" and Adams, who apparently made very few suggestions. As Jefferson wrote years later to Henry Lee, "I did not consider it any part of my charge to invent new ideas altogether, and to offer no sentiment which had ever been expressed before. . . . This was the object of the Declaration of Independence. Not to find out new principles, or new arguments, never before thought of, not merely to say things which had never been said before; but to place before mankind the common sense of the subject."

In Alonzo Chappell's oil painting *Drafting the Declaration of Independence* (from left) Robert R. Livingston, Roger Sherman, John Adams (standing), Thomas Jefferson, and Benjamin Franklin create the most historic document in our nation's history.

Adams was delighted with its "high tone and the flights of oratory with which it abounded," although he knew parts of it would not survive congressional debate, especially a section Jefferson included "concerning negro slavery, which, though I knew his southern brethren would never suffer to pass in Congress, I certainly never would oppose." He also wondered whether it was necessary to refer to King George as a tyrant, considering it "too passionate, and too much like scolding, for so grave and solemn a document."

On June 28 Jefferson delivered his draft, titled "A Declaration by the Representatives of the United States of America, in General Congress assembled." That certainly was among the very first times the phrase "United States of America" was used in an official document.

Congress spent two days editing and revising the draft. As Adams knew, the mention of slavery was eliminated completely to retain the support of the southern states. Overall, as much as a third of the document was eliminated or changed. On July 1, the first vote was taken. Nine states voted to approve it, Pennsylvania and South Carolina voted against it, New York abstained to await further directions from the state assembly, and Delaware did not cast a vote because its two delegates were split.

On July 2, an official vote was taken on Richard Lee's resolution. There were twelve yea votes, with New York abstaining. The thirteen colonies had united to declare their independence from Great Britain. Two days later, after about eighty minor revisions to the text of the declaration, it, too, was adopted. Jefferson, who took great pride in his effort, was reportedly furious at the number of changes, but the Declaration of Independence as adopted—with all of its compromises—has served as a model for other nations around the world. Those brave fifty-six men who affixed their signatures knew it was substantially more than an official document; for them it was a death warrant. With their signatures, they were committing treason.

John Adams wrote to Abigail, "The second day of July 1776 will be the most memorable Epocha in the history of America. . . . It ought to be commemorated as the day of deliverance . . . solemnized with pomp and parade, with shows, games, sports, guns, bells, bonfires and illuminations from one end of this continent to the other."

It is not surprising that several myths swirl around the story of the signing of the most important document in American history. First, while in re-creations of the day, the founding fathers lined up to sign the declaration, in fact no one really knows who signed it when. It is generally agreed that John Hancock, president of the Congress, was the first to sign on July 4, most others signed a parchment copy on August 2, and a few others added their signatures in the ensuing weeks and even months. Supposedly, when signing in bold strokes, Hancock explained that he was writing so large so that "King George will be able to read that." There isn't any evidence that he actually said these words or anything close. Also, in legend, Hancock acknowledged that all the signers would hang together, to which Franklin replied, "We must indeed all hang together, or most assuredly we shall all hang separately." That quote appeared in print for the first time half a century after the signing.

After Congress voted its approval, an estimated two hundred copies of the document, bearing only the names of Hancock and the secretary of the Congress, Charles Thomson,

Signers of the Times

On the twenty-fifth anniversary of the signing of the Declaration of Independence, Dr. Benjamin Rush wrote to his close friend John Adams, "Do you recollect the pensive and awful silence which pervaded the house when we were called up, one after another, to the table of the President of Congress to subscribe to what was believed by many at that time to be our own death warrants? The silence and the gloom of the morning were interrupted, I well recollect, only for a moment by Colonel Harrison of Virginia, who said to Mr. Elbridge Gerry at the table, 'I shall have a great advantage over you, Mr. Gerry, when we are all hung for what we are now doing. From the size and weight of my body I shall die in a few minutes, but from the lightness of your body you will dance in the air an hour or two before you are dead.'"

The British had made it clear that affixing one's signature to the Declaration of Independence was a treasonous act, punishable by hanging. Each of the fifty-six delegates who signed it knew the risk he was taking, and doing so at a time when few people believed the colonies could defeat the mighty British army. And while the names of many of these founding fathers live in our history—men like John and Samuel Adams, John Hancock, Benjamin Franklin, Thomas Jefferson, and Richard Henry Lee—many others have been largely forgotten. But these were all men of substantial achievements, some of whom went on to make additional small marks in history, while others met a sadder fate.

Among the lesser-known signers was the thoroughly abrasive delegate from Maryland, Samuel Chase, who was known to his fellows as Old Bacon Face. Chase was a renowned orator of the time and credited with convincing

Maryland to vote for independence—although he personally did not sign the document until August 2. As a member of the Continental Congress, he was suspected of using inside information to corner the flour market and eventually lost his seat, but his tarnished reputation was restored when Washington appointed him to the Supreme Court. It was as an associate justice that he gained another kind of recognition—becoming the only Supreme Court justice to be impeached. The House claimed he allowed his political bias to affect several lower court decisions; but in fact this was a political maneuver by President Jefferson to remove Federalists from the bench. The effort failed when Chase was acquitted by the Senate, a result that many historians believe helped guarantee an independent judiciary.

Connecticut's Samuel Huntington has lived in history as the answer to a tricky trivia question: Who really was the first president of the United States? Huntington may have been the only delegate to the Continental Congress who had no formal education; he was raised on his family's farm and became a cooper, or barrel maker, and eventually a practicing attorney and judge. In 1779 he was elected president of the Congress and was serving in that position on March 1, 1781, when the Articles of Confederation were officially adopted, transforming the thirteen sovereign colonies into the United States of America. On that day his new title became president of the United States in

Samuel Huntington

Congress Assembled. While he did have a few powers as the leader of this new nation, in fact the executive office wasn't created until the Constitution was ratified in 1787.

It is probable that no delegate traveled a longer distance to independence, both literally and figuratively, than Pennsylvania's George Taylor. Born in Ireland, making him one of the eight foreign-born signers of the Declaration of Independence, he immigrated to Pennsylvania in 1736. He paid for his passage by becoming indentured, or bound, to a Philadelphia iron maker until he had worked off his debt. He rose from shoveling coal into the furnace to bookkeeper, and, when the iron maker died, he married the widow and took control of the business. He expanded the works and, as a successful businessman, was elected to the Pennsylvania Assembly. When five Loyalist representatives to the Continental Congress were forced to resign before the vote for independence, he was one of the men appointed to replace them. Signing the Declaration of Independence on August 2, 1776, may have been the first thing he did in Congress; seven months later he was replaced. But he did make one additional contribution to freedom: his furnaces produced grapeshot, cannons, and cannonballs, in addition to other weapons. He died at age sixty in 1781—before the war was won.

While none of the signers was punished by death for treason, Virginia's George Wythe was the only delegate to be murdered. Wythe was considered among the brightest and most respected members of the Congress; Jefferson

George Wythe

referred to him as "my second father" and "my faithful and beloved mentor in youth, and my most affectionate friend through life." He also was a leader in the debates about how best to respond to the British acts and was considered an important adviser to James Monroe, John Marshall, and Henry Clay. He, too, signed the Declaration of Independence in August, then left Congress to work with Jefferson in creating a constitutional system in Virginia. Accepting a job offer from the College of William and Mary, he is recognized as the nation's first law professor. In keeping with his commitment to human rights, he freed his own slaves, although two of them remained in his house to care for him in his dotage. Wythe had provided for both of them in his will, although his grand-nephew was to inherit the bulk of his estate. This grand-nephew also would inherit the bequest to the former slaves if they died before Wythe.

One morning Wythe's housekeeper saw this grand-nephew furtively throw a piece of paper in the fire and later that day, after drinking coffee,

Wythe and his two helpers were felled by terrible stomach pains. One of the former slaves died and Wythe lingered for weeks in terrible pain before finally crying out, "I am murdered" and dying. The grand-nephew was arrested for using arsenic to poison two people, disposing of the packet in the fire. Ironically, because black men and women were not legally permitted to bear witness against whites, the killer was acquitted. A legal technicality allowed Wythe's murderer to get away with his crimes, although he was disinherited.

Only a few men who signed the Declaration of Independence actually suffered because of it; among them were New Jersey delegates "Honest John" Hart and Richard Stockton. Hart was an uneducated New Jersey farmer admired for his common sense and plainspoken manner. After casting his vote for independence, he was elected the speaker of New Jersey's first assembly. In December 1776, as British troops approached his farm, the recently widowed Hart sent his children to live with friends, then escaped into nearby Sourland Mountain. According to legend, for the next few months the sixty-five-year-old Hart survived in the wild, sleeping in caves and snow-covered forests, for a time finding shelter in a natural rock formation known as the Rock House. When the patriots defeated the British at Princeton, they began to withdraw, allowing Hart to return. Although his home and lands had been plundered, he was able to rebuild and resume his position in the New Jersey legislature.

Richard Stockton was considerably less fortunate. Unlike Hart, Stockton was born into wealth—his father donated the land where Princeton University stands—and he became a well-known lawyer, horse breeder, and art collector. But he was as committed to the cause of freedom as Hart and drew up a plan that could have avoided the war by allowing America to become a self-governing British Commonwealth, like Australia. When his plan was rejected by the king and Parliament, he became more active in the fight, donating substantial sums to feed, supply, and arm Washington's soldiers. After signing the Declaration of Independence, Stockton returned to his family's palatial estate, known as Morven, which in later years served as the official residence of New Jersey's governor. When the British invaded the state, he remained there until every soldier in the area was safely gone before

Contrary to the legend in which the fifty-six signers of the Declaration lined up on July 4, 1776, and one-by-one risked death by affixing their names to it, many weeks passed before the document was finally signed.

fleeing with his family to stay with friends thirty miles away in Monmouth. But someone betrayed him and he was arrested by Loyalists, put in irons, and eventually imprisoned in New York. Congress passed a resolution urging Washington to take whatever steps necessary to secure Stockton's release; and while the legend is that he was freed in a prisoner exchange, there also is evidence that General Howe pardoned him after Stockton signed a document in which he swore allegiance to the king and agreed to cease involvement in the war. If he did sign such an agreement— and no one knows for certain what papers he signed—he was the only man who recanted his signature, but he did so only after suffering in prison. He returned home considerably weakened and was soon diagnosed with cancer. Those people who knew him well continued to support him, and after his death at age fifty in 1781, Washington wrote to his widow, "Be assured we can never forget our friend at Morven."

Ironically, among this group of lesser-known signers, Georgia's Button Gwinnett has gained the most fame. Gwinnett must have had quite a winning personality, because before entering politics he accomplished little other than borrowing considerable sums of money and losing it. He convinced various

people to loan him money to immigrate to America from England—he was one of only two signers born in England—open a business in South Carolina, and buy a Georgia plantation, without ever repaying anyone. He also convinced Georgians to send him to the Continental Congress, where he voted for and signed the Declaration of Independence, and then, upon the death of the state's governor, to make him acting governor. A feud with Colonel Lachlan McIntosh, commander of Georgia's Continental

Button Gwinnett

Army militia, was settled with a duel, which resulted in Gwinnett's death from gangrene. But what has made Gwinnett so memorable, besides the several places in Georgia that bear his name, is not what he did but rather what he did not do—he did not sign his name to many documents other than the Declaration of Independence. In fact, only about fifty examples of his signature are known to exist, apparently most of them IOUs, making it the rarest and most expensive autograph of all the signers—and a great prize for collectors. Most of his autographs are owned by libraries and museums. A document he signed was sold in 2011 for $722,500—among the most valuable signatures in history.

The men who signed the Declaration of Independence were rich and poor; they were among the best educated and least educated people in the country; they were native born or immigrants from Europe; they were brave and . . . less brave; they were lawyers and ministers, farmers and coopers. Twenty-six-year-old Edward Rutledge was the youngest to sign and seventy-year-old Ben Franklin the oldest. In other words, they were as different as any group of more than fifty people might be. But one thing brought them together: the courage to risk their lives to declare America a free and independent nation.

were printed and distributed to newspapers throughout the thirteen colonies. Because signing it was an act of treason, the names of the signers were kept secret until the following year. On July 8, the document was read publicly for the first time. On the ninth, George Washington read it to many of his troops gathered in Bowling Green, Brooklyn, and ordered his brigade commanders to read it to those who could not attend; in response, his army pulled down an equestrian statue of King George III, ripped off its head, and carried it high atop a pole through the narrow streets of the city. That statue subsequently was melted down to provide more than forty-two thousand musket balls and bullets of "melted majesty," as one patriot described them. Similar acts of defiance took place in cities throughout the states as these newly anointed "Americans" celebrated by tearing down British signs, knocking over statues, ringing the bells of freedom, and lighting great bonfires.

The announcement that the Declaration had been signed was greeted by celebrations throughout the colonies. In this fanciful 1776 engraving, turbaned black men, presumably slaves, pull down a statue of King George III in Bowling Green, New York City.

And as the newly proclaimed nation celebrated, the massive British fleet began lifting anchor.

It took more than a month for news of the Declaration of Independence to reach England. On August 10 the *London Gazette* reported that a letter from General Howe read, "I am informed that the Continental Congress have declared the United Colonies free and independent states." By that point shots already had been fired in New York.

On July 12, Lord Richard Howe, or "Black Dick," as he was known, had dispatched the forty-four-gun *Phoenix* and twenty-four-gun *Rose* to probe American shore defenses along the Hudson River. The ships sailed several miles inland, to Tarrytown, as soldiers on land watched in awe. As they turned and began cruising back to New York, Lieutenant Alexander Hamilton, commander of a battery built on Bayard's Hill, the tallest point on Manhattan Island, ordered his men to fire on them. His gunners loaded and lit their nine-pounders. These were the first rounds ever to be fired in defense of the United States of America—and one of the cannons blew up. The misfire killed six of Hamilton's men. This was a disaster for the twenty-year-old Hamilton, whose excellent work had previously caught the attention of General Washington.

Alexander Hamilton was an unlikely American leader. He had been born on the West Indies island of Nevis, the illegitimate son of a Scottish merchant and a divorced young woman. He proved to be a brilliant student and at seventeen was sent to the colonies by several patrons to further his education. He settled finally at King's College, which is now Columbia University, in New York. In 1775, his passions aroused by the growing demands for freedom, he dropped out of school and organized his own volunteer militia unit. When the sixty-four-gun British man-of-war *Asia* sailed for Halifax in late August of that year, his unit was ordered to seize a battery of twenty-four cannons seemingly abandoned on the southern tip of Manhattan. In fact, the British had set up a clever ambush. As Hamilton's unit moved into the fort, redcoats waiting on a patrol barge floating just offshore opened fire on them with their muskets. The militia returned fire, killing one soldier. The *Asia* returned, letting loose a thirty-two-gun broadside. One shell went through the roof of the famed Fraunces Tavern. Hamilton proved his cool under fire, continuing to labor until he and the men with him successfully hauled away twenty-one cannons.

Hamilton's mathematical prowess earned him a reputation as an outstanding artillery officer, capable of plotting and adjusting the trajectory of his cannons. In March 1776, New York appointed him captain of its new artillery unit and allowed him to recruit twenty-five men. When Washington's army arrived to prepare the city for battle, Hamilton and his men constructed such a splendid fortification on Bayard's Hill that Washington praised them "for their masterly manner of executing the work." Hamilton clearly was a young officer to watch—until his cannon exploded. There were some reports that his men had been "at their cups," meaning their celebration had continued too long and they were drunk.

Whatever the truth of it, there was little Washington could do. A great army sitting offshore was preparing for battle and he needed every man. Earlier in the summer he had contemplated launching his own offensive on the British troops that had landed on Staten Island, catching them before their preparations were complete. Major General Lord Stirling apparently had drawn up a plan of attack, but a lack of able men and sufficient boats prevented him from going ahead.

On August 8, Washington put his army on twenty-four-hour watch, warning them, "The movements of the enemy and intelligence by deserters give the utmost reason to believe that the great struggle in which we are contending for everything dear to us and our posterity, is near at hand. . . . The fate of unborn millions will now depend, under God, on the courage and conduct of this army. . . . We have therefore to resolve to conquer or die."

The British kept their powder dry. While American history tends to portray them as ruthless aggressors, they actually made substantial efforts to prevent more bloodshed. Admiral Howe, who years earlier had become close with Benjamin Franklin and almost seemed sympathetic to the colonial cause, had tried to avoid this battle. Twice in July he had sent a letter addressed to George Washington, Esquire, in which he offered a basis for reconciliation, offering a pardon for everyone who professed loyalty to the king. Washington's aide, Colonel Joseph Reed, would not accept the letter, pointing out that it was improperly addressed and explaining that there was no such person in the camp of that name, the only Washington being His Excellency General George Washington. A second letter, this one addressed to "George Washington, Esquire and etc. etc." also was refused. Washington finally agreed to meet with Howe's adjutant, Colonel James Patterson, on July 20.

Patterson brought the letter with him. He regretted that General Howe was powerless to use that title because doing so meant he was endorsing the legitimacy of the rebellion. He suggested that "etc. etc." meant "everything" that would follow. Washington countered that it also could be construed to mean "anything." Patterson made the offer of pardons and again Washington corrected him, pointing out that Americans had done nothing wrong; they simply were defending their rights. Thus, as they had committed no crimes, they had no need of a pardon. Patterson continued to search for a means to resolve the conflict short of battle. Washington refused to relent. For a man facing an army of forty thousand professional soldiers supported by a great naval armada with less than half that number of men, it was a remarkable display of courage. The letter sat unopened.

In a final effort, while thousands of British troops were stepping ashore on Staten Island, Admiral Howe had a copy of the letter delivered to his friend Benjamin Franklin, who thanked him for the offer but rejected it respectfully, because it contained only "offers of pardon upon submission." Howe responded by claiming that he had the king's authority to negotiate "a lasting peace and reunion" if only the Americans would acknowledge the supremacy of the king.

Washington was a realist, yet the victory over a superior force in Boston must have emboldened him. In a letter to Hancock earlier in the summer he had written, "If our troops will behave well . . . [the British] will have to wade through much blood and slaughter before they can carry any part of our works, if they carry 'em at all."

Washington's commanders were not so certain. General Nathanael Greene, who commanded the troops on Long Island, proposed withdrawing the army and burning the city, depriving the British of its benefits, and saving the army to fight again under more favorable conditions. Washington admitted that he had considered that possibility but had decided to make his stand there.

By mid-August Howe's army had made camp on Staten Island. Watching this vast army prepare for battle, an American captain named Nathan Hale wrote to his brother, "For about six or eight days the enemy have been expected hourly, whenever the wind and tide in the least favored. . . . We hope, under God, to give a good account of the enemy whenever they choose to make the last appeal."

John Adams wrote Abigail, "The eyes of the world are upon Washington and Howe and their armies."

On August 22, Howe ferried twenty-two thousand troops and forty pieces of artillery across the Narrows from Staten Island to Gravesend Bay, in Brooklyn. They marched six miles inland, making camp at the village of Flatbush. Washington felt certain that the main assault would be made on Manhattan and that this was a bluff, intended to draw his troops out of their well-defended positions. He had put fewer than three thousand men and thirty-six cannons in Brooklyn, spread out in four shabbily constructed forts, connected by four miles of entrenchments. When he was notified that Howe's troops had landed there, he sent an additional fifteen hundred to join General Greene's forces.

All attempts at making peace had failed, and Howe prepared for battle. He would not repeat the mistakes he'd made in Boston. This time he would seize the offensive with an overwhelming army and continue fighting until the rebellion was crushed. On the night of August 27, he walked into William Howard's Halfway House, and sometime later he walked out with Howard and his son, who would guide his men through the night.

Howe's column was two miles long, led by guides followed by "pioneers," who were to saw down any trees that blocked the passage of cannons. His men had left their campfires burning to deceive any Americans who might be watching. Soon into their journey, five American guards, who mistakenly believed the approaching troops were friendly, were captured without a shot being fired.

Just before midnight on August 26, the first shots of a battle that was to become known as both the Battle of Brooklyn and the Battle of Long Island were fired. The British began the frontal assault through the Gowanus Pass, one of the four routes into Brooklyn. The Americans, occupying the high ground, fought back ferociously. Washington's strategy was to meet the initial assault, then have his men retreat into the fortifications on Brooklyn Heights—knowing that the British would pursue them right into his cannons. The superior position on top of the hill would give the Americans a strategic advantage.

At precisely 9:00 a.m. Howe fired his cannons, the signal that the flanking attack was about to begin. At that moment Hessian troops began a frontal assault on the center of Washington's defenses. At about the same time Washington accepted that he had been wrong, that this was the real attack, and ordered more troops to move quickly to Brooklyn. The Americans initially were able to blunt the attack, not yet aware of Howe's flanking maneuver. But as the battle raged, Howe's trap was revealed. The American troops were blocked on three sides, and the only possible escape was across the eighty-yard-wide Gowanus Creek. With no other option available, and some of his units now outnumbered by as much as ten to one, Washington ordered a retreat to the fortifications on Brooklyn Heights.

As the main elements of the American army desperately withdrew, Lord Stirling's 1st Maryland Regiment, known as the Maryland 400, held the line against the overwhelming British force for more than a half hour at a place known as the Old Stone House. The regiment made as many as six counterattacks on troops commanded by General Charles Cornwallis, trying to break through the lines. The Hessians took no prisoners, bayoneting even those men who threw down their muskets and surrendered. A British regular wrote in his diary, "We took care to tell the Hessians that the rebels had resolved to give no quarter to them in particular, which made them fight desperately, and put all to death that fell into their hands."

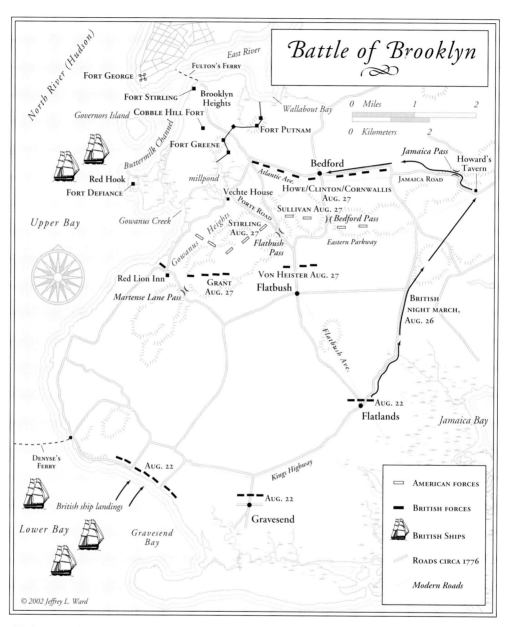

This map of the Battle of Brooklyn, also known as the Battle of Long Island, includes numerous details about the fighting in which the British conquered New York.

Watching this battle at a distance, General Washington remarked with great sadness to one of his commanders, General Putnam, "Good God, what brave fellows I must this day lose."

After more than 3,000 men had successfully escaped the trap, the surviving Marylanders made a break for it, trying to get across the creek. Many of them got bogged down in the mud and only 12 men made it safely back to American lines. More than 360 Americans died that day and another 1,100 were wounded or captured. Lord Stirling was surrounded and taken prisoner, but his courage and that of his men, who sacrificed themselves for this new country, had saved Washington's army. In reports of the battle one newspaper referred to him as "the bravest man in America."

The American losses had been catastrophic. According to General Howe's reports, the British had lost only 367 men.

With his victory assured, Howe made a fateful decision. The American fortification on Brooklyn Heights was about two miles across and one mile deep. A frontal assault would cost hundreds, perhaps thousands of lives. So rather than pressing his attack as his staff suggested, Howe ordered his army to halt. With his army in front of the entrenched Americans and the Royal Navy blocking the East River at their rear, there appeared to be no escape for the patriots. Howe ordered his cannons brought forward, stretched his lines to encircle Washington's troops, and settled in for a siege, confident that Washington's army must either surrender or die on the heights.

Once again, though, the weather intervened unexpectedly. A nasty rainstorm accompanied by unfriendly winds on the twenty-eighth made it impossible for the British fleet to sail up the East River, which separated Washington's troops in Brooklyn from the safety of Manhattan. While the British built earthworks in preparation for their eventual attack, Washington spent that day visiting camps and encouraging his men, trying to raise their battered morale. But as the toll of the battle became clearer to him, he accepted the vulnerability of his position. Somehow he had to get his men across the river directly under the watchful eyes of the enemy. To make that feat possible, he turned to Colonel John Glover and his "Marvelous Men from Marblehead," the 14th Continental Regiment, consisting almost entirely of Massachusetts fishermen.

John Glover had been serving in the militia since 1759. During the Siege of Boston, Washington had chartered Glover's schooner, the *Hannah*, to harass and raid British supply ships. The *Hannah* was the first privateer in the service of the Continental army, and it has been celebrated as the first ship of the United States Navy. Washington told Glover that somehow, in the dark of night, he and his men had to ferry the entire American army across

General Howe's victorious
army lands in New York in
September 1776, beginning
an occupation that was to last
seven years.

the river. An aide, Colonel Benjamin Tallmadge, later wrote of the situation in a letter: "To move so large a body of troops, with all their necessary appendages, across a river a full mile wide, with a rapid current, in the face of a victorious, well-disciplined army nearly three times as numerous . . . and a fleet capable of stopping the navigation so that not one boat could have passed over, seemed to present most formidable obstacles."

No one knows for certain how Glover was able to assemble his makeshift armada within a few hours. And yet he did it, pulling together a miniature fleet of rowboats, sailboats, one schooner, and numerous flat-bottomed craft capable of carrying horses and artillery.

In addition to somehow hiding this massive operation from the enemy, they had to overcome three natural factors: time, tides, and the wind—and any of them could prevent or end the operation. Washington was depending on the dark to conceal the evacuation, and the late August night was one of the shortest of the year. Any man left on shore at sunrise would be lost. Unfriendly tides might make rowing more difficult, and a lack of wind would make sailing impossible.

But Washington had no choice. Suspecting that spies in his camp would see Glover's boats gathering and give away his plans, he devised a clever ruse. He sent a message to General William Heath in Manhattan, advising him, "We have many battalions from New Jersey which are coming over this evening to relieve those here. You will please, therefore to order every flat-bottomed boat and other craft fit for transportation of troops down to New York as soon as possible." If that message was intercepted, as Washington thought it would be, Howe would believe the boats were to carry reinforcements to Long Island rather than ferry Washington's army to Manhattan. To get his men ready without disclosing the plan, he ordered his commanders to prepare them for a nighttime attack.

The storm remained stationary over the area, the thick, dark clouds blocking the moon and intermittent rain obscuring visibility for more than a few feet. One of the most unusual episodes of the Revolutionary War began at ten o'clock. The troops were told unit by unit that they were being relieved and sent back to Manhattan, so none knew that the whole army was retreating. They were ordered to leave their fires burning and their tents in place, cover their wagon wheels with rags to muffle their sounds, and then proceed briskly and silently to the river.

Glover had managed to assemble a fleet of oars and sail, manned by the seamen of Marblehead. For the first few hours the evacuation went well, and the cooperating winds and tides enabled the boats to make the two-mile round-trip without difficulty. But after midnight, with half the army still on Long Island, the winds shifted and an unusually strong ebb tide made the trip long and difficult for rowboats and sailing ships alike. The sailors struggled through the night, and a few hours before sunrise the winds shifted once again and caught the sails. It was an efficient operation, but as dawn approached Washington realized it had not been good enough. The rearguard was still waiting on the shore for transport and there were only minutes until the sun revealed their presence.

In many of his letters and diary entries during the war, Washington made reference to Providence, the hand of God or nature that had helped deliver his men. This certainly was one of those instances. As the sun rose on the morning of the twenty-ninth, a dense blanket of fog rolled in and covered the entire area, saving hundreds of men. It would take more than an hour before the sun would burn it off, and by then all nine thousand troops and almost all of the horses, supplies, powder, and cannons were safely across the river.

Washington and Colonel Benjamin Tallmadge were among the last men to leave. Tallmadge regrettably had to leave his favorite horse tied to a tree—but when he reached the

After being defeated in the Battle of Long Island, Washington successfully saved the remnants of his army with a daring retreat, pictured here, across the treacherous mile-wide East River. If Howe had been able to prevent this withdrawal, the revolution might have ended on the shores of Long Island.

other side he decided to go back and get it. "I called for a crew of volunteers to go with me," he wrote, "and guiding the boat myself, I obtained my horse and got off some distance into the river before the enemy appeared in Brooklyn."

Later that day the British fleet sailed up the East River, but the miraculous escape was a complete success. In only nine hours, Washington's army had been saved.

The question became what to do now. From the high points the British now occupied in Brooklyn, Howe's artillery could reach much of the city. Within hours they could reduce it to rubble or burn it to the ground. Washington did not believe either was likely. With so many Loyalists still living in the city, Howe would not dare destroy it, and his troops would need the houses and buildings through the winter months. He would have to attack, Washington knew, and drive the American army out of the city.

Perhaps more than anything else at that moment, Washington needed reliable intelligence. He needed to know what Howe intended to do and when he would strike. He needed to know the disposition of his forces and the level of his powder and supplies. What Washington needed was a reliable spy.

At the time, spies were considered men without honor or integrity. Most often they were civilians living behind enemy lines who would pass along intelligence because they believed in the cause, were paid, or were threatened. Washington had previously sent several spies on missions but had received only sketchy and somewhat dubious information from them. But he was desperate. With his army outnumbered, and soldiers deserting in growing numbers, his only chance for victory was to learn the enemy's plans. As he complained on September 6, "We have not been able to obtain the least information as to the enemy's plans."

Finally Washington turned to Thomas Knowlton, who, a month earlier, had been promoted to lieutenant colonel and authorized to form a small and select unit to carry out specialized reconnaissance missions. This consisted primarily of going out well in front of the army and observing enemy movements through a telescope. Knowlton's Rangers were America's first unit of elite troops. Knowlton himself had already distinguished himself on special missions. During the Siege of Boston, Washington had sent him into the city to burn the buildings at the base of Bunker Hill that provided cover for the redcoats and to capture a British guard for interrogation. Knowlton accomplished that mission without being detected.

Among the men Knowlton selected for his Rangers was a twenty-one-year-old school-teacher named Nathan Hale. After graduating from Yale University, Hale had taken a position at a public school supported by "the gentlemen of New London, Connecticut." Like so many other young men, he shared the dream of freedom. He had already joined the local militia. Days after Lexington and Concord, he stood up at a meeting in church and proclaimed,

"Let us march immediately, and never lay down our arms until we obtain our independence." Hale was determined to finish the last few months of his contract at the school, but then he received a letter from his classmate and friend, Benjamin Tallmadge. "Was I in your condition," Tallmadge wrote, "I think the more extensive service would be my choice. Our holy religion, the honor of our God, a glorious country, and a happy constitution is what we have to defend." The next day Hale resigned his teaching position and accepted a commission as first lieutenant in the 7th Connecticut Regiment. He served loyally through the opening months of the war but saw no combat. When offered the opportunity to join Knowlton's unit—possibly because he was one of the few Yale graduates serving on the front lines—he accepted the challenge. He was put in command of a reconnaissance company watching the Westchester and Manhattan shorelines. It was important but tedious work.

In early September Washington had called upon Knowlton to find a volunteer willing to put on civilian clothes and go behind the English lines to gather intelligence. It isn't known if Washington found it necessary to remind the colonel that the ignoble penalty for spying was death by hanging. Knowlton gathered his officers and told them about this conversation, then asked if there was a volunteer. After several seconds of absolute silence, Nathan Hale spoke up, the only person to do so, volunteering, "I will undertake it."

Another classmate from the university, William Hull, tried to talk Hale out of what he believed to be a suicide mission. It was a dangerous job, Hull said, and Hale lacked the experience and the necessary tools. He had no training for the work, nor did he have the nature for it: Hale was "of too frank and open a temper to act successfully the part of a spy, or to face its dangers; he was too open to deceit and disguise, and it probably would lead to an ignominious death." Hull pleaded with him to "abandon the enterprise . . . for the love of country, for the love of kindred." The risk was too great. Live; and fight for the country!

Hale listened politely to his friend, then explained, "I wish to be useful, and every kind of service necessary to the public good becomes honorable by being necessary. If the exigencies of my country demand a peculiar service, its claims to perform that service are imperious." He had spent more than a year in service, and he had been paid, but had made no accomplishment worth mentioning. As he had wished, he finally was getting the opportunity to do something meaningful for his country.

While there is no official record of Nathan Hale meeting with General Washington, which is not surprising considering the highly secretive circumstances, the story has been told that they did indeed meet privately. And undoubtedly Washington praised his courage and outlined his needs for information. No one knows if Washington watched Hale depart.

Crossing the Delaware

German artist Emanuel Leutze's circa-1850 painting of George Washington crossing the ice-covered Delaware River may be the best-known image from the Revolutionary War. In this painting General Washington is standing nobly in the front of a small boat as oarsmen push large chunks of ice away, while other boats are slightly in the distance behind him. It is indeed a stirring image, although it bears little resemblance to what actually happened. The real story is far more heroic than the artist portrayed.

By the end of 1776 a series of defeats had pushed Washington's army out of New York and New Jersey. The once promising lamp of freedom had

Washington Crossing the Delaware, oil on canvas, Emanuel Leutze.

dimmed. It was becoming clear that this colonial army was no match for the haughty British and their Hessian allies. In late December the patriots were camped in Delaware with little hope of victory. The army was already weak and under-supplied and many men intended to go home when their enlistments expired at the end of the month. There was a small boost in morale in late December when Washington ordered Thomas Paine's stirring new pamphlet, "The American Crisis," read to his troops: "These are the times that try men's souls," Paine wrote. "The summer soldier and the sunshine patriot will, in this crisis, shrink from the service of his country; but he that stands it now, deserves the love and thanks of man and woman. Tyranny, like hell, is not easily conquered; yet we have this consolation with us, that the harder the conflict, the more glorious the triumph."

But Washington knew that far more than inspirational words were necessary. His men needed the hope that only a military victory could provide. While the enemy sat safe and secure in his winter headquarters, Washington knew that he had only one significant advantage: surprise. And so he planned one of the most audacious, difficult, and unexpected attacks in military history. It was a bold stroke and the outcome of the war might depend on his success. Under the cover of night he intended to row and pole thousands of troops across the swollen Delaware River to surprise the Hessian troops warmly encamped in Trenton. The password for attack was straightforward: "victory or death."

Washington's troops certainly must have been stunned that Christmas Day when informed at regular afternoon muster that they were about to embark on a secret mission. They marched silently to the river and waited till dark—and as they did the weather turned on them. The wind began to blow and it started snowing. Rather than the daylight crossing in fair weather depicted in Leutze's painting, the extraordinarily dangerous crossing was made during a raging storm in the night.

An estimated twenty-four hundred men, eighteen cannons and ammunition, and as many as seventy-five horses made the crossing, engineered by Colonel Henry Knox. Supposedly among them were future presents James Monroe and James Madison, future Supreme Court justice John Marshall, and Alexander Hamilton and Aaron Burr. Rather than the shallow rowboat in the painting, they used flat-bottomed freight boats and almost definitely Washington remained seated; if he had attempted to stand up in a small boat while crossing an ice-filled river in a storm, the result most probably would have been disastrous.

Other details in the painting also are inaccurate, among them the fact that the flag being carried in the boat actually wouldn't exist for another six months and that chunks of ice did not clog the Delaware.

But the defiant spirit conveyed by Leutze is absolutely accurate. Washington certainly understood what he was risking that night. Three contingents were scheduled to cross the river, but only the largest group, led by Washington, successfully made the crossing. Washington decided to proceed with his mission, a direct attack on the Hessian camp at Trenton. One of the soldiers who made that crossing later wrote, "Our horses were then unharnessed and the artillery men prepared. We marched on and it was not long before we heard the out sentries of the enemy . . . retreated firing, and our army, then with a quick step pushing on upon both roads, at the same time entered the town. Their artillery taken, they resigned with little opposition, all Hessians, with 4 brass field pieces; the remainder crossing the bridge at the lower end of the town escaped."

While popular history infers that Washington caught the Hessians stuffed, drunk, and sleepy from a night of celebrations, respected historians report no evidence of that. In fact, fife player John Greenwood wrote, "I am certain not a drop of liquor was drunk during the whole night, nor, as I could see, even a piece of bread eaten, and I am willing to go upon oath that I did not see even a solitary drunken soldier belonging to the enemy."

The surprise attack had been a complete success, catching the enemy unprepared. The Hessians fought bravely but briefly before surrendering. A reported twenty-two Hessians were killed, eighty-three wounded, and almost nine hundred men captured, in addition to a substantial store of weapons and supplies. Two Americans died from frostbite because they had no shoes and eight others were injured in the fighting, among them future president James Monroe, who nearly bled to death. While the plan originally called for Washington's army to march on Princeton and New Brunswick after capturing Trenton, the failure of the other two elements to reach their objectives made that impossible. Washington wisely withdrew with his prisoners—and his victory.

While the capture of almost a thousand men surely was significant, the victory's greater value was in boosting morale. It demonstrated that ordinary Americans could defeat the previously feared Hessians. General Howe supposedly was stunned that his elite—and expensive—soldiers could be so easily captured by the rebels. Some historians believe the Battle of Trenton may have even marked the turning point of the war. Congress, greatly buoyed by the success, agreed to pay a $10 bonus to each man who agreed

This heroic portrait of Washington about to dismount and join his army in crossing the Delaware River was painted in 1819 by famed American portrait artist Thomas Sully.

to stay for an additional six weeks after his enlistment ended. As the soldier Elisha Bostwick recorded, "I engaged to stay that time and made every exertion in my power to make as many of the soldiers stay with me as I could, and quite a number did engage with me who otherwise would have went [*sic*] home."

The monumentally large romantic painting *Washington Crossing the Delaware* is twelve feet by twenty-one feet and was painted in Düsseldorf, Germany. When it was exhibited in 1851, more than fifty thousand people came to see it. It is now on display at the Metropolitan Museum of Art in New York.

CHAPTER 6

Benedict Arnold

American Traitor

General Howe's army had been settled in New York City for only a few days when the great fire began during the afternoon of September 21, 1776. It was believed to have been ignited near the Fighting Cocks Tavern, a bar and brothel in the lower part of the city not far from Whitehall Slip in the Battery. It raged throughout the night, spread by a southwest wind. By the time it burned itself out, more than five hundred buildings, as much as a quarter of the entire city, had been destroyed.

The British immediately suspected arson. Alarm bells had disappeared, handles had been cut off fire buckets, and many of the city's cisterns were mysteriously empty. Even as new fires appeared to spring up without cause, incensed soldiers raced through the city arresting—or killing—suspects. "Some of them were caught with matches and fire-balls about them," wrote an eyewitness to the Great Fire of New York, Ambrose Serle. "One man, detected in the act, was knocked down by a grenadier and thrown into the

🖎 A mezzotint of Colonel Benedict Arnold, "who commanded the Provincial Troops sent against Quebec through the wilderness of Canada and was wounded in storming that city under General Montgomery," published in 1776, oddly, in London.

flames for his reward. Another, who was found cutting off the handles of water buckets to prevent their use, was first hung by the neck till he was dead and afterwards by the heels upon a signpost by the sailors. Many others were seized . . . and, but for the officers, most of them would have been killed by the enraged populace and soldiery."

Officially the cause of the fire was never determined. But the royal governor, William Tryon, blamed Washington, claiming, "Some officers of his army were found concealed in the city." Among them was Nathan Hale.

Disguised as a schoolteacher seeking employment, supposedly carrying his Yale diploma, Hale had spent several days behind British lines gathering information. His notes and hand-drawn maps were concealed in the soles of his shoes as he waited on the Brooklyn shores to meet the boat that would carry him to safety. It isn't known how Hale was captured. There were claims he was recognized and exposed by a Loyalist cousin, Samuel Hale. But most

This hand-colored French etching from about 1778 depicts the looting and violence that took place during the great fire that destroyed almost one quarter of New York only days after the British occupied the city.

likely he was caught by Robert Rogers, the founder of the legendary Rangers who had laid the foundation for modern-day special operations during the French and Indian War. Hale had attracted Rogers's curiosity and, after Rogers falsely professed to be a patriot spy to gain his confidence, admitted his mission.

Hale was arrested while smoke from the great fire was still rising over the city. No evidence was found that he was an arsonist. But he was caught up in the British fury over the fire. Several days earlier the Americans had caught a lieutenant colonel named Ledwitz, trying to sell information to the British; he claimed in a letter to Howe found on his person that he had joined Washington's army only to save himself and his family. While the penalty for treason was death, a military court-martial voted to spare his life. Nathan Hale was not so fortunate.

He was locked in the brig aboard the *Halifax* and transported to the city. On the afternoon of September 21 he was brought in front of General Howe. Apparently he identified himself and admitted his mission. Howe pronounced the only penalty permitted: Hale would be hanged the next morning. While dozens of men and women all over the city were being detained, arrested, or even killed on suspicion of being involved in the Great Fire, there is no indication that Howe believed Hale was involved.

Nathan Hale spent some of his last night alive with Howe's chief engineer, Captain John Montresor, who later remembered, "He was calm, and bore himself with gentle dignity, in the consciousness of rectitude and high intentions." At about eleven in the morning he was marched to a nearby apple orchard. A rope was thrown over a heavy branch and then placed around his neck. A small crowd gathered to watch the American spy hang, among them the engineer Montresor. Provost Marshal William Cunningham, known to be an especially hard and brutal man, asked Hale if he had any final words. And then Nathan Hale did or did not say the words that have been etched into history: "I only regret that I have but one life to lose for my country."

There is no actual record of Hale's final words. Apparently the day of the hanging, Howe sent Montresor to deliver a message to Washington. Traveling under the protection of a white flag, he met Hale's friend, William Hull, and informed him of what had happened, then quoted those last words. The statement actually was paraphrased from Joseph Addison's 1712 play, *Cato*: "What a pity it is / That we can die but once to serve our country." The well-educated Hale would have read the play or seen it performed. So it certainly is possible, but there are several other equally probable stories that quote far different words.

For example, British lieutenant Frederick MacKensie wrote in his diary that same day that he had been told by a witness, a farmer named Tunis Bogart, that Hale "behaved with great composure and resolution, saying, he thought it the duty of every good officer, to obey

On the night of September 22, 1776, General Howe wrote in his orderly book: "A spy from the enemy by his own full confession, apprehended last night, was executed this day at 11 o'clock in front of the Artillery Park"—thus coldly recording the fate of the patriot Nathan Hale.

any orders given him by his commander in chief; and desired the spectators to be at all times prepared to meet death in whatever shape it might appear."

The first newspaper report of the hanging appeared less than a year later in the *Essex Journal*, which reported that his final words were, "You are shedding the blood of the innocent. If I had ten thousand lives, I would lay them all down, if called to it, in defense of my injured, bleeding country." And in 1781 the *Independent Chronicle and the Universal Advertiser* quoted another version of Hale's last words, closer to the ones that have been made famous. "I am so satisfied with the cause in which I have engaged, that my only regret is that I have not more lives than one to offer in its service."

Whatever his actual words, his patriotism could not be questioned. And because of that, Nathan Hale, a young man who failed to complete his only mission as a spy, has earned a place in American history.

After his execution his body was left hanging for three days, until it was cut down and buried in an unmarked grave. If that was intended to serve as a message to would-be spies, it failed.

Hale's death apparently caused barely a ripple among American troops. Few people knew him, much less his mission, and its impact seemed minor measured against the great events of those days: the burning of the city and Washington's fear of another British assault.

But Washington still had a desperate need for reliable information. Greatly outnumbered by better-trained and -equipped troops, his only hope for victory was to gain early knowledge of the enemy's plans and the disposition of his forces. To accomplish that, he turned to his aide, Colonel Benjamin Tallmadge, who had been a Yale classmate of Hale's. Tallmadge, who had been born on Long Island, had established a small spy network on the island and in New York that became known as the Culper Ring, consisting mostly of friends from schooldays and ordinary citizens committed to the Revolution. Using clever methods to relay information—for example, the female member of the ring, Anna Strong, would hang a black petticoat on her clothesline when there was a packet of documents to be picked up on her farm—the group was responsible for alerting Washington that Howe intended to attack newly arrived French troops at Newport, Rhode Island. It also detected a massive British counterfeiting operation. But the group's signature success was uncovering Major John André and General Benedict Arnold's plot to surrender the vitally important fort at West Point to General Howe.

Throughout all the wars of American history, few stories are as compelling, as complex, or as mystifying as that of Benedict Arnold, whose name was to become synonymous with betrayal. For a time, Benedict Arnold was a true hero; he began the war as a patriot and his courage and leadership in battle contributed significantly toward the eventual victory. But obviously heroism is not his legacy.

Most Americans know the end of the story—Benedict Arnold's betrayal of Washington. But what is it that would cause a man of proven courage and honor to give up his most closely held beliefs and betray those people closest to him?

Nothing in Benedict Arnold's early life suggested that he would become the most notorious traitor in American history. Like so many military officers of that time, Arnold was born into privilege. His father was a wealthy Connecticut businessman who sent his son to prestigious schools in Canterbury in the expectation that eventually he would attend Yale. He was considered to be smart and clever and his path seemed laid out nicely for him. But when three of his sisters died of yellow fever, his father began drinking excessively, which led to financial ruin. Benedict's life changed quickly and drastically; his father had lost the family fortune and, with it, his son's future. Rather than head to the leafy walks of Yale, Arnold was withdrawn from secondary school and apprenticed to his cousin's successful apothecary business. As a sixteen-year-old, he took a brief leave from the business to join the Connecticut militia in the French and Indian War, but returned within weeks without being involved in any action.

Those who have looked for reasons why Arnold chose to betray his country often begin with this sudden change of circumstances. But at first he appeared to have adjusted well, and even prospered. After concluding his seven-year apprenticeship, he opened his own apothecary and bookstore in New Haven with his only surviving sister. That shop was so successful that he eventually purchased a share in three merchant ships carrying goods from the West Indies. Arnold had learned life's hard lessons and had a reputation as a tough man who would not back down. He was reputed to be an excellent shot and a strong and relentless fighting man. He often commanded one of his ships and supposedly once challenged a British captain named Croskie to a duel after being insulted as a "damned Yankee, destitute of any good manners or those of a gentleman." He wounded his opponent, who apologized after Arnold threatened to kill him.

When the British trade acts drove him into debt, Arnold became a skillful smuggler. Once again he was threatened with losing everything that mattered to him. But his aptitude for business eventually enabled him to prosper, and he became one of New Haven's most successful and respected merchants. He owned ships, wharves, shops, and even slaves and servants. He lived with his wife and their three children in what was described as one of the finest mansions in the city.

But like so many colonists, Arnold became angrier with each British slight. He was trading in the Caribbean when news of the Boston Massacre reached him. Knowing only the most basic facts, he reportedly was stunned that the British had started shooting protesters. As he wrote to a merchant friend, "Good God! Are Americans all asleep and tamely giving up their glorious liberties, or are they all turned philosophers that they don't take immediate vengeance on such miscreants?"

In response Arnold became active in the Sons of Liberty and was elected a captain of the militia. As politics moved seemingly inevitably toward war, he spoke publicly for liberty from the British oppressors and prepared his men to fight. Few men so openly challenged British rule.

After news of the battle at Lexington and Concord reached New Haven, the citizens voted narrowly to stay out of the fighting. But Arnold gathered about sixty men, who vowed to march to Boston to give support to the cause. The following morning he led his militia to the city's armory where the gunpowder was stored. When the commander of the local militia warned him that he was not permitted to hand over the keys without orders, Arnold reportedly responded, "Regular orders be damned and our friends and neighbors being mowed down by redcoats. Give us the powder or we'll take it!" When the commander continued to resist, Arnold warned, "None but the Almighty God shall prevent my marching!"

With their fill of powder, they marched to Boston and helped enforce the siege.

Samuel Adams and other colonial leaders believed General Gage would try to lift the siege by bringing troops down from Canada. If he was able to relieve his troops in Boston, Gage also might successfully isolate the New England colonies—those places stirring the pot of rebellion. The quickest way to get the British into the fight was to bring them down through Lake Champlain to Lake George and then to the Hudson River. There was at least one good way to prevent that—take Fort Ticonderoga.

Fort Ticonderoga—"Ticonderoga" was an Iroquois word meaning "between two waters" or "where the waters meet"—was strategically located between the western shores of Lake Champlain and Lake George, and offered access to the Hudson River. Originally known as Fort Carillon, it had been built by the French in 1755 and was considered "the gateway to the continent," the most heavily contested piece of land during the French and Indian War. The British suffered more than two thousand casualties in an unsuccessful attempt in 1758 to take the fort—the bloodiest battle of that war—although they did return and drive out the French a year later. But before the French withdrew, they blew up the fort's magazine. In the ensuing years, with the French no longer a threat, the fort fell into disrepair. But colonial leaders understood its potentially vital strategic location—and even more important, they had heard tantalizing stories that the British kept a large amount of artillery there.

Arnold had traveled extensively through the region and was aware that the fort was ideally located and lightly defended. He convinced the Massachusetts Committee of Safety to fund a secret mission to capture the fort. The committee commissioned him a colonel and authorized him to recruit as many as four hundred men to capture the fort and return with any materials that might prove useful.

Arnold was not the only person to recognize Ticonderoga's value. Ethan Allen— frontiersman, land speculator, homespun philosopher, writer, politician, and eventually a founder of Vermont—also knew those woods well. Years earlier he had raised a small militia, known as the Green Mountain Boys, to protect and defend disputed lands in an area known as the New Hampshire Grants—which were later to become Vermont. Ethan Allen and about a hundred Green Mountain Boys took off to capture the fort before Arnold and his men could get there.

Arnold and his Massachusetts militia caught up with Allen en route. The men argued about who had the right to take the fort: Arnold said he had been ordered by the legal authorities to capture it. Good for you, Allen told him; his Green Mountain Boys weren't taking orders from no fancy-pants. The two men reached an uneasy truce and agreed to lead the expedition together—and they rode side by side to make certain neither one of them looked to be in charge.

One of Allen's men had snuck into the fort disguised as a peddler. He reported that its walls were deteriorating, the garrison was undermanned, what powder they had was wet— and they were expecting reinforcements within days. The two commanders agreed to attack. In the early brush of sunrise on May 10, 1775, a small force warily approached the fort; by all reports, they were stunned by the British response.

The one guard watching the wide-open gate tried to fire his musket, but his powder was wet. He dropped his musket and ran. Allen's Green Mountain Boys walked uncontested into the fort and quickly rounded up the sleeping soldiers. They learned later that the British had neglected to inform this garrison that shots had been fired in Massachusetts, so the troops there were completely unprepared to resist. Supposedly, when the fort's commanding officer asked from behind a locked door what they were doing there, Allen responded that he had taken the fort, "in the name of the Great Jehovah and the Continental Congress," although another report claimed he simply said, "Come out, you old rat."

The greatest danger in the capture of Fort Ticonderoga came later, when Allen's men discovered and helped themselves to the liquor stores and almost came to battle with Arnold's troops.

This was Arnold's first victory. The artillery captured there would later force the British to abandon Boston. After Allen's men departed, Arnold set about rebuilding the fort's defenses, fully aware of its value. Within weeks Connecticut sent an estimated one thousand troops to prevent a British drive from the north. Apparently Arnold was furious when Colonel Benjamin Hinman arrived and tried to take command. He resisted until delegates from the Committee of Safety informed him that he was to serve under Colonel Hinman. In response Arnold resigned his commission, disbanded his militia, and went home.

Although both Allen and Arnold wrote extensive reports about the events for the Committee of Safety, it appears they received only Allen's glorified version, which barely mentioned Arnold. In fact, when Allen later published his memoir, he didn't even mention Arnold.

This was the beginning of a pattern that was to repeat itself several times. Benedict Arnold would take great risks for the cause in which he so fervently believed—and then his accomplishments would be ignored or he would be set aside. It's unclear why Arnold was regularly denied the credit he had earned. According to some descriptions, while he had substantial leadership skills, he had an abrasive personality, lacking the political charm that others used so well to gain prestige and power—sometimes beyond their actual accomplishments. This might well be the source of the bitterness that resulted in his turning. Remarkably, his talents allowed him to rise high in the ranks without his rancor being detected.

George Washington's respect for him began with Arnold's mission to Quebec. With each succeeding colonial success, it seemed more and more likely that British troops then in Canada would be summoned south to help end the rebellion. In July 1775, the Continental Congress authorized New York general Philip Schuyler to invade Quebec. Arnold, greatly disappointed that he was not put in command, went directly to Washington and proposed a second offensive aimed specifically at Quebec City. With Schuyler's support, Washington approved the plan—and commissioned Benedict Arnold a colonel in the Continental army.

Arnold marched north with eleven hundred men. The route through the Maine wilderness proved far more difficult than had been anticipated. The lack of food and supplies caused more than three hundred men to turn back, while about two hundred men died of disease and starvation, perished in the swamps, or were carried away in river rapids. This was still mostly an unsettled and unmapped country and men like Arnold risked their lives, facing unknown dangers day after day. By the end of this march, which turned out to be more than twice as long as originally anticipated, Arnold's men, as he wrote to Washington, "were almost naked and in want of every necessity." It was a substantially weakened force that finally made contact with General Richard Montgomery's troops outside Quebec City in late December. Montgomery's army had been far more successful, capturing Montreal on its march into Canada.

Although Arnold would not learn of it for several weeks, he'd been promoted to the rank of brigadier general.

Quebec City was well fortified, defended by about five hundred regular troops and an equal number from the local militias. The assault began in a snowstorm on December 31. It was a disaster. Montgomery was killed early in the battle, and Arnold suffered a serious leg wound. The British held the city, killing or capturing more than 350 Americans. Arnold was given command of Montreal. When the British finally began their advance in the summer and fall of 1776, Arnold distinguished himself in several battles that delayed the British long enough to allow an orderly patriot retreat. But he resented the way the war was being conducted. Complaining of the difficulties he faced as a commander, Arnold purportedly wrote to Continental Navy Captain David Hawley, "When you ask for a frigate, they give you a raft. Ask for sailors and they give you tavern waiters. And if you want breeches, they give you a vest."

The Last Portage of the Great Carrying Place depicts some of the hardships endured by Arnold's troops on their incredible 1775–1776 march to Quebec.

In the ensuing months Arnold once again was caught up in military politics as other officers, men he viewed as far less deserving, were promoted over him as the Congress attempted to balance the number of generals from each state. Arnold again threatened to resign. Washington was sympathetic and wrote to Congress in his behalf, and as a result Arnold received his promotion to major general—but not the seniority he strongly felt he deserved.

It was at the crucial Battle of Saratoga, in September 1777, that Benedict Arnold distinguished himself as an American military hero—and faced the greatest humiliation of his career. The previous June, General John Burgoyne had begun the British offensive from Canada, leading eight thousand troops armed with more than 130 artillery pieces from Quebec down the Hudson River toward Albany, where he was to link up with General Howe's troops moving north from New York. If this maneuver succeeded, New England would be isolated from the rest of the states and the war might rapidly be brought to an end. In July, "Gentleman Johnny" Burgoyne shocked the Continental Congress by successfully recapturing strongly fortified Fort Ticonderoga. As a result, Washington replaced Schuyler with General Horatio Gates as commander of the northern army.

Washington had seen far too much of officers who led from behind; to blunt the British offensive, he needed men who weren't afraid to fight, men who took the battle directly to the enemy, men like Arnold. At Washington's request, General Arnold withdrew his resignation and joined Gates at Saratoga in upstate New York. Initially the two men got along, but hostility set in when the first battle of Saratoga began on September 17. At Saratoga, the cautious Gates spread his ten thousand men across an area known as the Bemis Heights, overlooking the west bank of the Hudson River. Arnold was given command of the left flank.

Burgoyne decided to initiate his attack from that left flank, hoping to get behind Gates's army on the heights. In anticipation, Arnold requested permission to attack before Burgoyne was prepared. Gates refused; a former British officer, he still harbored great respect for that army and preferred to maintain his secure position. He would defend the heights. But he allowed Arnold to send out elements of his own division for reconnaissance. The advance units of both armies came together at Freeman's Farm. Both sides quickly sent reinforcements into the fighting—although Gates refused to commit his main force, certain Burgoyne would make a frontal assault. The battle raged through the afternoon; one of Arnold's men, Captain Ebenezer Wakefield, reported watching his commander, "in front of the line, his eyes flashing, pointing with his sword to the advancing foe, with a voice that rang clear as a trumpet and electrified the line." When the fighting was done for the day, Burgoyne's forces had won but had paid a terrible price. More than six hundred men were killed or wounded, almost twice the casualties suffered by Arnold. It turned out to be more than Burgoyne could afford.

Several days after the battle, Arnold confronted Gates in his tent. In addition to refusing to provide reinforcements, in the report of the fighting that Gates sent to Congress, he did not mention Arnold or his men. In legend Arnold slashed open Gates's tent with his sword. While that's probably apocryphal, he did storm into Gates's tent and confronted him. The two men screamed at each other, reportedly employing "high words and gross language." The imperious, infuriated Gates relieved Arnold of his command. Arnold responded by writing a note in which the first signs of his bitterness were revealed, claiming that despite the "ingratitude of my countrymen, every personal interest shall be buried in my zeal for the safety and happiness of my country." Arnold also requested permission from Gates to leave the camp and report to Washington. It was granted, but Arnold hesitated; the battle was about to be renewed and he intended to fight alongside his men.

When word of this confrontation spread to the troops, Arnold's men circulated a petition demanding that he be reinstated. But before Gates could respond, Burgoyne attacked.

The first battle of Saratoga had left Burgoyne in an untenable position. He had won, but he had lost whatever advantages he once had. He had no choice but to press the attack, to smash through Gates's line and get to Albany, but he lacked sufficient forces to properly support the effort. On October 7 Burgoyne marched two thousand men back to Freeman's Farm. When Arnold, who no longer had command authority, practically begged Gates to send a force to meet the attack, Gates told him, "General Arnold, I have nothing for you to do. You have no business here."

Benedict Arnold was not going to let Gates's hesitancy cost his men victory again. He rode into the battle. By the time he arrived, the Americans had counterattacked and were overrunning British lines. Arnold raced to the front. Screaming, "Come on brave boys, come on!" he led a charge into the center of the redcoats' position. Finding a gap in the line, he charged through it, then turned left to get behind the defenders. Bullets were whizzing by him. He was hit again in his left leg. His horse was hit and went down, crushing his already wounded leg. The battle continued all around him, as Burgoyne desperately withdrew his troops. That day more than eight hundred men had been killed, wounded, or captured. Burgoyne tried to make a stand in the town of Saratoga, but Gates encircled him. Burgoyne had no choice but to surrender his army.

Answering to Parliament at a later time, Burgoyne admitted he had expected Gates to defend his superior position, but "Arnold chose to give rather than receive the attack." While General Nathanael Greene credited Arnold and Major General Benjamin Lincoln for much

Only a month after the British had captured Philadelphia in September *1777*, General Gates revived patriot morale by defeating General Burgoyne at Saratoga. Burgoyne's surrender, pictured here, convinced French king Louis XVI to provide support for the revolution.

of the success, a gold medal in Gates's honor was authorized by the Congress. As a direct result of the success at Saratoga, the French decided to enter the war to support the American army. For France, which had lost its foothold in the new country in the French and Indian War, this was a satisfying outcome.

Benedict Arnold spent months in the hospital; his leg was saved but was never again truly serviceable. When British general Henry Clinton was ordered to withdraw his troops from Philadelphia, Washington rewarded Arnold by appointing him military commander of that city. It was a safe and plum post that offered numerous possibilities to a man who understood business. And by this time, Arnold had experienced far too much to remain an idealist. For him this war was no longer about breaking the bonds of British tyranny. The fact was that Philadelphia would be a lucrative post for him.

Philadelphia was a place in turmoil. The patriots, who had left hurriedly when the British had taken control of the city in September 1777, now returned, while the Loyalists either fled or lived in fear of retribution. Washington ordered Arnold to provide equal "security to individuals of every class and description," but that proved a difficult task. When Arnold took the necessary steps to protect Loyalists and their property, he was viewed with suspicion by patriots who began to wonder about his true sympathies.

In the chaotic economic circumstances, a lively black market developed—and this was exactly the type of commerce Arnold understood. Years earlier in New Haven he had made his fortune in a similar situation. Not surprisingly, he began to prosper. Among other questionable activities, he was involved in the lucrative smuggling business and also profited from buying confiscated Loyalists' property at greatly reduced value, then selling for a substantial profit.

Finally away from the battlefields, Arnold found his pleasures in Philadelphia society. His first wife had died years earlier, so he was open to the charms of the most eligible women in the city, finally settling on eighteen-year-old Peggy Shippen, the lovely daughter of wealthy merchant, judge—and Loyalist—Edward Shippen. They married in April 1779. Peggy Shippen was young but not naive. During the British occupation she had found favor with British major John André, and even after the British had withdrawn from the city she had maintained contact with him. A Philadelphia shopkeeper, Joseph Stansbury, was known to carry messages between them.

It never has been determined precisely when or even why Benedict Arnold made his decision to betray his country. Certainly it may have been as simple as money: Life in Philadelphia with his lovely, much younger bride turned out to be far more expensive than Arnold had expected and once again he had fallen deeply into debt. His weakness for the gambling tables may have contributed to those losses. His wife was likely a factor. Peggy Shippen was said to be a sensual woman with expensive tastes; she also was a Loyalist with strong ties to her ex, André. She might easily have swayed her already bitter husband—and undoubtedly her already established contacts facilitated his betrayal. Or the repeated slights accumulated, culminating with being insulted by the man he most admired, George Washington.

Arnold's often-suspect business dealings eventually brought disfavor on him, and in 1779 he was charged with thirteen counts of profiteering, including the misuse of government property. Those charges infuriated Arnold, who already believed he had been robbed of much of the credit he had earned for his courage and leadership. He was court-martialed and wrote to Washington, "Having become a cripple in the service of my country, I little expected to meet

*Miss Margaret Shippen
daughter of Chief Justice Shippen*

This 1778 pencil drawing by Major John André captures the beauty of eighteen-year-old Peggy Shippen, rumored to have been his paramour, who became Benedict Arnold's second wife—and may have led Arnold to betray his country.

[such] ungrateful returns." A Philadelphia diplomat named Silas Deane informed General Greene that General Arnold was embittered more by the "wounds his character has received, from base, and envious men, than those he received, in defense of his country." Although a court-martial acquitted him of eleven of those charges—he was convicted of two minor infractions—as part of his penalty Washington publicly rebuked him, writing in his General Orders on April 6, 1780, "The Commander in Chief would have been much happier in an occasion of bestowing commendations on an officer who has rendered such distinguished services to his country as Major General Arnold; but in the present case a sense of duty and a regard to candor oblige him to declare, that he considers his conduct in the instance of the permit as peculiarly reprehensible, both in a civil and military view, and . . . imprudent and improper." Arnold responded to Washington's censure by resigning his post in Philadelphia.

By that time, though, Arnold already had committed treason. It appears that at some point while awaiting his court-martial, Arnold had begun his correspondence with André, who by then had been placed in charge of British secret intelligence in America. John André

The nineteenth-century print *The Treason of Arnold* illustrates Benedict Arnold persuading Major John André to conceal the plans for West Point in his boot. Had André remained in uniform he would have been treated as a military prisoner when captured. Instead he changed into civilian clothes and was hanged as a spy.

was an enlightened man. He was fluent in four languages and could draw, paint, sing, and write. During the occupation of Philadelphia he had become a favorite of high society. And undoubtedly he appreciated the value of turning a man like Benedict Arnold.

By May 1779, Arnold had made his intentions known to André, demanding payment and an equivalent rank in the British army in exchange for information. While André was the spymaster, decisions concerning Arnold were to be made by the commander in chief of North America, General Sir Henry Clinton. Clinton and André responded by offering Arnold fair payment and establishing the method of communication: Arnold would send seemingly ordinary letters through Stansbury, but they actually would include messages written in invisible ink, or transmitted by code and cipher. Blackstone's *Commentaries on the Laws of England* would serve as the key.

While negotiations continued over terms, Arnold proved his value by providing intelligence about troop dispositions and movements and the anticipated arrival of the French fleet—including six warships and six thousand troops—in Newport, Rhode Island. At some point André apparently suggested that Arnold approach Washington about assuming command of the fortifications at West Point. General Clinton was extremely interested in obtaining the plans and details about its defenses.

The importance of that strategic location to either the Americans or the British cannot be overstated. Sitting on a plateau in upstate New York, West Point commanded a critical choke point on the Hudson River. Its defenses included artillery batteries, an almost impregnable fortress manned by a full contingent of three thousand troops, and a five-hundred-yard-long sixty-five-ton iron chain stretching across the Hudson from West Point to Constitution Island to prevent ships from slipping through. Any ship trying to break through would inevitably be hung up on the chain—each link weighed 180 pounds—then blasted into smithereens by the artillery. Washington considered it his "most important post in America . . . first in magnitude and importance," and warned that if the British gained control they could "interrupt our easiest communication between the eastern and southern states, open a new source of supplies to them, and a new door to distress and disaffect the country."

It isn't known precisely why Washington decided to give Arnold command of that fortress. Obviously he had not lost respect for him after his conviction and continued to value his proven courage and leadership on the battlefield. In fact, he wrote to Arnold promising, "as far as it shall be in my power, I will myself furnish you with opportunities for regaining the esteem which you have formerly enjoyed." In 1780, when Washington began planning an assault on the British army entrenched in New York, he offered Arnold command of the left wing. It was the kind of prestigious position Arnold had been desperate for in the past, but the offer came much too late. Washington was quite surprised when Arnold turned down this offer, writing, "His countenance changed and he appeared to be quite fallen and instead of thanking me . . . never opened his mouth." Arnold later claimed that his injured left leg would not permit him to lead troops in battle. But eventually he did make a request of Washington; he would like to be put in command of West Point.

In fact, it made sense. It was a position that had to be held at all costs and Arnold long ago had proved himself. It was a stationary post, so Arnold's disability would not be a problem. And there was something else: starting earlier that year there had been persistent rumors that a British spy had infiltrated Washington's command. To try to identify him, Benjamin Tallmadge reactivated the Culper spy ring, which had been dormant for some time. While they kept few records, for obvious reasons, they must have enjoyed at least some success, because in June Tallmadge warned one of Washington's closest advisers, Jonathan Trumbull, of an insider plot to attack West Point. Assuming Washington also had knowledge of these rumors, it makes sense that he would put someone he trusted completely—like General Arnold—in charge.

In June, Arnold stopped at West Point on his way home to Connecticut to make a thorough inspection, and he prepared a detailed report of his visit. By then Arnold obviously was committed to this plot, as he arranged through friends in New York to begin transferring his assets to London. In early July, Arnold sent a message to Clinton that he was to be given command of the fortress, offering to provide "drawing of the works . . . by which you might take [West Point] without loss." The price for his betrayal, he wrote in a second letter, was £20,000, more than a million dollars today. On August 3, his appointment as commander of West Point, in addition to several other posts along the Hudson, was made official. Two weeks later he received a letter from André agreeing to most of his demands. The plot was put into action.

There is some evidence that by August Arnold's letters were being intercepted, although there is no hint that anyone could link them directly to him. What is known is that some of Arnold's letters never got to Clinton, that someone had tampered with at least one letter that did get through to make the message illegible, and that Tallmadge was becoming suspicious of Arnold.

After taking command, General Arnold immediately began weakening West Point's defenses. Needed repairs on the chain were postponed. The garrison was reduced by sending troops to other river posts or detailing them to Washington. Supplies of necessities were cut back so drastically that some of his officers wondered if he was selling them on the black market.

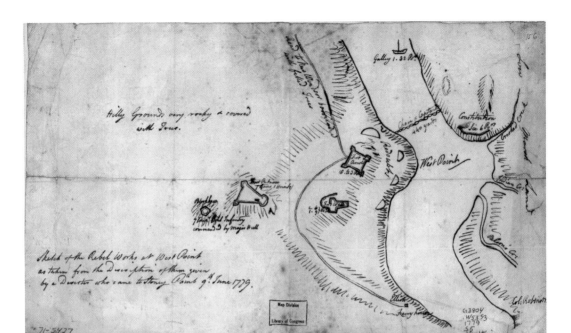

This 1779 sketch, made from a description provided by a deserter, shows the positions of the defenses at West Point.

General Clinton, meanwhile, began preparations to launch his attack on West Point. His plan was to sail up the river and land his army, knowing that Arnold would put up little more than a token defense before surrendering. Apparently Clinton already had in his hands a great deal of intelligence detailing the weakest points of the fort. Rather than risk an attack before all the pieces were in place, he decided to wait until André was able to coordinate a time and date with Arnold. While a meeting between the men was risky, the stakes were so high that it was worth it. Clinton was reluctant to permit André to meet with Arnold, and allowed the encounter only after the major agreed he would not take off his uniform, he would not go behind enemy lines, and he would not carry any incriminating documents. The first meeting, planned for September 11 near the town of Dobbs Ferry, was called off when British gunships mistakenly fired at the boat carrying André.

The second meeting, the final meeting, was scheduled for September 23. On the seventeenth, Arnold dined with Joshua Hett Smith, a New York businessman whom many people suspected of being a Loyalist but who also may have been for sale to either side. There is

A steel engraving made from a sketch provided by Major Charles L'Enfant showing the fortress at West Point as it looked in 1780, overlooking the Hudson River. West Point was considered the most vital strategic position on the river. Slightly more than a decade later, L'Enfant would create the city plan for Washington, D.C.

some evidence that he was a double, or even a triple agent, and his involvement—whether intentional or not—led directly to the failure of the plot.

On the eighteenth Arnold met with Washington and came away confident that his superior harbored no suspicions. What Tallmadge knew, if anything, at this point is unclear. Most probably the unmasking of Arnold's deception was the result of chance, but if there had been a plan in place to foil Arnold's plan without divulging sources of information, it certainly could have proceeded this same way.

On the twentieth, the sloop HMS *Vulture* secretly carried Major André up the river. The following evening, at Arnold's request, Smith rowed to that ship and brought back a man identified to him as John Anderson. "Anderson" spent much of the following day meeting with General Arnold at Smith's home in West Haverstraw. Smith later claimed he had not been privy to any of their discussions. The *Vulture* was supposed to wait at anchor for André to return, but on the morning of the twenty-second, shore batteries opened fire and the ship was unable to wait for him.

In Smith's confession, which he made to Alexander Hamilton, he claimed he was suffering from "the fever and ague [shaking]," and was therefore unable to row "Anderson" back to the ship without making any reference to the shelling. But after the ship left, Smith rode with Anderson and put him on the road toward White Plains. He also testified that Anderson was wearing an officer's red coat and, at Arnold's request, he gave him civilian clothes to wear. This proved to be very important; the fact that André was caught behind enemy lines wearing civilian clothes identified him as a spy rather than a prisoner of war and therefore made him eligible to be hanged. For some never-disclosed reason, rather than showing "Anderson" the most direct route south, Smith instead took him north into American-patrolled territory. "The circuitous route . . ." André later said, "was imposed without alternative upon me." On the road they met several people and passed successfully through two checkpoints. They spent the night in a farmhouse. The next morning Smith left him at a fork near Tarrytown, telling him which path to take. "Anderson" obviously didn't trust him, instead taking the other path.

Gangs of bandits, highwaymen, and militiamen were known to roam those woods. Later that morning, as he got close to British lines, André was stopped by three men. They could have been bandits or militiamen; in any case, their allegiance was to the Americans. One of them was wearing a Hessian's coat and, because they were near a British camp, André initially identified himself as a British officer. When he realized his mistake he tried bargaining, showing them a pass written by Arnold; when that failed, he offered them his horse, his

A classic 1845 Currier & Ives print of the capture of Major John André. The papers in his boot have been discovered and he is now dressed as a civilian—sealing his doom.

watch, whatever he had to bargain with. When the men searched him they found six pages of maps, diagrams, and papers hidden in his boot. While only one of the men could read, they all certainly could recognize the plans for West Point. Rather than taking a substantial bribe or André's valuables, they decided to deliver him to the closest American post. Maybe it was loyalty, maybe it was because they believed they would receive a larger reward—or maybe there was a more complicated reason.

They delivered André to their local commander, Colonel John Jameson, who decided to send him back to Arnold under guard with a note explaining he had been caught carrying important papers. But he sent the "parcel of papers taken from under his stockings . . . of a very dangerous tendency" to Washington. At that moment, André probably figured he was safe.

Hours later Tallmadge learned of the events. When he saw the papers taken from André, who was traveling with a pass from Arnold, he knew he had identified his traitor. He ordered Jameson to send a fast rider to bring back André, but Jameson, fearing he was caught between two officers, insisted that his note be delivered to Arnold. There was nothing Tallmadge could do to prevent that.

Coincidentally, Arnold was to host Washington for breakfast at West Point that very morning. He received Jameson's note shortly before the general was due to arrive. He went upstairs, kissed his wife, and fled. When Washington arrived and found Arnold was not there to greet him, he apparently was upset at the absence of proper military protocol. Most reports indicate he was still at West Point when Jameson's "parcel of papers" arrived. The following day Washington made Arnold's betrayal public, including in the General Orders, "Treason, of the blackest dye, was yesterday discovered. General Arnold, who commanded at West Point—lost to every sentiment of honor, of private and public obligation—was about to deliver up that important post into the hands of the enemy. Such an event must have given the American cause a deadly wound, if not a fatal stab."

Arnold's treachery actually served the American cause by inspiring a renewed anti-British fervor. Arnold was reviled throughout the states, and effigies of him were hanged and burned. The morale of the army, which had been lagging due to the long and inconclusive war, picked up substantially. Riflemen were said to take target practice on his image.

While General Arnold successfully escaped to New York, which was occupied by the British, André was convicted of being a spy. A board of officers, including fourteen generals, ordered that "Major André, Adjutant General to the British Army, ought to be considered as a spy from the enemy; and that, agreeable to the law and usage of nations, it is their opinion he ought to suffer death." Sir Henry Clinton beseeched Washington to spare him but reportedly refused when Washington offered to trade him for Arnold, explaining that doing so would prevent any man from ever again changing sides. At Clinton's request, Arnold threatened Washington if André was executed, writing, "I call heaven and earth to witness, that your Excellency will be justly answerable for the torrent of blood that may be spilt in consequence." During André's captivity, as was true during Nathan Hale's, André earned the respect of his enemy; Hamilton wrote, "Never perhaps did any man suffer death with more justice, or deserve it less."

André was hanged on October 2. Supposedly many witnesses cried. His last words, carefully recorded, were, "I pray you to bear me witness that I meet my fate like a brave man." Several decades later his remains were sent to England, where he was buried in Hero's Corner in Westminster Abbey.

Smith, whose role in this story remained murky, also was tried, but he was acquitted because of a lack of evidence. Peggy Arnold was never charged with any complicity and Washington permitted her to join her husband in New York.

Arnold received his promised commission in the British army and returned to the battlefield. American leaders had orders to hang him immediately if he was captured. He led an invasion force into Virginia and briefly held—and looted—Richmond, then attacked and burned New London, Connecticut, while his troops massacred captured militiamen. Even after British forces were defeated at Yorktown, he urged the king to renew attacks, with greater force, but the British never embraced him. While he served their objectives, his treason was never completely overlooked, and many people held him responsible for the execution of the revered major, John André. Arnold actually tried several times to rehabilitate his reputation, writing letters to newspapers in which he claimed that it was his conscience, not the monetary rewards, that motivated his actions.

Arnold spent the remainder of his life earning and losing fortunes, at one point owning more than thirteen thousand acres in Canada, but he was always looking for his next war. Ironically, while trading in the Caribbean he was captured by the French and presumed to be a British spy. In that instance he again escaped the noose, this time by squeezing through a cabin window and sliding down a rope to a raft, which he managed to row to a British warship. When he died in England in 1801, he was given a state funeral—but without the military honors he would have wished. His wife spent the last years of her life settling all of his debts—except the biggest one of all, to America, which could never be repaid.

Foreign Aides

George Washington must have truly despaired at dinner on the evening of August 5, 1777, when he was formally introduced to the nineteen-year-old Marquis de Lafayette. That morning he had been informed that 250 British ships, carrying as many as eighteen thousand troops, were en route to Philadelphia where his under-equipped, poorly trained, and dispirited army was on the verge of collapse. And yet he was forced to spend his evening entertaining this extremely wealthy teenager.

Marie-Joseph-Paul-Yves-Roch-Gilbert du Motier de La Fayette, one of the richest young men in France, had purchased his own boat, hired his own soldiers, and, against the explicit orders of King Louis XVI who did not want to threaten France's fragile peace with England, sailed to America. Some historians believe his purpose was to avenge the death of his father, who had been killed by British soldiers in the 1759 Battle of Minden. It was a ludicrous situation that might well have been imagined by the satirical novelist Henry Fielding; although Lafayette spoke almost no English and had no experience in battle, the Continental Congress had awarded him the rank of major general. The problem was that while the Congress intended the commission to be purely honorary, Lafayette had very different expectations: he was determined to fight the British.

Washington had no idea what to do with this pleasant but inexperienced and determined teenager. He wrote to Virginian Benjamin Harrison for advice, complaining, "What line of conduct I am to pursue, to comply with [Continental Congress's] design and his expectations, I know no more than the child unborn, and beg to be instructed."

Lafayette was only the latest of many Europeans who had come to America. Since the beginning of the war, American agents in Europe had been trying to recruit experienced military officers who could help transform the disparate militias into an army. Mostly they had succeeded in sending to Washington a series of nondescript counts, barons, chevaliers, and veteran military officers of low repute who desired to use this war for personal gain. At first, Lafayette appeared to be just another dilettante to be kept out of danger while he helped fund the patriotic cause.

But as Washington—and the world—would learn, Lafayette was one of a small group of extraordinary European soldiers—among them the Prussian baron Friedrich von Steuben, and Polish officers Tadeusz Kościuszko and Kazimierz Pulaski, whose courage and capabilities contributed significantly to the American victory and the birth of the revolutionary spirit that was to resonate across their own continent.

A letter of recommendation from Benjamin Franklin, who was in Paris trying to persuade the French to enter the war, convinced Washington to find a place on his staff for Lafayette. The young Frenchman began proving his value in early September at the Battle of Brandywine. When Washington's right flank was threatened, he sent Lafayette into battle with Major General John Sullivan's 3rd Pennsylvania Brigade. Although wounded in the calf, Lafayette distinguished himself by forsaking treatment in order to organize an orderly retreat. As a result, he was cited for bravery and given a command.

It was during the infamous winter of 1777–78 at Valley Forge that Lafayette proved his mettle to Washington. The two men became close friends and allies. As Lafayette wrote to his wife in France, Washington "finds in me a trustworthy friend in whom he can confide and who will always tell him the truth. Not a day goes by without his talking to me at length or writing long letters to me. And he is willing to consult me on most interesting points." Living and suffering through the coldest days of that bitter winter alongside the troops, Lafayette bought uniforms, weapons, and supplies for the army—but, more important, he continued to urge the French government to support the Revolution. Sent north in early February by the Congress to invade Canada so it might be returned to France, Lafayette abandoned that mission in Albany when more than half the troops and the supplies he had been promised failed to arrive, and he returned to Valley Forge.

Washington's confidence in Lafayette continued to grow. In May, Washington ordered him to take twenty-two hundred troops toward Philadelphia to try to ascertain British general William Howe's intentions. General Howe must have been quite pleased to learn of Lafayette's presence; capturing this aristocrat would send a strong message to the French government about the consequences of interfering in this conflict. Howe sent more than

Washington and the newly arrived twenty-year-old Marquis de Lafayette,
pictured during the terrible winter at Valley Forge by John Ward Dunsmore.

twelve-thousand troops to trap Lafayette in an area called Barren Hill. Lafayette
skillfully managed to escape, with his force suffering only minor casualties.

After serving at Washington's side in several other small battles, Lafayette
sailed to France in 1779, creating a stir in Paris when he appeared in court
wearing his Continental army uniform. But his reports helped convince the king
to send the French fleet north from the Caribbean and commit six thousand
troops and supplies to the war. Washington reported this success by his protégé
to Congress, writing, "During the time he has been in France, he has uniformly
manifested the same zeal in our affairs, which animated his conduct while he was
among us; and he has been upon all occasions an essential friend to America."

Lafayette returned to America in 1781 and distinguished himself in a
campaign against British forces led by the traitor General Benedict Arnold.
In October, the French support he had helped muster made the difference in
the climactic Battle of Yorktown: While five thousand American troops under
Lafayette's command blocked Lord Cornwallis's escape routes, Washington's
twenty-five hundred soldiers joined four thousand French troops and the

French fleet to completely encircle the British. After British efforts to relieve Cornwallis failed, the general finally agreed to surrender his eight thousand men and a strong naval force, marking the end of fighting on American soil. Lafayette stood with Washington to accept the British surrender.

At the conclusion of the war, Lafayette served nobly in the French Revolution. As commander of the French National Guard, he tore down the Bastille, sending the key to its west portal to Washington at Mount Vernon. Celebrated in America for his contributions, in 1824 the Marquis de Lafayette became the first foreign dignitary invited to address Congress, and upon his death a decade later John Quincy Adams said, "The name of Lafayette shall stand enrolled upon the annals of our race, high on the list of the pure and disinterested benefactors of mankind."

In contrast to the young and inexperienced Lafayette, forty-seven-year-old Friedrich Wilhelm Ludolf Gerhard Augustin von Steuben brought with him to America more than three decades of military experience in the Prussian army when he arrived in December 1777. After having served as quartermaster general and adjutant general on the personal staff of Frederick the Great, in 1764 he was made Baron von Steuben.

The American Revolution provided great opportunity for soldiers from several foreign countries. The British, whose armies were spread thinly throughout the world, hired as many as thirty thousand soldiers from Hesse-Cassel and other German states, paying the leaders of their principalities for their services. Veteran officers from other parts of Europe, left without a cause after the end of the Seven Years' War, also looked to America for employment. Among them was Baron von Steuben, who approached Franklin in Paris after failing to find a position with other foreign armies. When the Continental Congress would not provide any guarantees of pay, rank, or command, Steuben traveled to America and volunteered his services to Washington in exchange for his expenses. "The object of my greatest ambition is to render your country all the service in my power," he wrote, "and to deserve the title of a citizen of America by fighting for the cause of liberty."

The Continental army was in shambles when Steuben joined Washington at Valley Forge in late February 1778. In addition to lacking arms, ammunition, food, shelter, and morale, the army had no orderly military structure, no formal training system, and no organized administration procedures. The troops didn't even know how to march in formation. Steuben immediately began imposing the lessons he had learned in the Prussian military on the encampment, attempting to transform a willing but untrained assembly of militias into an army in a matter of months. The fact that he didn't speak English only made the already seemingly impossible task just a little more difficult.

Steuben attacked the problem by creating a model company of slightly more than a hundred men, then began drilling them in the full range of military skills from marching to fighting with a bayonet. Creating the prototype of the tough drill sergeant, he made his men relentlessly practice reloading and firing, reloading and firing, until the process became natural and efficient. He taught them basic tactics and simple maneuvers. As a veteran officer described Steuben's impact, "Discipline flourishes and daily improves under the indefatigable efforts of Baron Steuben—who is much esteemed by us." In addition to personally demonstrating these techniques, he spoke to Alexander

Due to a scarcity of paper, Baron von Steuben's command and drill manual was printed on blue paper. The fundamental principles explained in "The Blue Book," as it became known, have remained the foundation of the American military for more than two centuries. The model company he formed also remains in existence and is known as the The President's 100.

Hamilton and General Nathanael Greene in French and they translated his comments into English. When harsher language became necessary, he employed Captain Benjamin Walker to curse at the troops for him.

Once these men were sufficiently trained, they began passing along their knowledge to other groups, and the effect rippled through the entire army. This training regimen eventually was turned into the classic manual *Regulations for the Order and Discipline of the Troops of the United States.* The *Blue Book*, or *Steuben's Regulations*, served as the basic training program, manual of arms, and organizational structure for generations of American soldiers—and remains the foundation for the professional army.

Von Steuben also instituted strict sanitation regulations, introducing the novel concept of latrines to soldiers who had no understanding of sanitary conditions, then established a standard layout of the camp in which orderly rows of tents were separated from the kitchens and latrines. Within months of his arrival, Washington had named Steuben inspector general of the army with the rank of major general.

Almost single-handedly Steuben brought professionalism to the colonial army. His training began paying off during the Battle of Monmouth in June, when retreating colonial troops stopped and formed an orderly battle line and, for the first time in the entire war, fought the British to a draw in a static battle. In subsequent battles the colonists stunned the British with their rapid and orderly response to commands, their newfound ability to maneuver, and their deadly use of the bayonet. Washington eventually gained such confidence in Steuben that during the decisive Battle of Yorktown, he put Steuben in command of one of three American divisions.

After the victory Baron von Steuben became an American citizen, settling on sixteen thousand acres of land in upstate New York given to him by a grateful government.

Among the other idealistic Europeans who came to America to fight for human rights was the young Polish military engineer Andrzej Tadeusz Bonawentura Kościuszko. To an army lacking just about every form of military expertise, Kościuszko's arrival in the summer of 1776 proved incredibly fortuitous. Initially a volunteer paid by Benjamin Franklin, who recognized the importance of his unique skills, in October he was commissioned a colonel. His first challenge was building fortifications along the Delaware River to prevent a British advance toward Philadelphia. He attracted Washington's attention the following spring at Fort Ticonderoga when he urged General Arthur St. Clair to situate a battery on a nearby hilltop. Two months after St. Clair refused to act on his suggestion, British general Burgoyne installed artillery on that high point, forcing the Americans to abandon the fortress. As the American army retreated south, Kościuszko was ordered to somehow delay the enemy pursuit. By cutting down trees to block roads, destroying bridges, and damming streams to bog down the British army, Kościuszko gave St. Clair the time needed to successfully withdraw.

A greatly impressed General Gates assigned Kościuszko to find the best defensive position for his army to make a stand. Kościuszko finally found that place—an area overlooking the Hudson River called Bemis Heights, not too far from the town of Saratoga. He designed an almost impregnable array of battlements there—which later enabled Gates's army to repulse several British attacks and led directly to Burgoyne's surrender. Gates reported in admiration, "The great tacticians of the campaign were the hills and forests, which a young Polish engineer was skillful enough to select for my encampment."

Kościuszko designed the fortifications at West Point that Benedict Arnold sold to the British, and when Major John André was captured with those plans, it was Baron von Steuben who supervised his hanging, turning down André's request to face a firing squad.

Kościuszko later fought in the campaign in the south, selecting positions for both camps and ambushes that provided a natural advantage, fortifying bases, running an intelligence network, and even leading men into battle. At one point, during Cornwallis's frantic pursuit of General Nathanael Greene's retreating army through the forest and across the rivers of the Carolinas, Kościuszko's preparations proved instrumental in saving the southern army. At the end of the war Congress promoted him to brigadier general.

While traveling to join the army in South Carolina, Kościuszko had paused in Virginia to fulfill one of his greatest desires—meeting Thomas

Jefferson. He and Jefferson eventually became good friends and faithful correspondents and Jefferson once said about him with admiration, "He is as pure a son of liberty as I have ever known."

After the American victory was secured, Kościuszko returned to Poland to lead the fight for freedom in his native country, eventually leading an unsuccessful uprising against occupying Russian forces. For his valor he was awarded his country's highest military honor. He returned to America in 1797 and, before departing for the final time to join the French in their fight against the Russians, he named Jefferson the executor of his estate, which was to be used to purchase the freedom of black slaves—including Jefferson's—and to educate them so they might live as free men. It was a request Jefferson was unable to fulfill.

Some foreign soldiers gave their lives to the revolutionary cause, among them the Polish aristocrat Kazimierz Pulaski. After leading Polish forces in an unsuccessful attempt to free his country from Russian and Prussian influence, he was exiled to France, where Lafayette and Benjamin Franklin strongly recommended him to Washington. "Count Pulaski of Poland," Franklin wrote, "an officer famous throughout Europe for his bravery and conduct in defense of the liberties of his country against the three great invading powers of Russia, Austria and Prussia . . . may be highly useful to our service."

Pulaski was a fighting soldier, a skilled horseman who had earned great respect for leading the cavalry into battle. While awaiting his commission he wrote to Washington, "I came here, where freedom is being defended, to serve it, and to live or die for it." He gained Washington's respect in September 1777 at the Battle of Brandywine, when he led a charge into British lines that averted a disastrous defeat of the Continental army's cavalry—and may have saved the commander in chief's life.

Until that time Washington used his few hundred mounted troops mostly for scouting, but after Congress appointed Pulaski brigadier general in charge of the army's four horse regiments, they began engaging in battle. "The Father of the American Cavalry," as he became known, created the Pulaski Legion, the country's first trained cavalry corps, and employed classic tactics in a series of battles, twice courageously leading charges into British lines. At the Battle of White Horse Tavern, his men alerted Washington that Howe's army was on the march, allowing the colonists to take strong defensive positions to prevent the attack. Other officers considered him quarrelsome, but no one ever questioned his courage in battle. In October 1779, during the Siege of Savannah, he was struck by grapeshot while leading a full-scale cavalry charge into British fortifications—and became one of the few European officers to lose his life in the cause of freedom.

The soldiers of Europe joined the fight for independence for many reasons, but without their combined contributions both on land and at sea, the outcome of the Revolutionary War might well have been very different.

Washington with the soldiers from Europe who helped create the victorious army: Washington (at left); Major General Baron Johann de Kalb, who had arrived with Lafayette; Von Steuben; Pulaski; Kościuszko; Lafayette; and the Lutheran pastor American-born Peter "Teufel Piet" (Devil Pete) Muhlenberg, who had served briefly in the German dragoons.

CHAPTER 7

Francis Marion

American Guerrilla Fighter

In late August 1780, elements of His Majesty's 63rd and Prince of Wales Regiments settled in for the night on the overgrown grounds of Thomas Sumter's abandoned plantation at Great Savannah, keeping careful watch over the 150 colonial prisoners captured at the Battle of Camden. The next day they would take them down the Santee Road to the prison ships docked in Charlestown. They put out sentries but expected no difficulty; they were in friendly territory and the colonial army was in tatters. General Gates had been badly beaten at Camden, and Sumter's men had been decimated at Fishing Creek. The British were so confident, in fact, that many of the troops slept inside the manor house, leaving their weapons stacked outside. But all around them, Colonel Francis Marion's militia was moving unseen and unheard through the South Carolina woods. It's possible the redcoats may have heard the forest whistling a conversation, but, if so, they did not understand the meaning.

☜ The elusive General Francis Marion relaxing in camp with his men. The Swamp Fox, whose guerrilla tactics confounded the British, prevented the enemy from securing gains in the Carolinas, thereby keeping a sizable number of troops in the south.

Marion's men slowly tightened their knot. They waited patiently for darkness. The night woods were their home; surprise was their ally. Marion detailed sixteen men to guard the escape route over Horse Creek. When a British sentry spotted them, he frantically fired a single warning shot. The alert sent the camp scurrying into action but it was too late; it was much too late. Marion's raiders, swinging swords and firing their muskets, raced out of the woods. Within minutes, twenty-two British regulars and two Loyalists had been killed or captured. One of Marion's riders had been mortally wounded and one prisoner had suffered a head wound.

The colonial prisoners were freed—but when asked if they wanted to join the raiders who had saved them, many of them looked warily at this ragged band of forest men and instead decided to take their chances in Charlestown. Francis Marion let them go. His men gathered the British weapons and supplies and faded back into the comfortable darkness of the woods.

Francis Marion, the Swamp Fox, is remembered today mostly by America's toughest and bravest warriors, who often honor him as the "Father of Special Operations." In a war that was fought mostly according to the traditional principles of battle—long static lines marching nobly into the battle—Francis Marion broke the rules. According to another redcoat who unsuccessfully pursued him, Lieutenant Colonel John W. T. Watson, Marion "would not fight like a gentleman or a Christian," and by doing so Marion introduced a new type of warfare.

With his small band of untrained and unpaid fighting men, who lived and fought in the swamps and forests of South Carolina, Marion successfully harassed the British army for almost three years, helping disrupt General Clinton's strategy of conquering and cutting off the southern states. Then the Swamp Fox moved north. Like American Robin Hoods, his men traveled like ghosts, appearing suddenly and creating havoc—and then just as quickly were gone.

The legend of the Swamp Fox was born in late 1780. After several encounters in which Marion's outnumbered forces humiliated British regulars at places like Blue Savannah, Black Mingo Creek, and Tearcoat Swamp in South Carolina—employing what decades later would be known as "guerrilla tactics"—Lord Cornwallis ordered Banastre "Bloody Ban" Tarleton to take his dragoons into the countryside and bring an end to Marion's shenanigans.

After several days the notorious "Tarleton's raiders" finally caught Marion's tracks. Although Marion was a daring and courageous man, this time too many men were pursuing him, and he fled. He and his men led the British on a spirited chase for more than seven hours, racing through as much as twenty-five miles of South Carolina wilderness. As the afternoon stretched into the early evening, Tarleton was forced to end his pursuit at Ox Swamp,

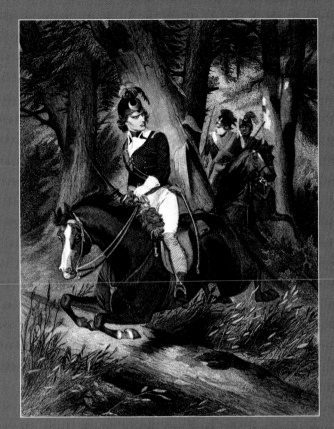

General Francis Marion (left), considered one of the fathers of guerrilla warfare, led his small band of patriots in the hit-and-run attacks that frustrated the imperious redcoats.

The despised British colonel Banastre Tarleton (at right) earned the nicknames "Bloody Ban" and "Butcher" after slaughtering surrendering troops at the Battle of Waxhaws. He pursued Marion through the Carolina swamps throughout 1780 without catching him, giving Marion the nickname by which he became known when he said, "as for this damned old fox, the devil himself could not catch him."

admitting bitterly that he had been unable to catch "that damned old fox," adding, "the devil himself could not catch him."

Renowned poet and journalist William Cullen Bryant would later celebrate the exploits of the Swamp Fox in his 1858 poem, "Song of Marion's Men":

> Our band is few, but true and tried,
>   Our leader frank and bold;
> The British soldier trembles
>   When Marion's name is told.
> Our fortress is the good greenwood,
>   Our tent the cypress-tree;
> We know the forest round us,
>   As seamen know the sea.
> We know its walks of thorny vines,
>   Its glades of reedy grass,
> Its safe and silent islands
>   Within the dark morass.

The battle for the south is often overlooked in history books, but it played a significant part in the outcome of the war. The British decision to maintain control of the southern colonies had drained them of soldiers and supplies that might have made a significant difference in the north, where George Washington's army was struggling. As Washington wrote despairingly in 1780, "We have been half our time without provision and are likely to continue so. We have no magazines, nor money to form them. And in a little while we shall have no men, if we had money to pay them. We have lived upon expedients till we can live no longer. In a word, the history of the war is a history of false hopes and temporary devices, instead of system and economy."

The British decision to greatly expand the war to the American south had been made two years earlier. After more than two years of battling the Continental army around the great northern cities of Boston, New York, and Philadelphia, in 1778 General Clinton switched tactics: he would attack those southern states that had a substantial Loyalist population and emancipated slaves, believing the men there would rise to his cause. Rather than chasing Washington's army through the states where the rebels enjoyed the fullest support, he would draw those soldiers south, where the population was far more favorable to the Crown. Once those states were subdued and again under Loyalist control, he would be free to turn his full attention to the north.

The British had launched this southern strategy by capturing the deep-water port of Savannah, Georgia, in December 1778, allowing them to safely land an army and all the necessary supplies. In late 1779, a fleet of ninety British ships carried fourteen thousand troops under the command of Generals Clinton and Cornwallis to Johns Island and Seabrook Island in South Carolina. General Clinton marched his troops overland across several rivers until he reached the south's largest port, Charlestown. The Siege of Charlestown lasted six months; in May 1780 patriot general Benjamin Lincoln surrendered the five thousand troops trapped there. But for an odd stroke of fate, one of them would have been Francis Marion.

One night in March 1780, Lieutenant Colonel Francis Marion, commander of the 2nd South Carolina Regiment, had joined his fellow officers in bitter revelry. Months earlier, when patriot general Benjamin Lincoln's offensive to retake Savannah had been repulsed with substantial losses, Marion had swallowed defeat for the first time. And now, as thousands of

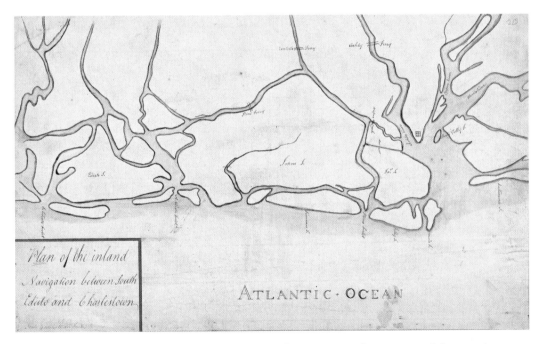

The inland waterways of South Carolina created a network of swamps and forests that served as barriers to the British but allowed local militia to move safely and secretly.

redcoats were moving to attack the city, he was in no mood for celebration. He had mostly de-clined to participate in the many rounds of toasts. Finally, his reluctance noted, he decided to leave. But in keeping with tradition, the doors had been locked—no one was permitted to go until the last glasses were raised. So Marion instead opened a window. He was on the second floor, but the drop to the ground didn't seem prohibitive. He eased himself out the window and fell awkwardly, badly damaging his ankle. The injury made him temporarily unfit for duty, so he went back to his farm outside Charlestown to heal. The city and its five thousand men fell while he was recuperating, leaving most of the Carolinas in British hands. It would be

many months, even years, before the American army could mount an effective offensive in the south. And so Marion began his own war, a war he was well suited to fight.

The details of Francis Marion's childhood are sketchy. He was born on a plantation near the town of Cordesville, South Carolina, hard on the banks of the Copper River, to Gabriel Marion Jr. and his wife, Esther. He was the last of seven children and was described as puny. One report said that as a baby he was smaller than a New England lobster and would fit easily into a cook pot. Apparently he had little formal schooling, spending much of his childhood hunting and fishing in the Low Country forests, swamps, and marshes. It was probably

Alonzo Chappel's engraving *Charleston: Siege 1780* depicts the beleaguered city from British lines.

during this time that he became especially close to a young slave named Oscar Marion, a boy about his own age who explored the woods with him. The great adventure of Francis Marion's life began at age fifteen, when he hired onto a merchant ship running the trade route to the West Indies. Just as in the stories of young lads trying to make their way in the world that Robert Louis Stevenson would write a century later, Marion's ship sank on his first voyage, supposedly after being struck by a whale. Six members of the crew managed to get into a lifeboat. Two men apparently died of exposure while praying to be rescued, and after a long week in the blazing sun the rest of them were saved. For the next decade Francis and his older brother, Job, managed the family plantation. But when the campaign against the Cherokee began in 1757, Captain John Postell recruited the brothers for the South Carolina militia.

The French and Indian War, or the Seven Years' War, as the British refer to it, matched the British colonies and their Indian allies against the French colonies and their Native American allies. Both nations committed regular military units to the fight for the natural riches of North America. Rather than the pitched battles common in European wars, much of the fighting was done in unsettled regions. To survive, Francis Marion had to learn how to mimic the Indian techniques: always moving rapidly in small forces, respecting the wilderness and living off its bounty, striking quickly and unexpectedly, and avoiding static battles against larger forces. The Cherokee lived in harmony with nature, and their ability to strike when and where they chose caused a fear in their enemies far greater than their actual numbers would have inspired, a lesson Marion learned well. By the time his war ended, Francis Marion had been promoted to lieutenant.

After the war he settled on his own plantation; it was on the Santee River and he named it Pond Bluff. He lived there peacefully with his wife and children, having seen enough of fighting in the French and Indian War. For a time, at least, he was far from the bickering taking place way up north. But in 1775 he was elected to the South Carolina Provincial Congress, where representatives were talking about wanting more independence from Parliament. For men like Marion, who had fought valiantly and loyally for the king only a few years earlier, this could not have been an easy decision to make. But when the fighting started in Massachusetts, the South Carolina Congress commissioned three state regiments and appointed him a captain. His allegiance was to the land he knew, South Carolina, rather than to a nation he had never seen.

Captain Marion spent the first years of the Revolution at Fort Sullivan, helping repulse the British attack on Charlestown in June 1776. With the exception of the ill-fated Siege of Savannah, he saw no more action—until the British captured Charlestown in May 1780.

The Liberty Flag, one of our first national flags, flew for the first time during the June 1776 siege of Sullivan's Island. By repulsing the attack, the small garrison inside Fort Moultrie successfully prevented the British fleet from capturing Charleston.

After the fall of the city, American reinforcements who had been on their way to assist the garrison there turned back. Some of them, however, were caught by British regulars led by Banastre Tarleton near Lancaster, South Carolina. There are many different reports about what actually happened in the Battle of Waxhaws, but the result was a massacre, as British troops, swinging their sabers, brutally murdered 113 patriots and severely wounded another 150. While Tarleton always insisted the massacre had taken place without his knowledge or authority, it gave rise to the expression "Tarleton's quarter," which meant that the victorious side would take no prisoners. "The loss of officers and men was great on the part of the Americans," Tarleton admitted, "owing to . . . a report amongst the [British] cavalry, that they had lost their commanding officer, which stimulated the soldiers to a vindictive asperity not easily restrained." In simpler words, his men believed he had been killed in the fighting and went crazy. Whatever the truth, the damage was done and many more men would die because of it.

In subsequent southern battles, countless wounded or surrendering soldiers were slaughtered in retribution. While the Waxhaws massacre was a military victory for the British, it proved to be a far more important rallying cry and propaganda victory for the Continental army.

Once General Clinton had secured Charlestown, he sent troops out into the countryside to apprehend separatist leaders. Marion, who would have spent the rest of the war sitting in a British prison if he had not fallen and injured his ankle, instead fled to General Horatio Gates's camp near Charlotte, North Carolina. He received a message there from the men from the Williamsburg district who had formed a militia and wanted him to lead them. At that time Gates had neither the men nor the supplies to sustain an offensive, so he ordered Marion and his Williamsburg men to attack British boats and communications on the Santee River.

Though clearly a man capable of inspiring others, Francis Marion did not look the part of a leader. While tall, impressive men like Washington were considered role models, Marion, according to Colonel Henry Lee, who fought at his side, was "in stature of the smallest size, thin as well as low. His visage was not pleasing, and his manners not captivating. He was reserved and silent, entering into conversation only when necessary, and then with modesty and good sense. He possessed a strong mind, improved only by his own reflections and observations, not by books or travels. His dress was . . . plain, regarding comfort and decency only. . . . He was sedulous and constant in his attention to the duties of his station, to which every other consideration yielded. . . . The procurement of subsistence for his men, and the contrivance of annoyance to his enemy, engrossed his entire mind." In other words, like most great leaders, he led by example: "Never avoiding danger," Lee continued, "he never rashly sought it; and acting for all around him as he did for himself, he risked the lives of his troops only when it was necessary." In fact, he apparently cared so little about his appearance that even after his leather regimental cap was partially burned, he continued to wear it.

Marion had fewer than one hundred men and limited supplies when he set out in the summer of 1780, but he did have one advantage: his men knew the land. This was their home. They had hunted these woods and fished the rivers; they had camped there and knew the dangers of the swamps. They knew the solid paths and they knew the soft bogs. And having grown up in those parts, they were well practiced with a long gun. In fact, while Marion often wore a sword when in battle, he was never known to use it. That turned out to be fortuitous. One day while cleaning his equipment, he tried to draw his sword—only to discover it was rusted to its scabbard.

At first, Marion's attacks were little more than irritants. His men disrupted supply lines, harassed troops, picked off stragglers. They barely accomplished enough to be noticed and were little more worrisome than the pesky mosquitoes that infested the southern swamps. Cornwallis's attention was focused on Gates, who commanded the last sizable Continental force in the Carolinas. Gates, perhaps emboldened by his prior success at Saratoga, began marching his four thousand men toward Charlestown. As much as possible, Marion and several other detachments softened their route. But Gates had little knowledge of the terrain or the elements or reliable intelligence about the enemy. The blistering hot weather, a lack of sufficient fresh water, dysentery, and even stomach ailments caused by green corn reduced his army by almost half. Among those men still able to fight were hundreds of untrained, terrified militia.

Cornwallis came out to meet Gates at Camden. When the first shots were fired, Gates's lines collapsed, as countless militia fled the battlefield. It quickly turned into a rout, and in less than an hour of fighting the Americans had suffered more than two thousand casualties. Gates himself had fled when his left flank crumbled. With the loss at Camden, the irregulars under the command of Lieutenant Colonel Francis Marion were about the last remnants of

Lord Charles Cornwallis by Thomas Gainsborough. After successfully capturing New York, Cornwallis was appointed commander of the British army in the south. Ordered to Yorktown, Virginia, by General Clinton with the promise he would be resupplied and reinforced there, he was forced to surrender his army to Washington when that assistance failed to arrive.

Washington's army left in South Carolina. They had no source of resupply, no safe havens to provide shelter, no hope of reinforcements. They were alone.

Washington, in fact, had little hope that Marion might accomplish anything of significance, yet he desperately needed him and other South Carolina militia to keep Cornwallis occupied to such an extent that he could not confidently move his army north without risking his southern base. As Washington wrote to John Rutledge, "[You] may rest assured that I am fully impressed with the importance of the southern states, and . . . the necessity of making every effort to expel the enemy from them. The late unlucky affair near Camden renders the situation more precarious. . . . Our endeavors in that quarter should be directed rather to checking the progress of the enemy by a permanent, compact, and well-organized body of men, than attempting immediately to recover the state of South Carolina by a numerous army of militia, who . . . are too fluctuating and undisciplined to oppose one composed chiefly of regular troops."

The Swamp Fox and his men moved like shadows through the countryside, cutting British lines of communications, disrupting shipping on the river, and continuing to harass Cornwallis's army. Marion began to focus his attention on Nelson's Ferry, where he embarrassed General Clinton by freeing 150 prisoners and capturing 22 men. Marion's first great victory came several days later. After handing over his 22 prisoners at Brittons Neck, his 52 men rode hard to make good their escape. More than a week later they ran into a much larger Loyalist force commanded by Major Micajah Ganey at Blue Savannah. In a brief skirmish that morning, Marion's band had routed Ganey's advance guard, but rather than pressing their luck, they had retreated into the countryside. Ganey wanted revenge and his whole force of two hundred men joined the pursuit. They raced through the afternoon, determined to punish the impudent Americans.

Marion watched contentedly as Ganey rode right into his trap. After Ganey's militia had raced past his position, he ordered his men to move in behind the much larger force. They stayed behind them until late in the afternoon, and when the pursuers paused to figure their position, Marion sprang his ambush. Ganey's men, exhausted and confused, panicked as volley after volley of shots came from all around them. As Colonel Peter Horry described the fighting years later, "In a moment the woods were all in a blaze. . . . Down tumbled the dead; off bolted the living; loud screamed the wounded; while far and wide, all over the woods, nothing was to be heard but the running of tories, and the snorting of wild bounding horses." They fled without any semblance of order into the swamps, suffering substantial casualties. Marion lost three men in the fighting.

That night the militia celebrated their victory with a rare large meal of roasted pigs, turkey, and "fine old peach brandy" that the British had been enjoying until attacked. "Ah, this brandy," Marion supposedly said, "was the worst foe these poor rogues ever had. But I'll take care it should be no foe to us."

The following morning Marion and his men moved into the swamps to round up any British survivors. As legend has it, they came upon the body of one of Ganey's men, but upon inspection they found no obvious wounds. They were mystified as to what had killed this soldier—until one of them saw a rattlesnake crawling into the undergrowth. One of them quickly raised his rifle to eliminate the threat, but another man stopped him, pleading for the reptile's life. They agreed to grant the snake a fair chance to live. A noose was fashioned and it was quickly captured. To decide its fate, they convened a court-martial. The snake was accused of the murder of a British soldier. There was a body of evidence to prove its guilt. But its defense attorney made a sensible plea: "If this creature is a murderer, then so are we all. This snake has killed one British soldier; we have killed many. This is not a murder, gentlemen. This is war!" The jury found the defendant not guilty, and it was released from captivity.

News of Marion's success spread rapidly through the South Carolina countryside. For the colonists this was the first bit of good cheer they had enjoyed in months. From that time forward they would seek Marion out, or his men, to inform him or warn him of British movements. For example, about a week after the victory at Blue Savannah, Marion was warned that a large force had made camp near Black Mingo Creek, outside the town of Hemingway. Rather than fading into the protection of the swamps, which was what he would be expected to do when facing a substantially larger force, Marion decided to attack. Perhaps he figured he would have the advantage of surprise. He led his men more than seventy miles through the countryside before finding Colonel John Cummins Ball and at least 150 Loyalists camped at Shepard's Ferry. Just before midnight Marion began his attack. Surprise was lost when a British sentry heard the lead horses crossing Willtown Bridge, which was north of the camp, and fired warning shots.

Marion never hesitated; he broke his men into three units and attacked from the center and both flanks, holding a substantial number in reserve. The British waited too long, until Marion's men were less than thirty yards away, then fired their first volley. Before they could reload, the militia was on them. When they came around the right flank, the Tories broke formation and ran for their lives. Ball's force broke apart. Three men were killed and an additional thirteen were wounded or taken prisoner. Two of Marion's men were killed, six were wounded. The skirmish had lasted no longer than fifteen minutes. The militia also captured as many as a hundred horses with new saddles and bridles, guns and powder, and even several fiddles and bows left by the fire. Among the horses was Colonel Ball's own mount; Marion claimed it for himself, named it Ball, and rode him through the next several months of the campaign. And another important lesson was learned: from that night forward Marion's men never crossed a bridge in the night until it had been covered with blankets to muffle the sound.

As was common, after this skirmish several members of the militia took leave and rode to their homes to tend to their personal affairs, while the rest of Marion's "Brigade," as it was being called, went back to their camp on Snow's Island, a desolate parcel of land in Florence County accessible only by boat. Its isolated location made it the perfect hideout for Marion's men between forays. No one could reach it without being spotted a great distance away. The number of men on Snow's Island at any particular time varied greatly as the size and the makeup of the militia were changing continually. There never was a steady number; volunteers came from far and wide. For example, after the fight at Black Mingo Creek five of Ball's men who had been captured volunteered to join the militia. With each success, country men would somehow find them and stay and fight awhile, then up and leave. Some returned; others did not. There was never a commitment asked or given. There was no discrimination among them; the militia consisted of black and white men, farmers and merchants, Irish immigrants and third-generation settlers, all brought together by their disgust for British intrusion into their lives. But among those men who stayed with Marion throughout his entire campaign was his slave, Oscar Marion.

To enlist slaves in the fight, especially in the south, in 1775 Lord Dunmore granted freedom to "all indentured servants, negroes, or others . . . that are able and willing to bear arms, they joining his majesty's troops."

Throughout the war Washington tried to walk the very narrow path between enlisting free black men and slaves, but the result was that African Americans in substantial numbers fought for both sides, in a great variety of roles in both the army and naval forces. And among them was Francis Marion's friend Oscar.

Oscar Marion was said to be Francis's aide, servant, chef, bugler, oarsman when necessary, and fighting man. As if they were writing a story of friendship that would be told centuries later, the two men fought side by side for seven years and, in fact, were depicted together in several noted paintings. In one painting, in which Oscar appears to be wounded, he and Marion are riding a white horse that has stopped for water at the Pee Dee River; in another he is shown hiding in the swamps with the rest of the brigade, and in still another he is rowing their boat. Perhaps the most famous painting, John Blake White's *General Marion Inviting a British Officer to Share His Meal*, which has hung in the US Senate since 1899, shows Oscar Marion in the background cooking a meal of sweet potatoes. According to the legend, a British officer under a white truce flag was brought blindfolded to the camp to discuss a prisoner exchange, and during that meeting he joined the rebels in a meal consisting solely of those roasted potatoes. When he returned to his lines, he resigned his commission, stating he could no longer engage in war against an enemy with the determination to keep fighting while having so little to eat. Or so the story goes.

At times the brigade was also joined by Marion's teenage nephew, Lieutenant Gabriel Marion, who had served in several of his uncle's campaigns. But that ended one terrible night in mid-November 1780. Marion had planned an attack on the village of Georgetown, a village on Winyah Bay, which was rich with needed supplies. While the main body waited in

John Blake White's 1820 painting *General Marion Inviting a British Officer to Share His Meal* depicts Marion with his slave, friend, and aide, Oscar Marion.

the swamps, he sent out two patrols to gather intelligence. Gabriel Marion was riding with Captain John Melton when they learned that Loyalists had made camp at a nearby place called "The Pens." As they passed through an overgrown swamp, they crossed paths with a Loyalist patrol. Both sides opened fire. In the melee Gabriel Marion was caught, and enemy soldiers started clubbing him with their muskets. As they beat him with the stocks of their long guns, Gabriel saw a familiar face, a man who before the war had often shared meals with his uncle. He ran to the man and threw his arms around him, beseeching him to help. There was nothing this man could do, although it is believed he spoke up on the young lieutenant's behalf. One of the Tories answered disgustedly that Gabriel "was one of the breed of that damned old rebel." His uncle's friend was warned to step off, or he would be killed, too. He had no choice. He moved away and Gabriel was shot through the chest.

Francis Marion was distraught when he learned of his nephew's death. Supposedly, in the next few days his killer was caught in another raid. Marion had promised that no harm was to come to him while in captivity. But when several prisoners were being moved across the swamps off the Black River, an officer rode right up to the man, lifted his weapon, and killed him on the spot. Marion was furious, ready to punish that deed; although he had been told that this Tory had murdered his nephew, "as a prisoner, his life ought to have been held most sacred; especially as the charge against him was without evidence, and, perhaps, no better than conjecture. As to my nephew, I believe he was cruelly murdered: but living virtuously, as he did, and then dying fighting for the rights of man, he is, no doubt, happy: and this is my comfort." The men who rode with Marion often said this was the only time they had seen him broken.

Francis Marion became a legend not only because of what he accomplished but by the way he accomplished it. Even though up north Ethan Allen and his Green Mountain Boys employed many of the same techniques as Marion's men, they were able to sustain their attacks for only a brief period of time. And eventually Ethan Allen was captured. The Swamp Fox was able to continue this mode of battle for many months, several times while large British forces were searching for him. In October Marion learned that Lieutenant Colonel Samuel Tynes had organized and was training a Loyalist militia consisting of many conscripted men in the hills near Tearcoat Swamp. The camp was established in the fork of the Black River; Tynes believed the swamp created an impassable natural barrier behind his men. Marion decided to attack and "break up the party, before its newly made converts should become confirmed in the principles they had unwillingly adopted."

Covered by the night, Marion's men silently crossed the river and set up an ambush on all three sides. At his signal the attack was launched. It ended in minutes; the Loyalists had suffered six dead, fourteen wounded, and twenty-three men captured. The raiders lost two horses. In addition to eighty muskets and horses captured, they gained several prisoners, who opted to join Marion's men.

In addition to these raids in force, groups of Marion's men continued pecking away at the Loyalists, taking small actions as much to keep the enemy off balance as to inflict real damage. As Marion once explained, "The destruction of all British stores . . . is of the greatest consequence to us, and only requires boldness and expedition." Operating from his island base, he sent out small detachments to harass the enemy. While one squad destroyed "a great quantity of valuable stores . . . at Manigault's Ferry," for example, Marion and other men raided a wagon convoy near Moncks Corner and destroyed fourteen wagonloads of soldiers' clothing and baggage while taking forty prisoners without absorbing any losses. He was relentless, inflicting the death of a thousand small stings.

Marion's unconventional tactics continued to confound his enemy. After crossing bridges, he would destroy them. He would approach an unwary enemy force or avoid potential ambush by fording streams at the deepest point rather than the shallowest, with his horse Ball almost always leading the way. His men moved under the cover of night and slept in the hottest part of the day. His scouts, who would remain hidden in tall trees for long periods, communicated by a shrill whistle. And to ensure complete secrecy, he never confided his plans to anyone else, even his officers; instead he led them to the point of attack. He picked his fights carefully; when confronted by an overwhelming force, he would scatter his men, only to reassemble them days later and a distance away. And as was written in celebration of his life in the early 1800s, "A swamp, right or left, or in his rear; a thicket beside him; any spot in which time could be gained . . . were all that he required, in order to secure a fit position for fighting in."

Furious at their inability to catch Marion, the British took out their frustration on the local population. Cornwallis told his officers, "All the inhabitants of this province . . . who had taken part in the revolt, should be punished with the greatest rigor; that they should be imprisoned and their whole property taken from them and destroyed." In early November Marion's relentless pursuer, Banastre Tarleton, devised a clever plan to finally bring an end to the Swamp Fox and his infernal attacks. His force was near Santee, camped on the plantation of rebel general Richard Richardson, who had died several weeks earlier and was buried on his land. Tarleton began spreading the rumor that the main body of his forces had returned to Camden, leaving only a small force behind. He was hoping that this opportunity would lure Marion into an attack against an overwhelming force. The plan might actually have worked, had Mary Richardson not dispatched one of her sons to warn Marion. When the Swamp Fox was informed that more than a thousand men were awaiting him, he sent his men home and faded safely into North Carolina's Great White Marsh.

When Tarleton learned from a prisoner who had escaped from his camp that Marion had eluded him again, he had a pleasant dinner with Mrs. Richardson and then, as Governor John Rutledge informed Congress, he "exceeded his usual barbarity, for having dined in her house, he not only burned it, after plundering it of everything it contained, but having driven into the barn a number of cattle, hogs, poultry, he consumed them, together with the barn, and the corn in it, in one general blaze." According to some historians, even that wasn't sufficient punishment. To ensure that General Richardson was dead and hadn't in fact escaped, Tarleton purportedly led or dragged Mary Richardson to her husband's grave and forced her to watch as his coffin was dug up and opened, then made her look at his decomposing remains.

Banastre once again pursued Marion, and once again without any success. To retaliate, as Cornwallis had ordered, his officers set fire to a huge swath of South Carolina, burning homes and farms over an area covering the seventy miles from Kingstree to Cheraw. They burned plantations, they burned crops, they killed livestock—especially sheep because their wool provided warm clothing—and they burned the churches. The result was quite different than Banastre expected; rather than being terrified by him, many of the radicalized colonists with nothing more to lose joined Marion's growing brigade.

Early in December 1780, only months after General Nathanael Greene had presided over the trial and execution of the spy Major John André, George Washington named Greene commander of the southern army, which at that time consisted of about a thousand irregulars, plus Marion's Brigade and similar militias under Thomas Sumter and Andrew Pickens.

In recognition of Marion's continued success, Greene promoted him to the rank of brigadier general of the South Carolina militia and put him in command of those troops in the eastern part of the state. More than that, though, Greene gave Marion reinforcements, sending Lieutenant Colonel Henry "Light Horse Harry" Lee and three hundred infantry and cavalry to support his efforts. At twenty-five, Henry Lee—whose son was Robert E. Lee—was about half as old as Marion and, in contrast to him, was said to be tall and handsome. But beginning in January, they made a fine team, as this larger force finally was able to take the offense.

Marion and Lee began by planning an attack on the two-hundred-man garrison at Georgetown. The Swamp Fox divided his force into three elements; in the middle of the night Captain Patrick Carnes and ninety men sailed down the Pee Dee River, taking cover in a swamp just across the river from the town, remaining there in hiding throughout the day. Meanwhile, Marion and Lee moved into place on either side of the town, waiting for

Nathanael Greene (above) began the war
as a militia private but rose to become
a major general in command of fighting
in the south and one of Washington's
most trusted aides; Colonel Henry
"Light Horse Harry" Lee (right) waged
a successful campaign in the south under
Greene—and was the father of Robert E.
Lee.

nightfall. After dark Carnes's commandos rowed across the river on flat-bottomed boats and
captured the completely surprised British commander. Then they fired a signal shot to launch
the attack. From either side of the village, Marion and Lee closed in.

After briefly trying but failing to make a fight of it, the garrison barricaded themselves inside secure bastions, choosing not to fight back. Marion and Lee walked into a completely calm
town. There wasn't an enemy soldier to be seen. As they carried no tools for breaking down doors
or windows, there was nothing they could do. The commander was granted parole, an honorable practice recognized by both sides, in which he was released with the understanding that
he would no longer fight. More than twenty Loyalists were killed or wounded; Marion's men
suffered no losses. Before dawn, the Swamp Fox and his men were again safely in the marshes.

In March, when General Greene attempted to lure Cornwallis into North Carolina, Lee
temporarily rejoined his army, leaving Marion and his dwindling force on Snow's Island. Colonel Francis, Lord Rawdon, perceived this to be an opportunity to put an end to the Swamp

Fox. He planned to launch a frontal assault led by Lieutenant Colonel John Watson, and when the outnumbered Marion attempted to withdraw to North Carolina, he would be met by a second substantial force, waiting on the Pee Dee River to crush him.

Marion, who had been alerted that Watson was on the march, had his men prepare an ambush. They attacked him near Murrays Ferry, then lured him across the Santee River into the Wiboo Swamp. By the time Watson realized what was happening, his army was trapped on the wrong side of the river. For the next week they played a human chess game, two armies maneuvering for position. Meanwhile, Marion's sharpshooters picked off Watson's men, es-

William Ranney's circa 1850 painting *Francis Marion Crossing the Pee Dee* depicts the irregularly dressed militia in their most comfortable surroundings. Marion was so successful, Cornwallis complained "that there was scarcely an inhabitant between the Santee and the Peedee that was not in arms against us."

pecially his officers, one by one by one. Each time Watson attempted to break out, Marion would destroy the bridges he needed. Watson found himself trapped in the marshes and bogs between the Santee and Black Rivers, unable to move and running out of provisions. Watson finally made camp at the Cantey plantation, waiting, and hoping, for reinforcements that never arrived. When his men tried to forage for food, the sharpshooters were waiting for them. Watson finally was forced to stage a breakout, crossing the Sampit River under fire, then racing for the safety of Georgetown. His defeated army arrived there with wagonloads of casualties.

But Lord Rawdon had enjoyed one substantial success. While Marion had Watson's men pinned down, Rawdon's second force had landed unopposed on Snow's Island and burned the base there. All of Marion's supplies were destroyed, except what his men were carrying on their back. They were reduced to two rounds per man, not enough to repulse even a minor attack. Francis Marion had been fighting relentlessly for many months and now found himself without enough men, ammunition, supplies, or even a base. It was time, he understood, to consider disbanding his militia.

Before he could act on that notion, he received word that Light Horse Harry Lee was returning with Continental army reinforcements. The day after he arrived, on April 15, 1781, the combined force began a march on Fort Watson, a key point in the communications chain between North and South Carolina. Located just below the junction of the Congaree and Wateree Rivers, it was manned by 120 British troops and had been built on the highest point in the area, rising more than thirty feet above the plains. The land around it had been cut bare, making it impossible to move close under cover. The walls were steep and covered with three rows of sharpened stakes, which protruded from its sloping sides. Several weeks earlier the fort had successfully held out against an attack by Sumter's men, killing eighteen of them and suffering almost no losses. The fort seemed impenetrable.

But if Marion couldn't get in, he reasoned, the defenders couldn't get out. Freshwater ran into the fort from Scott's Lake. Marion's men dammed that source, shutting off the fort's water supply. Then they waited. The fort's resourceful commander responded by sinking a deep well, providing all the water the garrison would need.

The attack seemed blunted. The lack of cover prevented Marion's sharpshooters from getting close enough to the fort to keep the defenders off the walls. What followed was one of the most unusual events of the entire war. Colonel Hezekiah Maham proposed building their own fortification, a tower that protected Marion's riflemen as they sniped at the walls. Having no other solution, Marion agreed to try it. His men began cutting down green pine trees and carrying them closer to the fort. They laid them down as two long parallel trunks, but each level of two trunks crossed the last. It took five days to construct this thirty-foot-high rectangular tower, a Maham Tower, as it later came to be known. At its top they built a fully protected platform. In the dark night of the twenty-second, troops carried the tower into place.

When the sun rose on the morning of the twenty-third, the defenders were stunned to see a wooden tower in front of the fort. Sharpshooters inside the tower forced the defenders off the walls, allowing two "forlorn hope" teams—the leading attackers—to scale the walls without opposition. As an officer inside the fort later wrote, "cowardly and mutinous behavior of a majority of men, having grounded their arms and refused to defend the post any longer," caused the commander to surrender the fort. Marion lost two men and an additional three men were wounded, but he captured a vast amount of stores and ammunition. Two of the defenders were killed, six were wounded, and the thirty-six Loyalist militia were taken prisoner. The remaining troops were paroled. After the fort was emptied, it was pulled down, and an important link in the British chain of forts across South Carolina was gone.

General Greene's letter to General Marion about the victory remains one of the great tributes an officer has received from his commander:

> When I consider how much you have done and suffered, and under what disadvantage you have maintained your ground, I am at a loss which I admire most, your courage and fortitude, or your address and management. . . . History affords no instance wherein an officer has kept possession of a country under so many disadvantages as you have; surrounded on every side with a superior force, hunted from every quarter with veteran troops, you have found means to elude all their attempts, and to keep alive the expiring hopes of an oppressed militia, when all succor seemed to be cut off. To fight the enemy bravely, with a prospect of victory, is nothing; but to fight with intrepidity, under the constant impression of a defeat, and inspire irregular troops to do it, is a talent peculiar to yourself. . . . I shall miss no opportunity of declaring to Congress, and to the world in general, the great sense I have of your merit and your services.

The British attempt to bring South Carolina under their control had failed. Unlike those northern cities with large population centers, the geography and climate of the agrarian southern society and the already established tradition of fierce independence had presented obstacles Cornwallis had never truly understood, much less been able to conquer. Francis Marion's militia had provided the Continental army the time it needed to rebuild and return in force to the south. By early May, General Greene was finally prepared to meet the British at equal strength on a great battlefield—and drive them out of the Carolinas. In response, the British began fortifying the larger cities, such as Charlestown and Savannah.

As British forces withdrew into Charlestown, Marion's militia kept up its attacks. In late May, with Lee's Continental troops, they attacked Fort Motte, the main British supply depot between Charlotte and country outposts. The fort had been built around a large plantation house. Using bows and flaming arrows, the men set fire to the manor home, with all its supplies and the protection it offered. Attempts to douse the fire were met with cannon balls. The garrison had no choice but to surrender.

The once powerful line of British forts that stretched across the state fell like dominoes. Marion once again marched on Georgetown. This time, as he set up his siege lines, the redcoats boarded ships and sailed for Charlestown. His men marched in unopposed—and he celebrated by wearing a new uniform and taking two mules to carry his baggage.

In late August Washington and French general Rochambeau began marching seven thousand troops toward Cornwallis's army in Yorktown, Virginia, at the mouth of Chesapeake Bay. With British attention focused there, the battle for the south was nearing a conclusion. But the British had one more stand left in them. In September, the regular Continental forces and the various militias caught twenty-three hundred British troops camped by the Eutaw Springs in South Carolina. On the morning of September 8, a small Loyalist party out collecting yams encountered a colonial patrol. The Loyalists gave chase—right into Harry Lee's waiting ambush. Throughout the afternoon the fighting elevated into a pitched battle, with a British charge directly into patriot lines proving temporarily successful. It was an especially vicious battle at point-blank range and the blood was said to have been ankle-deep in places. The militias counterattacked, driving back the British—then actually settling into the redcoats' camp. Some men were finishing meals that had been left there by Loyalist troops when the British attacked—and a four-hour bloodbath ensued. It was a fury of death. And when the survivors left the battlefield, the outcome was ambiguous. While the British ended up holding the most territory, they had suffered grievous casualties: more than seven hundred men were killed, wounded, or captured. The patriots suffered, too, losing five hundred men killed, wounded, or captured. Many men were buried where they fell.

Neither side was left fit for more fighting. The British continued their retreat to Charlestown. And they prepared to move north to reinforce Cornwallis, who had stumbled into a trap at Yorktown. Washington surrounded Cornwallis's army with more than seventeen thousand French and Americans. Any escape over land was blocked by troops led by the Marquis de Lafayette; any attempt to flee by ship was blocked by the French fleet. On September 28, a massive and continuous bombardment began. For three weeks, day and night, infantry and naval artillery and cannons blasted the British position. Finally, on October 17, Cornwallis surrendered. For such a historic battle, the number of casualties actually was very light. Only 156 British men were killed, 326 wounded, and 70 men were missing. On the other side, 88 allied French and American men were killed and 301 wounded—considerably fewer than the mostly forgotten Battle at Eutaw Springs. Although the war continued for almost two more years, the victory at Yorktown marked the end of major combat in America.

There were repeated skirmishes as the war came slowly to an end. But Francis Marion, the Swamp Fox, had seen too much death. When told to attack a small British force gathering freshwater outside Charlestown, for example, he replied, completely in keeping with his character, "My brigade is composed of citizens, enough of whose blood has been

The bloody Battle of Eutaw Springs on September 8, 1781, was the last major engagement in the southern campaign. The outcome was indecisive: the British reported 85 men killed and 351 wounded, while the patriots lost an estimated 125 killed and 382 wounded. Afterward, the redcoats withdrew to Charlestown, unsuccessful in blunting the Americans, advance.

John Trumball's large painting *Surrender of Lord Wallis*, depicting the British laying down their arms at Yorktown in October 1781, has hung in the Capitol rotunda since 1820. Noticeably absent from that painting—as in real life—is General Cornwallis, who claimed to be too ill to attend.

shed already. If ordered to attack, I shall obey; but with my consent, not another life shall be lost. . . . Knowing, as we do, that the enemy are on the eve of departure, so far from offering to molest, I would rather send a party to protect them."

With the fighting done, the men of his militia went home, most of them to peacefully work their fields. In 1781 Marion was elected to the South Carolina Assembly, helping to forge a peace between the remaining Loyalists and the victorious Americans. While others cried for retribution, he championed conciliation, one time even stepping in to prevent the lynching of a former Tory commander.

Marion rebuilt his own plantation, reportedly with Oscar, who had been wounded but had healed. Eventually Francis Marion married his cousin and lived the remainder of his life in peace and relative obscurity.

Valley Forge

The British army had proudly marched into Philadelphia in September 1777. The Continental Congress had fled to York, approximately one hundred miles away. After defeats at Brandywine and Germantown, the battered remnants of Washington's army had settled in for the long, cold winter of 1777–78 at Valley Forge, a strong defensive position on the Schuylkill River. It would be during this terrible winter at Valley Forge that Washington molded his army and brought hope to what at times had seemed like a hopeless fight for freedom.

Valley Forge has become symbolic of the terrible conditions that had to be overcome in the fight to create a new nation. As the French volunteer, the Chevalier de Pontgibaud, wrote upon arriving there in December:

> My imagination had pictured an army with uniforms, the glitter of arms, standards, etc., in short, military pomp of all sorts; instead of the imposing spectacle I expected, I saw, grouped together or standing alone, a few militiamen, poorly clad, and for the most part without shoes. . . . I also noticed soldiers wearing cotton nightcaps under their hats, and some having for cloaks or greatcoats coarse woolen blankets, exactly like those provided for the patients in our French hospitals. I learned afterwards that these were the officers and generals. Such, in strict truth, was, at the time I came amongst them, the appearance of this armed mob.

When Washington's twelve-thousand-man army made camp, they were short of every conceivable provision, including food, clothing, and medicine. It is difficult to imagine the deprivations his army faced: an estimated two out of three soldiers lacked shoes, and even blankets were scarce. Men injured in battle couldn't be properly treated and many of them died from their wounds. For a time many of the troops were forced to subsist on a mixture of water and flour known as a "firecake." At first there was little shelter from the cold and wet. As a result, scores of men left when their enlistment expired and others simply deserted in despair. General Washington pleaded to Congress: "It is more alarming than you will probably conceive. . . . For some days past, there has been little less, than a famine in camp. A part of the army has been a week, without any kind of flesh, and the rest for three or four days. Naked

In his General Orders of March 1, 1778, Washington paid tribute to the men who had suffered the Valley Forge winter with him, seen in this Tompkins H. Matteson painting, writing "to return his warmest thinks to the virtuous officers and soldiery of this army for persevering fidelity and zeal which they have uniformly manifested in all their conduct. Their fortitude . . . under the additional sufferings . . . clearly proves them worthy the inevitable privilege of contending for the rights of human nature, the Freedom and Independence of their Country."

and starving as they are, we cannot enough admire the incomparable patience and fidelity of the soldiery." Rather than facing these problems directly, the Congress discussed replacing Washington with a more aggressive leader.

Incredibly, while Washington's men lacked provisions, great numbers of them apparently had an abundance of spirit and fortitude. Meanwhile, only twenty miles away, the British army was warmly entrenched in Philadelphia, passing the winter in a safe and civilized manner, hosting formal dinners, attending theater, awaiting the spring thaw to finish this war, suffering few if any hardships. While the British celebrated Christmas with feasts by blazing fireplaces, the colonists dined on rice and vinegar, covering their freezing feet with rags. Yet at the end of the winter, it was the colonial army that emerged stronger and ready to do battle.

There were several reasons for this turnabout. For one thing, Congress had finally taken Washington seriously when he decried, "Unless some great and capital change suddenly takes place . . . this Army must inevitably . . . starve, dissolve, or disperse, in order to obtain subsistence in the best manner they can." Congress began spending the funds necessary to properly feed and equip the army. By February more than two thousand basic eighty-log cabins had been constructed and provisions were arriving daily at the encampment. In addition, the Prussian drill master Baron von Steuben had arrived and, with Washington's approval, began implementing uniform training procedures that would rapidly transform the troops into a well-drilled army. Wives and families, the "camp followers," had come to support their men, among them Martha Washington, who organized the women into sewing and nursing groups. Perhaps most important, the French government, inspired by the American victory at Saratoga the previous September and October, finally entered the war, agreeing to send both troops and the French fleet.

Washington celebrated the French decision by pardoning two men sentenced to hang for desertion, giving his troops a day off and proclaiming that he wanted "to set apart a day for gratefully acknowledging the divine goodness" and allotting each man one "gill of rum."

The toll taken by the winter was enormous. Of the twelve thousand men who began the winter, an estimated twenty-five hundred died of wounds; diseases including smallpox, dysentery, typhoid, and pneumonia that raced through the camp; or simply malnutrition. Another two thousand had finished their enlistment or deserted.

Although Washington's army had been reduced significantly in size, it had become a tougher, more resilient, properly trained, and highly motivated force. Having been tested and persevered, the colonial troops were now ready to take the fight to the enemy.

The British army, meanwhile, had lost its edge. By the time Washington marched his men out of Valley Forge, the strategic situation had changed drastically. Fearful of being cut off by the French fleet, General Howe decided to abandon Philadelphia and marshal his forces in New York. Continental troops reoccupied Philadelphia in June 1778. A week later, the Congress returned.

The colonial army took the offensive. As the British marched the hundred miles overland to New York, Washington ordered an attack on Howe's rear guard. The Americans caught the British at the Monmouth, New Jersey, courthouse. The Battle of Monmouth raged throughout the blistering hot day of June 28. As cold as it had been in the depths of December, temperatures on this day exceeded 100 degrees Fahrenheit. It was during this battle that the legend of Molly Pitcher was born. A woman named Mary Ludwig Hays was among the camp followers who served during the fighting by bringing water from a nearby spring to the fighting men to quench their thirst and cool their cannons. According to the story, when her husband, an artilleryman, was either wounded or had been killed she took his place and continued firing, and his gun crew mates began referring to her respectfully as "Molly Pitcher."

While the British rear guard achieved its aims by successfully protecting its withdrawing troops, the colonial army considered Monmouth a great victory. Washington's men had stood up to the full might of the British for the first time and fought them to a draw. The hard-won lessons learned during the winter at Valley Forge had made all the difference.

CHAPTER 8

FORGOTTEN
Heroes

A silvery moon slipped out from behind a cloud, briefly illuminating the lone sentry. Forty-eight men, mostly from the 1st Rhode Island regiment, instantly fell silent in the shadows, watching and waiting. They were about to attempt one of the boldest raids of the war: they were going to kidnap British general Richard Prescott.

It was a seemingly impossible mission. Several months earlier Washington's second-in-command, General Charles Lee, had been captured. Military tradition of the time allowed officers of equal rank to be exchanged. When informers reported that General Prescott was staying in a farmhouse in Newport, Rhode Island, a daring raid was planned: a small party would row across Narragansett Bay, sneak onto the island, and, under the eyes of three thousand enemy soldiers, grab the general and return safely. "The

☞ Prince Whipple, believed to be the African-American in this painting, became a legendary figure. Once, while carrying a substantial sum for his master, he was attacked by two highwaymen. He struck one with a whip, shot the other one, and delivered the money safely.

The slave Jack Sisson was credited with heroics in the successful raid to kidnap British general Richard Prescott.

enterprise will be attended with danger," the commander, Major William Barton, had warned when asking for volunteers, "and it is probable some of us may pass the shades of death before it is accomplished." The whole regiment stepped forward. Barton chose forty men; among them was an African American named Jack Sisson. Little is known of Sisson, beyond the fact that he was tall and broad and muscular, and he was a slave owned by Thomas Sisson, who had died that year. Major Barton must have had great confidence in him, though, as he picked him to steer the lead boat across the bay and participate in the actual raiding party.

With oars muffled, the five whale boats rowed three-quarters of a mile across open water; after landing, the raiding party moved quickly and quietly through fields and pastures more than half a mile to Mr. Overing's farmhouse. As they approached the house, the sentry called out, "Who comes there?" One of Barton's men responded, "Friends. Have you seen any deserters tonight?" As the cautious sentry waited for the proper countersign, Sisson raced forward and brought him down before he could raise a signal. He was quickly bound. Barton and Sisson went into the house; they climbed the stairway and found Prescott's door locked. According to the *Pennsylvania Evening Post*, Sisson banged his head against the door and "with his head, at the second stroke, forced a passage." The door flew open and the two men quickly hustled the startled general outside. In addition to Prescott, an aide and the sentry were taken back to the boats.

The raiding party was halfway back across the bay when the alarm was raised. Artillerymen fired cannons to alert the Royal Navy, but it was too late. The raid was a success and Prescott was exchanged for General Lee.

Jack Sisson was only one of the estimated nine thousand African Americans who fought and distinguished themselves in both the army and the navy in the war. The role of African Americans in the Revolution has been largely ignored, but black men actually fought on both sides and participated in just about all the major events of the war. Crispus Attucks is acknowledged as one of the first fatalities, being shot and killed in the Boston Massacre. At least nine black soldiers were among the minutemen who stood up to the British regulars

Newton Prince, an African American eyewitness to the shooting of Crispus Attucks at the Boston Massacre, reported, "I saw two or three strike with sticks on the guns. I was going off to the west of the soldiers and heard the guns fire and saw the dead carried off."

at Lexington and Concord, and among the wounded that day was Prince Estabrook, who is credited by many as being the first black combatant of the war.

Prior to the start of the war, both free and enslaved African Americans had served in many local and state militias, and saw action in battles against Indians. When war broke out the militias joined Washington's army, putting many African Americans in the uncomfortable position of fighting for a country that considered them property and deprived them of most of those rights they were fighting for. Among these soldiers was Salem Poor, a former slave who in 1769 had purchased his freedom for £27, about a year's salary, and married a freewoman. He enlisted in 1775 and soon found himself in the middle of the chaos on Breed's Hill. As British regulars overran the patriots' position, Salem Poor was one of the last men to abandon their redoubt, giving other soldiers the chance to get away. Historian Sarah Bailey wrote in 1880 that Poor saw Lieutenant Colonel James Abercrombie, commander of the elite grenadiers, "mount the redoubt and wave his arms in triumph; the colored lad aimed and fired, and then watched the British officer topple over." While there is limited historical record to support Bailey's specific claim, Poor's actions on Breed's Hill were so courageous that fourteen officers noted his heroism in a letter to the General Court of Massachusetts, writing, "The subscribers beg leave to report to your Honorable House (which we do in justice to the character of so brave a man), that, under our own observation, we declare that a negro man called Salem Poor of Col. Fryes regiment . . . behaved like an experienced officer, as well as an excellent soldier. To set forth particulars of his conduct would be tedious. We would only beg leave to say in the person of this negro centers a brave and gallant soldier."

Another African American hero of that bloody battle was Peter Salem, who had been given his freedom in 1775 to enlist in the Continental army. On Breed's Hill that bloody day he is credited by many historians with killing Marine major John Pitcairn. For his bravery that day he was acclaimed as a hero of battle. Men like Poor and Salem proved without doubt that African Americans were the equal of their white comrades in battle, but their presence posed a dilemma for Washington. Colonists were frightened that slaves who were given weapons might someday rise and turn those weapons against their owners, while slave owners knew that slaves who served in the military did so expecting their freedom. Washington was a slaveholder, but he also was an especially benevolent man and his opinion on the matter has never been clear. His own servant, Billy Lee, rode at his side throughout the war, according to historian Fritz Hirschfeld, "in the thick of battle, ready to hand over to the general a spare horse or his telescope or whatever else might be needed." As a valued aide to the beloved Washington, Lee became one of the best-known African Americans of the time.

In his 1887 book, *History of the Colored Race in America*, William Alexander wrote that at Bunker Hill, as seen in this lithograph, "Peter Salem, also a colored man, who so gallantly manned and defended the slight breastworks, shot dead Major Pitcairn, of the British Marines, who, in the final struggle, had scaled the redoubt and shouted 'The day is our own!'"

The question of what to do with African American soldiers aroused complex political issues. While the men were needed desperately, Washington could not risk alienating the colonies whose economy depended on slave labor. Finally, in July 1775, he ordered recruiters to stop enlisting "any stroller, negro, or vagabond," although permitting any African American already serving to remain in the ranks until his term of enlistment ended. As might have been predicted, the northern colonies objected. As Massachusetts's militia general John Thomas wrote to John Adams, "We have some negroes ... I look on them [as] equally serviceable with other men ... in action; many of them have proved themselves brave."

In response, the following November Virginia's royal governor, Lord Dunmore, offered slaves who volunteered to fight for the British their freedom: "I do hereby further declare all

John Trumbull's 1780 portrait of George Washington accurately portrays Washington's servant and slave Billy Lee at his side, where he served proudly throughout the war. In Washington's will the only slave he freed was the loyal Lee.

indentured servants, negroes, or others, [appertaining to Rebels,] free, that are able and willing to bear arms, they joining His Majesty's troops." Only a few hundred African Americans joined in the British ranks and, rather than being integrated into the ranks, they were formed into the specially created Ethiopian Regiment. The reality of runaway slaves fighting for the British—and their freedom—further complicated Washington's dilemma.

Finally, perhaps after a meeting with young Phillis Wheatley, the African American teenage poet, who became famous in both the colonies and England when her first volume was published in 1773, and whose work was read at the funerals of patriots, Washington informed Colonel Henry Lee, "We must use Negroes or run the risk of losing the war. . . . Success will depend on which side can arm the Negroes faster." The final resolution was that free African Americans who had served would be permitted to reenlist, but slaves would not be allowed to serve. Ironically, Dunmore's offer actually provided some benefit to his enemy, as southern plantation owners, somewhat ambivalent about being drawn into what many believed was a northern war, suddenly saw their way of life threatened and offered support to the American army.

The slaves themselves faced a very difficult choice with no guarantees, no matter what decision they made. When slave owner William Whipple enlisted in Washington's army, he took his servant, Prince Whipple, to war with him. Along the way he told Prince that should they be involved in combat, William expected him to acquit himself with courage to defend

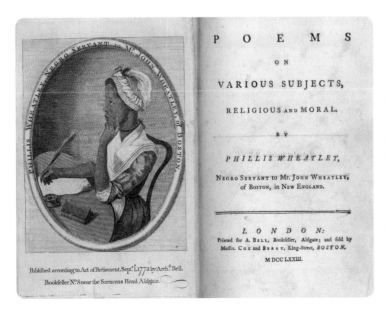

In 1773, eighteen-year-old slave Phillis Wheatley became the first black woman in America to have a collection of her poems published. The London publisher required the affirmation of eighteen important men, among them John Hancock, Reverend Samuel Mather, and royal governor Thomas Hutchinson that Wheatley actually was the author of these poems.

his country. The slave purportedly replied, "Sir, I have no inducement to fight; but if I had my liberty, I would endeavor to defend it to the last drop of my blood."

Hearing that, Captain Whipple freed him immediately. Prince Whipple enlisted in the army and eventually became an aide to George Washington. In fact, he is reputed to be the African American who is at Washington's side in the classic painting *Washington Crossing the Delaware*.

Only three colonies—Massachusetts, Connecticut, and Rhode Island—actively recruited African American soldiers, but there is no way of knowing precisely how many black soldiers were serving with the 1st Rhode Island Regiment at the Battle of Red Bank. Certainly it was a sizable contingent. One of them, it is known, was Jack Sisson. But whatever the number, the Continental troops made a historic and brave stand on October 22, 1777. After the British had conquered Philadelphia in September, Washington attempted to prevent them from being resupplied by blockading the Delaware River. He ordered two forts built downriver, Fort Mercer on the New Jersey side and Fort Mifflin on the opposite bank. As long as the Americans held those high points, no British shipping could reach the city. General Howe sent two thousand Hessian troops under the command of Colonel Carl von Donop to attack the four hundred men inside Fort Mercer. The colonel promised confidently, "Either the fort shall be called Fort Donop, or I shall have fallen."

Von Donop's prediction was accurate. The attack was repulsed by the courageous defenders of the fort and he was mortally wounded. In addition to 377 troops being killed during the battle, compared to 14 Americans, two British warships brought forward to support the attack ran aground and were set on fire and destroyed. It was the worst British defeat since Bunker Hill. Colonel James Varnum was so impressed by the courage displayed by his African American troops during the battle that he petitioned the Rhode Island Assembly to allow him to form an all-black regiment.

Varnum's timing was perfect. A shortage of troops had forced Washington to issue a quota to the states, allowing those states to determine who would be allowed to serve. The Rhode Island General Assembly permitted both free and enslaved African Americans to enlist, promising them that "every slave so enlisting shall, upon his passing muster before Colonel Christopher Greene, be immediately discharged from the service of his master or mistress, and be absolutely free." Their owners were to be paid the full market value, up to $400, for every slave who joined the fight. Eventually the 1st Rhode Island Regiment became the only majority African-American regiment in the Continental army.

The regiment first distinguished itself at the Battle of Rhode Island in late August 1778. This was planned to be the first battle in which colonial troops were supported by French

This Nathaniel Currier print features an unidentified black officer with Washington after he crossed the Delaware River. It is possible the soldier is supposed to be Prince Whipple or Washington's slave William Lee—or is simply intended to acknowledge the bravery of the black soldiers who fought in the Continental Army.

troops and the newly arrived French fleet. They were planning to attack the British garrison on Aquidneck Island, knowing that if they could capture the sixty-seven hundred soldiers there, General Clinton's position in New York would be desperate. But the French fleet was crippled by a storm and was unable to provide the promised assistance. General John Sullivan decided to press the attack and for several days the two sides traded artillery fire and met in occasional skirmishes. It became clear that without naval support Sullivan's army would not be able to advance. An orderly retreat began. Sullivan had to ferry more than five thousand troops across the Sakonnet River with six thousand enemy troops in pursuit. General Varnum's 1st Rhode Island was ordered to provide a defensive line across the island to prevent the British from attacking the retreating forces.

The battle raged through the day. The Hessians attacked the line three times and in hand-to-hand fighting were repulsed. As Samuel Greene Arnold wrote in his 1859 *History of the State of Rhode Island*:

> A third time the enemy, with desperate courage and increased strength, attempted to assail the redoubt, and would have carried it, but for the timely aid of two Continental battalions dispatched by Sullivan to support his almost exhausted troops. It was in repelling these furious onsets, that the newly raised black regiment . . . distinguished itself by deeds of desperate valor. Posted behind a thicket in the valley, three times they drove back the Hessians, who charged repeatedly down the hill to dislodge them; and so determined were the enemy in these successive charges that, the day after the battle, the Hessian colonel . . . applied to exchange his command . . . because he dared not lead his regiment again to battle, lest his men should shoot him for having caused so much loss.

Among the soldiers was an African American artillerist who was wounded in the arm. Rather than withdrawing, this soldier, whose name was not recorded, exchanged places with a white soldier, telling him, "I've got one arm to fight for my country." As he took his new position, he was shot and killed on the spot.

After their valiant stand on Aquidneck Island the 1st Rhode Island was sent to defend a position on the northern bank of New York's Croton River. On May 31, 1781, sixty cavalrymen and two hundred infantrymen of Colonel James DeLancey's Westchester Refugees launched a surprise attack on the camp. In the lightning raid, fourteen men of the 1st Rhode Island were killed, one hundred wounded, and thirty men were taken prisoner and later sold back into slavery in the West Indies. DeLancey's men suffered no casualties. Among the dead was the regiment's white commander, Colonel Christopher Greene, who was run through with a saber while still in his nightclothes, then thrown over a saddle and carried away. A contemporary account reported Greene's body was found about a mile away, cut and mangled "in a most shocking way." While there is no firm evidence to support it, the accepted belief at the time was that this raid was in retribution for Greene's fervent efforts in leading black soldiers against British troops.

While the 1st Rhode Island had suffered devastating losses it was rapidly reconstituted as a fighting force and within a few months was marching south under a new commander, Colonel Steven Olney.

The artist John Trumbull was an eyewitness to the Battle of Bunker Hill. This painting, circa 1820, depicts the death of General Warren. Trumbull became known for his painstaking research and visual accuracy. The African American on the right may have been Peter Salem or a slave belonging to the man in front of him, colonial officer Thomas Grosvenor.

Even among the numerous examples of extraordinary courage displayed by African American soldiers in combat, the actions of Jordan Freeman and Lambert Latham at the Battle of Groton Heights stands out. In September 1781, seventeen hundred British troops commanded by traitorous general Benedict Arnold landed near New London, Connecticut, and attacked lightly defended Fort Griswold. The estimated 185 patriots manning the fort, including both black and white soldiers, put up a spirited resistance, but had no chance of defeating the much larger force. As British troops led by Major William Montgomery scaled the walls, Jordan Freeman raced out to meet them. Out of ammunition, he bayoneted and killed Major Montgomery, then was himself killed.

After the fort had been taken, according to an eyewitness, a British captain demanded to know who had been in command of the fort. Colonel William Ledyard stepped forward, saying, "I did once. You do now." And then, according to an eyewitness, "at the same moment handing him his sword, which the unfeeling villain buried in his breast! Oh, the hellish spite and madness of a man that will murder a reasonable and noble-hearted officer, in the act of submitting and surrendering!"

In response, African American soldier Lambert Latham "retaliated upon the [British] officer by thrusting his bayonet through his body. Lambert, in return, received from the enemy thirty-three bayonet wounds, and thus fell, nobly avenging the death of his commander." The British response was to strike out against the survivors in what became known as the Fort Griswold Massacre. In fact, at the Battle of Yorktown, the Marquis de Lafayette purportedly led his men into battle with the war cry, "Remember Fort Griswold!"

The soldier at left in Jean Verger's 1780 watercolor featuring men who fought at Yorktown is a member of the 1st Rhode Island Regiment. While many colonials units were integrated, "the Black Regiment" is considered to be the first African American military force.

In addition to fighting on the front lines, many African Americans served in the Continental navy or filled a variety of other positions. Several men proved invaluable as spies, among them a slave named Pompey Lamb. In May 1779, Major General Sir Henry Clinton and forty-five hundred men captured the supply depot at Kings Ferry on the Hudson about twelve miles south of West Point, and the lightly defended forts at Stoney Point and Verplanck Point. It was an important position and he quickly reinforced it.

Clinton's plan was to try to draw Washington to him, but the colonial commander refused to take the bait. The problem was that these positions were almost impregnable; Stoney Point stood on a promontory about 150 feet above the Hudson River surrounded on three sides by the river and protected on the fourth side by a marsh. The British referred to it as "the Table on the Hill," and it could be reached only by traversing a causeway running through the marsh or by wading through the marshes at very low tide. A frontal assault would be close to suicidal; as Washington wrote to a friend, "An attempt to dislodge them . . . would require a greater force and apparatus than we are masters of." Rather than arms, he decided to use subterfuge. He sent several women to visit the position and their reports were disheartening; they saw no obvious weaknesses in the fortifications.

But when the British began using Stoney Point as a staging area for raids up and down the river, Washington knew he had to act. He assigned the task of taking the fortress to one of his bravest generals, "Mad Anthony" Wayne. Wayne commanded the Corps of Light Infantry, an elite group trained by Baron von Steuben to fight at close quarters, especially with a bayonet. The problem was getting close enough to the British troops to be able to use their bayonets.

The attack was planned for July 15. According to a now legendary story, one of the few people permitted regular passage into the fort was the slave Pompey, owned by a patriot known as Captain Lamb. Pompey would supply the garrison with locally grown berries, cherries, and vegetables. In early July, according to Wayne's plan, Pompey informed the soldiers that Captain Lamb needed him to work the fields during the day, but he would be pleased to make his delivery at night if he was given the password so he could get by the sentinels. The countersign on the night of the fifteenth was "The fort's our own." General Wayne was so pleased when he was informed of this that he made it the war cry of his attack.

Early that afternoon Wayne's men set out on a fourteen-mile march, reaching the fort after dark. This was to be a daring midnight attack made with bayonets, axes, and pikes. Muskets were not loaded. The attackers knew that if their approach was discovered before they reached the fort, they would be brutally cut down by British cannons. Fortunately, the weather was poor that night and clouds obscured the moon. The soldiers were each given a square of white paper to affix to their caps that would make them identifiable in the fighting. Wayne announced a bounty of as much as $500 to the first men to mount the breastworks. As the men prepared for what might be a suicide mission, many of them wrote final letters to their family; General Wayne wrote out his will.

Near midnight Pompey and two soldiers disguised as farmers, all of them carrying large baskets filled with fruits and vegetables, approached the first sentry on the far side of the causeway. After giving him the correct countersign, they were permitted to approach. As Pompey engaged the sentry in conversation, the soldiers seized and gagged him before he could sound a warning. They then proceeded to the causeway, taking the sentry with them. Several hundred men raced across the causeway while others waded through the marsh in water up to their chest. It was only as they approached the fort itself that pickets spotted them and raised the alarm, far too late for the deadly British artillery to be employed.

The battle began. It was brief but brutal, lasting only a half hour before the British surrendered. Some of Wayne's men had to make an extraordinarily difficult climb almost straight up the side of a cliff, but they made it. Wayne had lost 18 men, and 83 were wounded. Nineteen British soldiers were killed and 543 taken prisoner. Washington eventually abandoned the position because it required more men than he could spare to defend it, but before leaving, his army took a vast amount of stores and weapons.

It was in that same area, more than a year later, that an African American soldier supposedly helped foil the plot that might have changed the outcome of the war. On September 21, 1780, John Jacob "Rifle Jack" Peterson and a white soldier, Moses Sherwood, both members of the 2nd Regiment of New York, were stationed as lookouts at Croton Point. Peterson must have been recognized as a fine shot, as he carried a rifle rather than a musket. As they looked down upon the great Hudson River, they spotted a longboat carrying twenty-four men leave the British warship HMS *Vulture* and head directly for them. When the boat was close enough, the two men began firing, reportedly killing two soldiers. The boat turned around and hurried back to the ship. Within minutes the *Vulture* opened fire on Croton Point.

Peterson and Sherwood raced to nearby Fort Lafayette and reported the exchange. The commander of the fort dispatched two cannons and a howitzer to move within range of the ship. At dawn the next morning they opened fire, causing minor damage but forcing the *Vulture*'s captain to lift anchor and sail out of range—leaving behind the person it was there to collect, Major John André, who had just obtained from General Benedict Arnold the plans for West Point. Forced to return to New York on horseback, André was captured and then Arnold was revealed as a traitor.

Certainly one of the most important contributions made by an African American to the victory was the undercover work of James Armistead, a slave on the Armistead plantation in New Kent County, Virginia. By 1781 the war had moved to the south, and when General Lafayette's troops arrived in Virginia, James received permission from his master to join the Continental army. He eventually was assigned one of the most dangerous and difficult missions in the war—he was to become a double agent.

The details of his exploits remain sketchy, but there is no question about his courage or the results. Armistead successfully made his way into turncoat general Benedict Arnold's camp, claiming to be a runaway slave, and volunteered to work for the British. Supposedly he earned Arnold's trust by guiding his troops through the back roads of Virginia. African Americans were treated as invisible men in those days and officers didn't hesitate to speak freely in front of them. Armistead soaked up information, which was passed along to Lafayette. Eventually the British employed him as a spy, sending him back behind patriot lines—and he returned with false information given to him by Lafayette. When Arnold moved north, Armistead stayed in Virginia, talking his way into Lord Charles Cornwallis's headquarters. There he served as a waiter and, of course, passed along any intelligence he overheard to Lafayette. In the summer of 1781, Armistead learned that the British fleet was going to transport ten thousand troops to reinforce the garrison at Yorktown, Virginia, making it the center of their planned offensive. With this information, Admiral Comte de Grasse's French fleet got there first and successfully blocked the Chesapeake Bay, preventing British admiral Thomas Graves from delivering the vital reinforcements. Without those new troops, the outmanned Cornwallis eventually was forced to surrender.

While the Emancipation Act of 1783 freed slaves who had served as soldiers, because Armistead had been a spy, rather than a fighting man, he was returned to his owner. When Lafayette learned about this, he issued a testimonial, writing, "This is to certify that the bearer by the name of James has done essential services to me while I had the honour to command in this state. His intelligences from the enemy's camp were industriously collected and faithfully delivered. He perfectly acquitted himself with some important commissions I gave him and appears to me entitled to every reward his situation can admit of." As a result, in 1787 the Virginia General Assembly paid his owner for his freedom.

In appreciation James Armistead took the name Lafayette as his surname; he married, bought forty acres, and became a farmer. When the Marquis de Lafayette returned to the United States in 1824 at President James Monroe's invitation, he was honored in all twenty-four states. Huge crowds lined the streets to greet him. Supposedly, while in Virginia

This 1783 painting by Jean Baptiste Le Paon portrays the Marquis de Lafayette with his trusted spy, James Armistead, who successfully infiltrated Cornwallis's headquarters. It was intelligence provided by Armistead that enabled Washington to prevent the British from reinforcing Yorktown, leading to the colonists' historic victory.

to visit Washington's grave and give a speech to the House of Delegates, Lafayette ordered his carriage stopped when he saw Armistead Lafayette—a free man—standing among the crowd, and he got out and embraced him.

African Americans also fought bravely and successfully for the British. Historians estimate that as many as a hundred thousand slaves escaped their bondage during the war, but no one knows how many of them responded to Lord Dunmore's offer of freedom. Certainly the best-known—and feared—was Colonel Tye.

Titus Cornelius escaped from his owner in Monmouth County, New Jersey, in 1775, and eventually organized a guerrilla band of twenty-four mixed-race Loyalists known as the Black Brigade. While the British never formally commissioned black soldiers, rank was earned and bestowed out of respect for accomplishments. Colonel Tye first gained recognition in the 1778 Battle of Monmouth, when his band captured an officer of the Monmouth militia, but his real success began the following year when he launched a series of hit-and-run raids throughout that region. His brigade would appear suddenly, strike swiftly, then fade back into the safety of the county's swamps, rivers, and forests. These raids often targeted slave owners and were a lethal mix of revenge, military strategy, and commission—the British paid a bounty for each successful operation. His men struck throughout the summer of 1779; in July, for example, they attacked Tye's old town of Shrewsbury, capturing horses, cattle, and two men. That winter his men joined forces with the Queen's Rangers, an elite British guerrilla unit, to attack patriot strongholds around New York for desperately needed supplies.

Tye's attacks escalated the following summer, when the Black Brigade captured two New Jersey legislators, two militia leaders, and twelve of their men, rustled more than two hundred head of cattle, and began assassinating patriot leaders like Joseph Murray, who was known to brutally execute Loyalists. Tye became a local legend when in August 1780 he attacked a patriot named Joshua Huddy, in reprisal for Huddy's involvement in several hangings, at his tavern in Colts Neck. Huddy and a lady companion managed to hold off the band for several hours, firing preloaded muskets, until Tye's men set fire to the tavern. Huddy quickly surrendered in return for Tye's men putting out the fire and allowing his companion, Lucretia Emmons, to go safely.

Huddy was taken into custody but managed to escape the next morning when a patriot militia came upon Tye's band and opened fire. Either during the initial fighting or in this action, Tye was wounded in the wrist. While the wound itself was minor, over time it became infected and he died several weeks later. The death notice that appeared in a local paper described him as "justly to be more feared and respected than any of his brethren of a fairer complexion."

More than a year later, Huddy was captured by another African American Loyalist, a man known as Moses, and this time he was hanged.

The story of contributions made to the cause of American freedom by African American soldiers reaches a crescendo at the Battle of Yorktown, the climactic battle of the war. The arrival of the French fleet and fifty-five hundred well-trained and equipped troops under the command of the Comte de Rochambeau in the summer of 1780 had greatly bolstered Washington's army. At that time British forces were fighting on two fronts: General Clinton's troops were occupying New York while General Lord Cornwallis's southern army had successfully captured Charlestown and Savannah. Initially Washington planned to link up with Rochambeau to attack New York when the larger French fleet arrived. But when the fleet instead sailed south toward Chesapeake Bay, Washington changed his plans.

Under orders from Clinton to find a protected deep-water harbor for the British fleet in the lower Chesapeake Bay, Cornwallis had settled at Yorktown. Washington realized that Cornwallis had put himself in a precarious position, although it would take great luck, skill, and courage to exploit it. Rather than attacking Clinton, Washington would march south and trap Cornwallis's army. To ensure that Clinton stayed put in New York, Washington used subterfuge to convince him that he intended to attack New York. He had large brick bread ovens built, erected tents, and prepared false plans detailing the attack that spies carried into the city. Then, leaving a small force behind to show continued activity in the camp, Washington and Rochambeau marched to Virginia.

In early September the French fleet landed three thousand troops in the lower Chesapeake Bay, then fought off a British attack. When the British sailed back to New York, the French fleet established a blockade to prevent Cornwallis from being resupplied by sea. By the end of September, almost eighteen thousand American and French troops were only seventeen miles away from the eighty-three hundred British troops at Yorktown—among them more than a thousand escaped slaves. Cornwallis sent Clinton a message pleading for help. Clinton responded that a British fleet carrying five thousand soldiers would depart from New York in early October. Somehow Cornwallis had to hold out until those reinforcements arrived.

Cornwallis began establishing a secure defensive position, including ten redoubts, small enclosed artillery positions connected by trenches. On September 28, Washington's army arrived at Yorktown. They immediately began digging siege trenches eight hundred yards from the British line. When that digging was completed, artillery moved up and began a barrage that continued for nine days, knocking out much of Cornwallis's cannons.

It was sometime during that period that Cornwallis learned that Clinton had been delayed. The British fleet was not en route to relieve him. On October 11, Washington began digging a second trench, this one only four hundred yards from the British lines. But artillery fire from redoubts 9 and 10 prevented him from completing this second trench. As historian Samuel Greene Arnold wrote, "These were two very strong redoubts, in advance of their principal line, from which the British fire was most galling." Washington had no choice: he had to mount an assault directly into those guns. He and Lafayette determined that the French were to storm the stronghold to the left, while the reconstituted 1st Rhode Island Regiment—among them Jack Sisson—was to attack redoubt 10, on the right.

The attack began on the night of October 14. As Colonel Olney, later of the 1st Rhode Island, remembered:

> General Washington made a short address or harangue, admonishing us to act the part of firm and brave soldiers. . . . I thought then that His Excellency's knees rather shook, but I have since doubted whether it was not mine.
>
> The column marched in silence. . . . Many, no doubt, thinking, that less than one quarter of a mile would finish the journey of life with them. On the march, I had a chance to whisper to several of my men (whom I doubted,) and told them I had full confidence they would act the part of brave soldiers . . . and if their guns should be shot away, not to retreat, but take the first man's gun that might be killed.

The attack began when a small group raced forward to hack a path through the abatis, a line of fallen trees arranged so that their intertwined branches formed a sort of barbed-wire barricade. They came under intense British fire. As Olney wrote, "The enemy fired a full body of musketry. At this, our men broke silence and huzzaed; and as the order for silence seemed broken by every one, I huzzaed with all my power, saying, see how frightened they are. . . . We made out to crawl through or get over, and from the enemy's first fire, until we got possession of the redoubt, I think did not exceed ten minutes." Colonel Olney was shot and stabbed by a bayonet, but survived. The French took a full half hour to capture their objective, suffering fifteen deaths, while nine Americans died in the attack.

The second trench was completed the following day and, as Arnold wrote in his history, "The walls of Yorktown crumbled before the terrible fire of the besiegers. . . . The British fire slackened, their ammunition was nearly exhausted, and their artillery broken and dismounted." Cornwallis made a futile counterattack, which was repulsed, then attempted to escape by crossing the York River in small boats. But foul weather forced him to turn back. He had no choice but to ask for terms of surrender.

Four days later the British fleet arrived. When informed of the situation, the fleet returned to New York.

On October 19, 1781, American and French troops lined up facing each other on either side of a road, lines said to stretch more than a mile long. The British soldiers, drums muffled in black cloth, marched between them and laid down their weapons. Watching proudly were the men of the 1st Rhode Island, whose attack on redoubt 10 had played a vital role in the victory.

While the war continued for almost two more years, Yorktown was the last substantial battle on American soil. It would be poetic to claim that all of the African Americans who fought in the war then enjoyed their freedom, but that is far from reality. It is estimated by historians that only about a third of former slaves eventually lived as free men. Supposedly as many as twenty thousand African Americans sailed to England with the defeated redcoats, knowing that slavery had been outlawed there. Former soldiers also ended up in other parts of Europe, Canada, and the West Indies. Unfortunately, a substantial number appear to have once again been enslaved.

Several thousand men who had served in the British army were granted land in Nova Scotia, but when that acreage proved to have little value for farming, twelve hundred of them were transported to Africa, where they founded the aptly named community of Freetown, in the colony of Sierra Leone.

Yankee Doodle Dandy

◄►

Yankee Doodle came to town,

riding on a pony,

Stuck a feather in his cap,

and called it Macaroni...

◄►

Young Americans have been joyfully singing that playful verse— without knowing what it means—for more than 250 years. "Yankee Doodle" is certainly among the oldest and best-known songs in American history. In fact, it's difficult to even read those few words without the familiar tune bouncing in your head. But very little actually is known about the derivation of that song, and there probably are as many stories about it as there are verses.

The derivation of the word Yankee isn't even known, although the first known use of it in print was by British general James Wolfe, who referred to the colonists fighting alongside his troops in the Seven Years' War. While inside the United States it usually refers specifically to northerners, to the rest of the world it means all Americans.

The well-known tune is considerably older than the Revolutionary War lyrics, and some version of it is said to exist in work songs sung in the French vineyards; or Irish, Dutch, Hungarian, and English folk tunes, including the British ditty "Lydia Fisher's Jug." The first known sheet music was published in London in 1775, and was to be sung "thru the Nose, and in the West Country drawl and dialect." But most historians believe the "Yankee Doodle" lyrics apparently date back to the 1750s, when often-ragged colonial militiamen in their simply country clothing and tricornered hats joined the handsomely turned out, well-drilled redcoats to fight the French. The lyrics, supposedly written by British surgeon and musician Richard Schackburg, were intended to ridicule the American country bumpkins: A doodle was a foolish person, so a "Yankee Doodle" was a silly colonist. A dandy was a man who affected an overly elite persona in his dress, speech, and manners, a man pretending to be far more than he is in an effort to impress people.

Rather than being pasta, "macaroni" referred to an overly feminine style of dress and manners made popular in England by wealthy young men returning from Italy and France after completing what was then known as the "Grand Tour" of Europe. So the seemingly silly feather-in-the-hat line was meant to make fun of the naïve Americans, who supposedly were so silly that they thought simply by sticking an animal feather in their coonskin caps they could look like a sophisticated European.

The joke backfired. Rather than being insulted, the colonists adopted the tune and when the Revolution began added their own verses to it, often writing new stanzas to reflect the latest events of the war. When the colonists acquired new artillery, for example, someone wrote: "Every time they shoot it off, It takes a horn of powder; and makes a noise like father's gun, Only a nation louder."

Apparently both sides marched to it throughout the war. It was a tune easily played on a fife, and its often boisterous, colorful, and even risqué lyrics added to the flavor. One well-known British stanza told the story of a colonist named Thomas Ditson who was tarred and feathered for trying to purchase a musket: "Yankee Doodle came to town, For to buy a musket; We will tar and feather him, and so we will John Hancock!"

According to a Boston newspaper report, confident British troops apparently were singing a derogatory version of that song as they marched out of that city in April 1775 to relieve redcoats under attack at Lexington and Concord. And when they returned, having been stunned by both the ferocity and innovative tactics of the local militia, one soldier, when asked if he had changed his tune, replied, "D--n them, they made us dance it till we were tired."

It eventually became the most popular American song, and was adopted as the unofficial anthem. According to legend, when the British surrendered to Washington at Yorktown in 1781, they played the song "The World Turned Upside Down," while the victorious Americans avenged the slight from so many years earlier by responding with a lively version of "Yankee Doodle." If that were true it would make a perfect ending, though contrary to most reports it probably isn't.

A charcoal sketch by Norman Rockwell from his 1937 large mural *Yankee Doodle Came to Town.*

Tradition at that time allowed musicians from the surrendering army to play a march favored by the victors while its flags flew and troops walked forward and laid down their arms. But when General Benjamin Lincoln had surrendered to British general Clinton at Charlestown he was ordered to keep the American colors furled and prohibited from playing an English or German song. It was an insult Lincoln did not forget; when Washington chose him to negotiate the terms of the British surrender at Yorktown he insisted on including a clause reading, "The garrison of York will march out to a place to be appointed in front of his posts, at two o'clock precisely, with shouldered arms, colors cased, and drums beating a British or German march." And while records do appear to show that the victorious Americans played "Yankee Doodle" when General Burgoyne surrendered his 6,000-man army to General

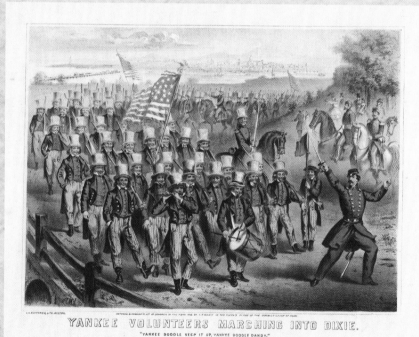

YANKEE VOLUNTEERS MARCHING INTO DIXIE.
"YANKEE DOODLE KEEP IT UP, YANKEE DOODLE DANDY."

Currier & Ives's 1862 hand-colored lithograph *Yankee Volunteers Marching into Dixie*, subtitled *Yankee Doodle Keep It Up, Yankee Doodle Dandy*, demonstrates the lasting popularity of the song.

Horatio Gates at Saratoga, there is no record of any music being played during the ceremony of surrender at Yorktown.

Rather than the popularity of the song ending with the conclusion of the war, as most wartime songs do, the ease with which new verses can be fit to it, as well as the seemingly nonsensical lyrics of the original version that have always appealed to children, have kept it popular. During the Civil War, for example, both Union and Confederate troops embraced it. While the Southerners pointed out in their song "Dixie Doodle," "Yankee Doodle had a mind, To whip the Southern Traitors; Because they didn't choose to live, on codfish and potatoes," the Northerners advised in the chorus of their version, "Yankee Doodle keep it up, Yankee Doodle dandy; Plant your bayonet on top, and with your gun be handy!"

The appeal of this simple song really has never ended.

A lobby card for the 1942 movie musical *Yankee Doodle Dandy*. James Cagney won the Academy Award as Best Actor for his starring role as the beloved entertainer George M. Cohan.

CHAPTER 9

President George Washington

FORGED IN CONFLICT

In the winter of 1786, George Washington stood silently at a large window, looking out onto the sprawling fields of his beloved plantation, Mount Vernon, wondering if he would be able to retain it. As was the case with so many people in this new country, his debts were growing rapidly and it had become far more difficult to pay them. But he must have realized how fortunate he was that at least his storehouses were well stocked. His Excellency had led the colonies to one of the greatest military victories in history, but the peace that followed was proving far more painful than anyone could have imagined.

The Revolution was over. It had been a long and bloody war, but the colonies had won their freedom. Now different battles had to be fought, with words and ideas rather than with muskets, to determine the kind of country so many men had died to create. The states had united for battle; now they had to form a nation.

Jean Ferris's painting *John Paul Jones at the Constitutional Convention* depicts the American naval hero entering Constitution Hall with Benjamin Franklin and George Washington.

General Washington had resigned his commission in December 1783. He was regarded throughout the new country with such great favor that he might have remained in command with any title of his choosing—there were some who would not have been disappointed if he had accepted a king's crown—but instead he chose to return to his former life as a benevolent plantation owner. He owned many thousands of acres and was known to treat his slaves fairly. To mark his resignation he had invited his officers to meet with him one final time at Fraunces Tavern in New York City. These were the men with whom he had fought through the hardest winters and the bloodiest battles. At this meeting, wrote Colonel Benjamin Tallmadge:

> His emotions were too strong to be concealed which seemed to be recip-
> rocated by every officer present. After partaking of a slight refreshment in
> almost breathless silence the general filled his glass with wine and turning
> to the officers said, "With a heart full of love and gratitude I now take leave
> of you. I most devoutly wish that your latter days may be as prosperous and
> happy as your former ones have been glorious and honorable." . . . General
> Knox being nearest to him turned to the commander in chief who, suffused
> in tears, was incapable of utterance but grasped his hand when they em-
> braced each other in silence. In the same affectionate manner every officer
> in the room marched up and parted with his general in chief. Such a scene
> of sorrow and weeping I had never before witnessed and fondly hope I may
> never be called to witness again.

And then he went home, leaving to others, he thought, the job of molding the separate states into a country. Few people realized how difficult a task that would prove to be. The cost of waging war had been extraordinarily high; it had left the new nation with massive debts. The colonies had struggled to pay for the war using a variety of methods to raise revenue: To support its militia, each state printed its own currency, taxed its residents, and even imposed duties on goods brought in from other states. In addition, the Continental Congress printed its own money but it had very questionable worth, as there was almost nothing of real value to back it, giving rise to the phrase "Not worth a continental."

The new country was fighting a different kind of war, and one that struck hard at every citizen; post–Revolutionary War America was suffering a devastating economic depression. During the war people had done business with trust, credit, and barter, but that had changed; merchants were insisting on hard currency. To settle their own debts they needed real dollars,

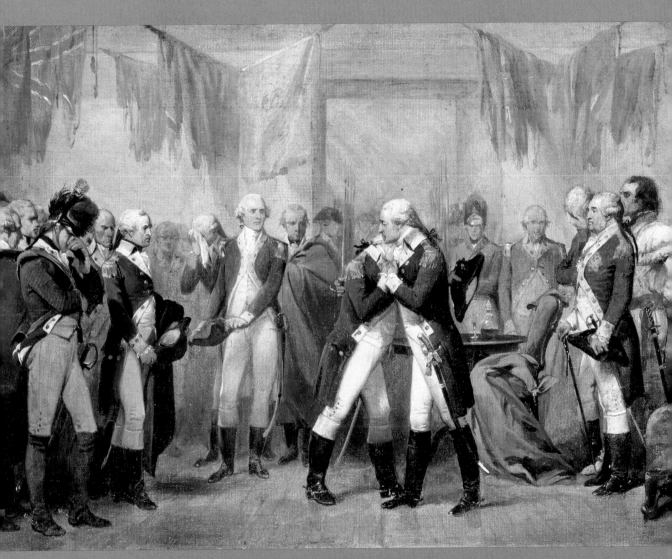

Alonzo Chappel's *Washington's Farewell to His Officers* captures the dramatic scene on December 4, 1783, when Washington gathered his staff at New York's Fraunces Tavern and announced his resignation. Finally, the war was over. Freedom had been won.

Among the first orders of business—literally—for the new country was the creation of a national currency. Until this time varied forms of exchange were common, from commodities to state-issued money to foreign coins and bills. The continental currency seen here was essentially worthless by the end of the war because the Congress devalued it by over-printing.

backed by gold and silver, but their customers just didn't have it. The farmers and tradesmen had little money to buy products, and so fewer people were employed to make those products. The manufacturing industry collapsed. The once thriving export market had shrunk drastically; Britain still dominated international trade and kept its markets mostly closed to Americans, especially the valuable West Indies trade, while at the same time dumping its own cheap goods, mostly in the south. The French were demanding repayment for their war expenditures while also protecting their own ports. American merchants, increasingly desperate for those foreign markets to be reopened, wanted taxes to be raised to settle those war debts. At the center of the problem was the fact that the country lacked a strong central government that could impose the policies necessary to deal with this crisis. The states were still almost completely autonomous, bound together only by a weak document called the Articles of Confederation.

Passed by the Continental Congress in 1777 and finally ratified in 1781, this treaty was intended to loosely bind the states together in a "perpetual union." It was drafted with great difficulty, as the states wanted to gain the benefits of a union without surrendering any of their individual powers. It contained thirteen articles, the first one bestowing on this confederation a name: "The stile of this confederacy shall be 'The United States of America.'" The other twelve mostly acted to limit the powers of the central government: The second article, arguably the most important, specifically did that, stating, unequivocally, "Each state retains its sovereignty, freedom, and independence, and every power, jurisdiction, and right, which is not by this Confederation expressly delegated." The government was given no power to mediate disputes between states. Also each state, regardless of its size, was granted one vote in Congress—and as unanimous consent was required to make any changes to this agreement, each state had complete veto power.

While it did grant some limited powers to the central government—for example, Article 8 stated that the expenditures of the central government would be paid by funds raised by state governments—it provided no mechanism to raise that revenue or enforce penalties. As a result, the very weak central government was helpless to deal with the current economic situation.

As Henry Knox described the problem in a 1786 letter to Washington, "Our political machine constituted of thirteen independent sovereignties, have been perpetually operating against each other, and against the federal head, ever since the peace—The powers of Congress are utterly inadequate to preserve the balance between the respective States, and oblige them to do [t]hose things which are essential for their own welfare, and for the general good. . . . The machine works inversely to the public good in all its parts. . . . [S]omething is wanting, and something must be done or we shall be involved in all the horror of faction and civil war without a prospect of its termination."

To raise desperately needed revenue, states had begun imposing taxes on their citizens—in some instances, ironically, at rates even higher than the British had once demanded. When farmers were unable to pay their debts or their mortgages or satisfy their tax bills, their homes, fields, livestock, and other possessions were seized. In a few places farmers who couldn't pay their debts—men who had fought for their country—were imprisoned. The farmers pleaded with their state assembly for relief, asking specifically for the state to lower taxes and issue more paper currency, but the merchants who dominated the legislature knew that would hurt their own interests and refused to consider it. Before the war, debtors had despised the tax collectors—now, after years of fighting, the only difference was who ended up with their money or property.

Once again anger was simmering in New England. These people had risen once before and been successful, and the memory was still quite fresh. Before the Revolution John Adams had written many critical articles under the pseudonym Humphrey Ploughjogger, meaning "the farmers," and while this time it probably was not the work of Adams, "Plough Jogger"—as this note was signed—reappeared in a local newspaper. "I have been greatly abused," he wrote, "have been obliged to do more than my part in the war, been loaded with class rates, town rates, province rates, Continental rates and all rates . . . been pulled and hauled by sheriffs, constables and collectors, and had my cattle sold for less than they were worth. . . . I think it is time for us to rise and put a stop to it, and have no more courts, nor sheriffs, nor collectors nor lawyers."

And just as they had two decades earlier, the protesters began taking action. In Massachusetts and Connecticut, farmers met tax collectors with force, seizing back their property and hiding livestock and other possessions. They prevented local courts, which were issuing writs to enforce debt collection, from meeting, and broke debtors free from jail. In response, state governments called out the militia—although in some instances that militia consisted of many of the same men participating in the protests. A fearful James Warren wrote to Adams, "We are now in a state of anarchy and confusion bordering on a civil war." Adams, a champion of liberty and individual rights, claimed the British were instigating treason and helped pass legislation in the state assembly suspending habeas corpus, allowing leaders of this growing rebellion to be jailed without a trial.

This growing rebellion found a leader in a farmer named Daniel Shays. His followers called themselves Regulators and sometimes marched with pine needles in their hats symbolic of the liberty tree. Shays was a farmer who had served as a captain in the Massachusetts militia during the war, seeing action at Lexington, Bunker Hill, and Saratoga before being wounded. Like so many other patriots, he never received the promised pay for his service and so was unable to pay his debts. In 1780 he was given an ornamental sword for his service— which he sold in an unsuccessful effort to settle those debts. In August 1786, Shays and an estimated fifteen hundred protesters successfully prevented the Northampton County Court of Common Pleas from hearing foreclosure cases. A week later the Worcester County Court was similarly stopped from meeting. For three days in late September Shays and six hundred farmers occupied the Springfield courthouse to ensure the Supreme Judicial Court could not meet. The county militia was called out to respond, but sympathetic members of that force refused to take arms against their friends and neighbors. In desperation, Governor James Bowdoin authorized General Benjamin Lincoln to recruit a private twelve-hundred-man militia, paid for by merchants, to protect the courts.

Until then, Shays's protests had been peaceful, but the presence of an armed militia changed the situation. To meet this new challenge, Shays planned to overrun a new federal arsenal at Springfield and seize all the arms and ammunition his growing army would need. They believed the defenders would also be sympathetic and stand aside. On January 25, 1787, two thousand farmers marched on the arsenal. The twelve hundred defenders stood their

The 1787 satirical engraving (top) gives some idea of all the problems local, state, and federal governments faced in establishing an equitable system. While focused on Connecticut politics, the wagon being pulled from either side as it sinks into the mud illustrated the difficulty in getting anything done. The woodcut (right) appeared on the cover of a pamphlet supporting Shay's Rebellion against economic injustice.

This illustration from an 1884 edition of *Harper's* depicts followers of Daniel Shays taking control of the Northampton, Massachusetts, courthouse to prevent judges from enforcing orders confiscating land from debtors. To the left, the proclamation signed by Benjamin Franklin offering a reward for the leaders of the rebellion.

ground. When Shays's Regulators continued to press forward, the guards fired warning shots; when that failed to stop them, they opened fire with artillery. Four men were killed and another twenty were wounded. Shays's army scattered, with Lincoln's militia in pursuit. Lincoln caught up with Shays at Petersham, capturing some of the protesters and causing most of the rest to return to their farms. Shays and some other leaders escaped into the independent republic of Vermont. The rebellion was finished.

Shays and other leaders eventually were granted amnesty; and while their protests failed, they had made their voices heard. In the next election, Massachusetts governor Bowdoin was easily defeated by the more conciliatory John Hancock. The newly elected Massachusetts legislature quickly cut taxes and suspended debt payments. The country began to climb out of its depression.

But the Shays Rebellion had made obvious the need for a stronger central government. The Annapolis Convention, meeting the prior September, had agreed to a constitutional convention intended to strengthen the Articles of Confederation. This meeting convened in Philadelphia in May 1787. Rhode Island, which had remained so aloof at times that it was referred to as Rogue Island, was concerned that strengthening the government would be harmful to its sovereignty and refused to send representatives.

Initially George Washington did not want to attend, convinced the states were not prepared to cede power to a stronger central government and nothing of value would be accomplished. As he wrote to Henry Knox, "I believe that the political machine will yet be much tumbled and tossed, and possibly be wrecked altogether, before such a system . . . will be adopted." It's also possible that Washington knew he would be elected the leader and did not want to appear to be grasping for power. But Knox, James Madison, and Benjamin Franklin, among others, prevailed upon him to attend, recognizing that he was the only man capable of bringing together a convention with so many competing interests.

At the beginning of the convention Washington was unanimously elected its president and it was agreed that the proceedings would be kept completely secret—to prevent outside pressure from being brought upon the delegates, none of the debates would be printed or communicated. The doors and windows were closed and few notes were taken. While apparently Washington was not an especially active participant in the debates, his presence in the hall, seated at the front in an ornate chair with a rising sun carved into its back, added the necessary solemnity to the proceedings.

It was a remarkable event. These men were attempting to achieve something that had never before been done: form a central government with sufficient power to rise above the states when necessary, while making certain those states maintained their sovereignty and that the individual rights of each citizen were protected. At that moment most people were far more loyal to their state than to the union. Citizens awaited eagerly to learn what type of government the convention would propose. Some people anticipated Washington emerging from behind those doors as the first king of America.

The framework for the convention was drawn from history. The representatives based their conclusions on British law and tradition, on arguments made thousands of years earlier by Greeks and Romans when debating the role of the state, and by their contemporaries from Germany and Holland who only recently had wrestled with the same complex questions. The debates were said to be long and at times angry. The desire to form a stronger nation certainly existed, but the lack of trust among the states created a roadblock. Washington's frustration

Junius Brutus Stearns's *Washington as Statesman* depicts the Constitutional Convention. Initially about the only thing on which the delegates could reach an agreement was the election of war hero Washington as the presiding officer.

was obvious, as he wrote to Alexander Hamilton, "In a word, I almost despair of seeing a favorable issue to the proceedings of the convention, and do therefore repent having had any agency in the business."

While supposedly this convention had been called to amend the Articles of Confederation, one of the first accomplishments was an agreement that an entirely new document be drafted, a document that would constitute the laws by which the united states would come together as one country.

The most difficult issue to be solved was how power would be shared by the central government and the states. Some representatives continued to insist that the rights of the individual states had to remain superior to any central government, while others, like James

Madison, wanted a strong national government. Many delegates were concerned that a strong central government could eventually lead to the same type of tyranny they had spent so many years and lives to overcome. In Madison's personal notes, he quoted New York's John Lansing, who summed up the feelings of those representatives defending states' rights: "Is it to be thought that the people of America, so watchful over their interests, so jealous of their liberties, will give up their all, will surrender both the sword and the purse, to the same body, and that, too, not chosen immediately by themselves? They never will. They never ought. Will they trust such a body with the regulation of their trade, with the regulation of their taxes, with all the other great powers which are in contemplation?"

Madison responded, "It will be said that, if the people are averse to parting with power, why is it hoped that they will part with it to a national legislature? The proper answer is that in this case they do not part with power; they only transfer it from one set of immediate representatives to another set."

James Madison had been among the first to arrive in Philadelphia and, while awaiting the others, had drawn up a government structure that became known as the Virginia Plan. Proposed to the convention by Edmund Randolph, it consisted of fifteen resolutions that were based loosely on concepts created by the French political philosopher Montesquieu and the British philosopher John Locke. Basically, it proposed a government elected by the citizens consisting of three branches; a legislature, a judiciary, and an executive, each with its own powers and some ability to provide checks and balances over the others. The legislature was to be divided into two houses; members of the House of Representatives would be directly elected by the people to three-year terms, and senators would be elected by state legislatures to seven-year terms. The plan did not include any suggestion over the composition of the executive branch.

Tempers frayed in the heat of the Philadelphia summer. To counter the Virginia Plan, which granted more power to those states with larger populations, the smaller states supported the New Jersey Plan, in which every state had one vote in a single legislative body. For a time compromise seemed impossible. At one point in the debate Delaware's Gunning Bedford Jr. rose and warned that if the large states tried to impose this structure, to protect their rights, "the small ones would find some foreign ally of more honor and good faith, who will take them by the hand and do them justice."

The suggestion that a state might need to turn to foreign nations for protection, so soon after the Revolution, was denounced as practically traitorous. Unfortunately, two greatly respected men who might have brought more order to the proceedings, Thomas Jefferson and

John Adams, were both in Europe trying to settle national debts and establish better relations. As Jefferson in Paris wrote to his close friend Adams in London, "I have news from America as late as July 19. Nothing had then transpired from the federal convention." Adding that while he thought it had been an "abominable" mistake keeping the proceedings private, he did suggest "all their other measures will be good and wise" because "it is really an assembly of demigods."

Jefferson's "assembly of demigods" debated and argued and reasoned and pleaded into the summer, searching for some compromise that would be agreeable to both large and small states. The larger states insisted that because they would be contributing more to the nation's finances and defense, they should have greater influence; the smaller states remained concerned that they would have no voice and demanded equal representation. Connecticut's Roger Sherman finally proposed a solution; the Great Compromise, as eventually modified, created a national legislature composed of two houses. The lower house would consist of representatives based on each state's population, while in the upper house every state would have two senators. The plan did not please everyone, but the delegates were sensible enough to understand, as Massachusetts's Caleb Strong warned before the vote was taken, "If no accommodation takes place, the Union itself must soon be dissolved."

After extended debate on July 16, the convention finally considered the compromise. It passed by one vote, arguably the most important single vote in American history.

There was still one additional and very complex problem to be solved: How would the lower house be apportioned? The southern states wanted nonvoting slaves to be counted when determining their population; the northern states wanted to include only free men. The balance of power in the government depended on the resolution; counting slaves the equal of free men would almost double the number of representatives from the southern states in this Congress as well as in the body that would elect the executive, the electoral college. It would tilt the balance of power in their direction.

In a brutal turn of logic, Massachusetts's Elbridge Gerry wondered, why "should the blacks, who were property in the south, be in the rule of representation more than the cattle and horses of the north?" The antislavery contingent also feared that allowing slaves to be counted would provide an additional incentive for the southern states to import more slaves.

The delegates finally agreed to recognize the existence of the slaves without making them the equal of free men. After considerable negotiation—all manner of ratios were considered, from one-quarter to three-fourths—they eventually settled on the Three-Fifths Compromise. One reason the South finally accepted this provision is that the convention also tied taxation to population. As Madison wrote later in his Federalist Papers, "By extending the rule to both [taxation and representation], the states will have opposite interests, which will control and balance each other, and produce the requisite impartiality."

New York's Gouverneur Morris was asked to write the preamble. He was given a draft of the ideas to be included, which began, "We the people of the states of New-Hampshire, Massachusetts, Rhode-Island and Providence Plantations, Connecticut, New-York, New-Jersey, Pennsylvania" and after much thought changed it to the now-familiar, "We the people of the United States, in order to form a more perfect union."

Patrick Henry rejected those words, instead wondering, "Who authorized them to speak the language of 'We the People,' instead of 'We the States'?"

It was Madison who responded, pointing to the defining philosophy that has made this Constitution so unique: "This is derived from the superior power of the people."

After considerable haggling, the delegates finally agreed on the basic principles that would bind the colonies together into a nation. The purpose of the Constitution, Morris's preamble continued, was to "establish justice, insure domestic tranquility, provide for the common defense, promote the general welfare, and secure the blessings of liberty to ourselves and our posterity."

The final draft of the document was the result of numerous compromises that left many of the men who drafted it dissatisfied. Benjamin Franklin may well have been speaking for the majority when he said on September 17, at the final meeting of the convention, "I confess that there are several parts of this constitution which I do not at present approve, but I am not sure I shall ever approve them . . . when you assemble a number of men to have the advantage of their joint wisdom, you inevitably assemble with those men, all their prejudices, their passions, their errors of opinion, their local interests, and their selfish views. From such an assembly can a perfect production be expected? It therefore astonishes me, Sir, to find this system approaching so near to perfection as it does."

Of the fifty-five delegates, thirty-nine signed the Constitution that day. George Washington pointed out that the Constitution had been accepted by the delegates from eleven states and Alexander Hamilton—the only one of New York's three delegates who had not left the convention in disgust. Washington was the first to sign. As the rest of the delegates signed, one by one, it was Benjamin Franklin, once again, who found the right words: "I have often and often, in the course of the session . . . looked at that [sun] behind the president, without being able to tell whether it was rising or setting: but now at length, I have the happiness to know, that it is a rising, and not a setting sun."

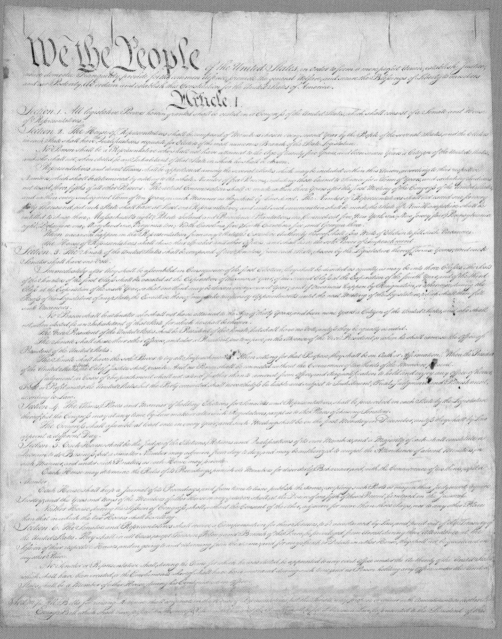

The Constitution of the United States was written by Jacob Shallus, the clerk of the Pennsylvania General Assembly. It was handwritten over a single September 1787 weekend with quill and ink on parchment. No one knows for certain how many handwritten copies of the original document were produced.

PRESIDENT GEORGE WASHINGTON

As Franklin left Independence Hall that September afternoon, a crowd had gathered outside to learn the result of the months of deliberations. Rumors had circulated, but overall the founding fathers had done a fine job maintaining secrecy. According to the notes of Maryland delegate Dr. James McHenry, Franklin was approached by an otherwise unidentified woman named Mrs. Powell who asked, "Well, Doctor, what have we got, a republic or a monarchy?" Franklin barely hesitated before responding, "A republic, if you can keep it!"

Before the Constitution became binding, it had to be ratified by at least nine of the thirteen states. Five states quickly did so; the others showed reluctance. Ironically, it was not so much what the document said as what it did not say that raised considerable alarm. Massachusetts, the birthplace of the Revolution, refused to sign the Constitution because it failed to reserve to the states all the powers not specifically granted to the national government. It also did not guarantee the political rights that in the past had proved so important: the freedoms of speech, religion, assembly, and the press. Only after Massachusetts and several other states were assured that those and other amendments would immediately be taken up by the new Congress did they agree to sign the Constitution of the United States of America. On June 21, 1788, New Hampshire became the ninth state to ratify the Constitution.

It was agreed that the new government would meet for the first time in New York on March 4, 1789.

In January of that year, George Washington, running unopposed, was elected the first president of the United States, receiving all 43,782 popular votes and 69 electoral votes. John Adams was elected vice president. There were no political parties and Washington did not campaign for the office; in fact, he had to be convinced to come out of retirement and accept the post. As he said somewhat ruefully, "My movements to the chair of government will be accompanied with feelings not unlike those of a culprit who is going to the place of his execution."

One of the first decisions Washington had to make was how he should be addressed. The Senate proposed he be called His Highness the President of the United States of America and the Protector of Their Liberties, but he opted for the far more modest Mr. President.

Although Washington was one of the richest men in America, his wealth was tied up in land. To pay the expenses of his move from Mount Vernon to the first presidential residence, at 3 Cherry Street in New York City, he was forced to borrow a substantial amount of money. Becoming president, he said, forced him "to do what I never expected to be driven to—that is, to borrow money on interest." The founding fathers had failed to determine the president's salary. While Washington considered rejecting any payment, concerned about the ethics of being paid for public service, he eventually agreed to accept $25,000 annually—although he still found it necessary to use his own money to cover all the household expenses.

As Washington's carriage took him from Virginia to New York, crowds gathered to offer their respects and warm hurrahs. On April 30, 1789, he was sworn into office on the balcony of Federal Hall, where the First Congress was meeting.

Washington was well aware he was setting the precedent for the nation's highest office, and while he brought dignity to the office, he was especially careful to avoid any of the trappings of a monarchy—although some traditions proved impossible to eliminate. For example, he set aside every Tuesday afternoon from three p.m. to four p.m. to meet with male visitors in his residence. Each week a long line of people waited to be formally introduced to him, and rather than shaking hands, they would bow respectfully. Members of Congress and other government officials or dignitaries were often invited to Thursday evening dinner. Martha Washington hosted Friday night levees. Both men and women were invited to these much less formal social events. At these dinners, guests were served by George and Martha Washington's slaves.

The most familiar legend about Washington tells of him cutting down his father's favorite cherry tree with a hatchet when he was only six years old, and when asked by his father if he had done it, replying honestly, "I cannot tell a lie. I cut down that tree." In truth, though, Washington was a smart, shrewd politician. He knew how—and when—to use his power to achieve his aims. Unlike Madison, Jefferson, Adams, and Franklin, Washington's name isn't closely attached to the important documents of that period, but his influence and his philosophy are present in every one of them.

During Washington's first two years in office, the new Congress was debating the initial amendments to the Constitution. In September, Congress passed the Bill of Rights containing twelve amendments, although the states ratified only the first ten: The First Amendment guaranteed freedom of religion, speech, and the press. The Second Amendment guaranteed that a well-regulated militia would provide security "and the right of the people to keep and bear arms." The Fourth Amendment prohibited the unreasonable search and seizures that had been so common during the British occupation. To prevent legal authorities from misusing their powers, the Sixth Amendment guaranteed that anyone accused of a crime would be given a fair and speedy public trial, and the right to legal counsel and a trial by jury. And the Tenth Amendment answered Massachusetts's fears, reserving all rights not specifically granted to the central government to the states. The Bill of Rights was ratified on December 15, 1791.

BARON STEUBEN.   GOV. ARTHUR ST. CLAIR.   SECRETARY SAMUEL A. OTIS.   ROGER SHERMAN.   GOV. GEORGE CLINTON.
         CHANCELLOR ROBERT R. LIVINGSTON.   GEORGE WASHINGTON.   JOHN ADAMS.   GEN'L HENRY KNOX.

WASHINGTON TAKING THE OATH AS PRESIDENT,

APRIL 30, 1789, ON THE SITE OF THE PRESENT TREASURY BUILDING, WALL STREET, NEW YORK CITY.

On the way to New York City's Federal Hall in April 1789, where he was to be inaugurated as the first president of the United States (at left) by Robert Livingston, Washington stopped in many towns—including (top) in Trenton, New Jersey—to share in the joy of this historic event.

The two amendments that were not ratified and so did not become part of the Bill of Rights prohibited a Congress in session from giving itself a pay raise and established a formula to be used to determine how representatives would be apportioned to the states. Incredibly, the amendment prohibiting Congress from raising its own salary did not have a termination date for ratification, so when a college student made that discovery in 1982 he began lobbying state legislatures—and eventually gained enough support to ratify it as the Twenty-Seventh Amendment.

Although there was no provision for it in the Constitution, Washington recruited a group of advisers to run various government departments for him. There was no official name for this group; it would be two decades before James Madison began referring to these advisers as his cabinet. Like the president, these first cabinet officials were building the foundation on which the future of the country would rest. They were making decisions that would resonate through the centuries, and a wrong choice could lead to ruin.

Alexander Hamilton, the first secretary of the Treasury, had to establish the economic policies for the new nation—while also handling the existing financial crisis. It was an especially difficult task, given that it had been England's repressive taxation that had ignited the Revolution. Hamilton advocated the creation of a central bank with the power to issue paper money. To gain support from the states, he proposed that this national bank assume the $25 million in war debts they were struggling to settle. To pay those debts, and finally put the United States on a sound financial footing, he proposed instituting excise taxes. It was a daring suggestion, especially when many Americans did not trust bankers. Benjamin Franklin argued that "the Colonies would gladly have borne the little tax on tea and other matters, had it not been the poverty caused by the bad influence of the English bankers on the Parliament, which has caused in the Colonies hatred of England and the Revolutionary War." And while Franklin may have feared the intrusion of bankers into the political arena, when the bank was chartered, he purchased one share or 0.01 percent ownership for $400 as a way of demonstrating his support. But many others fought against it.

Among the cabinet members who vehemently opposed Hamilton was the first secretary of state, Thomas Jefferson, who believed the creation of a national bank was unconstitutional—and the imposition of excise taxes had been the very reason the states had declared independence. As Jefferson remembered about those discussions, "Hamilton and myself were daily pitted in the cabinet like two cocks. . . . The president, on weighing the advice of all, is left free to make up an opinion for himself."

This was just one of many battles in the war between Hamilton and his followers, who believed in a strong central government, and Jefferson and his followers, who were wary of the tyranny of a too powerful national government. To gain support for his ideas, Hamilton had helped form the nation's first political party, the Federalists, in 1787.

Washington eventually supported Hamilton's proposal and the First Bank of the United States was chartered in February 1791. As a result, Jefferson began forming opposition parties, then known as Democratic-Republican Societies. While they existed under a variety of names—Democratic, Republican, True Republican, Constitutional, Patriotic, Political, Franklin, and Madisonian—they all supported strong state governments and were united as anti-Federalists. Basically, the Federalists consisted of northern businessmen, bankers, and merchants who believed that industry fueled the American economy, which in turn benefited everyone, whereas the Democratic-Republicans were mostly farmers and artisans who wanted government to just leave them alone. The founding fathers abhorred political parties. Washington warned against "factions" and Jefferson said, "If I could not go to heaven but with a party, I would not go there at all." But among their many extraordinary accomplishments was the creation of our current two-party political system.

Congress agreed to impose the first excise tax in American history, a tax "upon spirits distilled within the United States, and for appropriating the same." By far the most popular distilled beverage was whiskey, so this became known as the whiskey tax. The result was a very unusual event, the only time in American history that the president has led troops into a battle.

With the spirit of rebellion against a powerful government imposing burdensome taxes still very much in the air, farmers—especially those on the western frontier who had long been distilling their surplus corn, rye, and grain—strongly objected. While the owners of large distilleries, many of them in the east, could easily absorb this additional tax, it placed a terrible burden on smaller farmers who grew their own crops and operated their own small stills. In some places on the frontier, whiskey was used as a form of currency, making this essentially an income tax. For many of them it was proof they had been right to fight against giving up their rights to a government so far away.

At first, these angry citizens tried to fight the tax legally; they organized and sent petitions to the Pennsylvania State Assembly as well as Congress. As a result, the tax was reduced by a penny. That gesture wasn't sufficient and, just as had happened so many years earlier, the peaceful protests gradually became violent. In September 1791 protesters tarred and feathered a tax collector. When a court officer tried to serve assault warrants on the guilty people, he also was tarred and feathered. As a result of that and other threats, the tax was not collected for almost two years.

The resistance continued to escalate. More tax collectors were attacked. Letters written by "Tom the Tinker" threatening anyone who complied with the tax appeared in local newspapers. Hamilton began asking for military support to suppress the growing Whiskey Rebellion. It wasn't simply a matter of collecting unpaid taxes; it was a challenge to the right of the central government to enforce laws passed by Congress. Washington had no choice; he had to respond. Trying desperately to maintain peace, he issued a proclamation criticizing westerners for "tending to obstruct the operation of the laws of the United States" and calling it a "duty that every citizen owes to his country and to the laws, and of a nature dangerous to the very being of a government." He warned that if they refused to "refrain and desist . . . all lawful ways and means will be strictly put in execution for bringing to justice their infractors . . . and securing obedience."

Washington's threats were ignored. In July 1794, an estimated fifty armed men surrounded the home of John Neville, a wealthy distiller and the regional supervisor for tax collections in western Pennsylvania. They demanded that Neville resign his position and hand over all his tax records. There also is some speculation that a US marshal who had come to serve legal papers on several residents was hiding in Neville's house. It isn't known who fired the first shots, but one of the protesters was killed and four more were wounded.

The following day the farmers' army returned to Neville's house in force, this time bringing as many as six hundred men commanded by Revolutionary War veteran Major James McFarlane. Neville barricaded himself inside with several armed slaves and eleven soldiers from nearby Fort Pitt. After negotiations, several women and children were permitted to leave the house, and Neville himself managed to sneak out to safety. Then the shooting began. Eventually the rebels asked for a cease-fire—supposedly someone in the house had waved a white flag. But when McFarlane stepped out from behind cover he was shot and killed. In response the protesters burned the house, barns, slave quarters, and storage sheds. Several men died.

A violent protest army was gathering and becoming a serious threat to the new government. The anger was no longer confined to the whiskey tax but included other grievances against the government. As Washington later wrote in his diary, he was told "that it was not merely the excise law their opposition was aimed at, but to all law, and government, and to the officers of government." The leaders of this rebellion had taken the lessons of the Revolution to heart. In several towns Friends of Liberty groups were organized. Supposedly plans were being made to burn the homes of the wealthy. There were even rumors that western towns had approached representatives from France, England, and Spain for aid in organizing a

The spirit of rebellion was still alive in September *1791*, when this group of Whiskey rebels tarred and feathered a tax collector and forced him from his burning home in western Pennsylvania.

separatist movement. In August, more than seven thousand people attended a rally at Braddock's Field in Pennsylvania, then marched toward Pittsburgh, destroying considerable private property before disbanding.

Finally, Supreme Court Justice James Wilson affirmed that western Pennsylvania was in an active state of rebellion, which permitted President Washington to legally call out the militia. In his proclamation Washington noted the stakes, "the contest being whether a small portion of the United States shall dictate to the whole Union, and at the expense of those who desire peace, indulge a desperate ambition." This was the first test of the supremacy of the central government over a state government. Militias from Virginia, Maryland, Penn-

Braddock's Field, Pennsylvania, where more than seven thousand protesters gathered to protest the whiskey taxes in August 1794 before marching nine miles to Pittsburgh.

sylvania, and New Jersey joined to create a 12,950-man force that was ordered to Carlisle, Pennsylvania. Washington decided to lead the army; Hamilton went with him, as he felt responsible for the situation. General Henry Lee, then governor of Virginia, was put in command of the troops.

The president joined his army in Carlisle. He created a stir wherever he went, as younger Americans wanted to see the hero of the Revolution, the president of the United States, in person. He certainly was the nation's greatest celebrity. There was at least one benefit to his participation; as his secretary wrote to Henry Knox, "As the president will be going . . . into the country of whiskey he proposes to make use of that liquor for his drink." In fact, it was a difficult situation for Washington. As Pennsylvania Congress member William Findley recalled, "He was anxious to prevent bloodshed, and at the same time to enforce due submission to the laws, with as little trouble as possible." On September 19, he became the only president ever to lead troops in the field when they began a monthlong march over the Allegheny Mountains to the town of Bedford.

By the time they got there, the rebellion was collapsing. The leaders were fleeing to avoid prosecution. The Whiskey rebels had lost their spirit, and the soldiers returned to their farms and homesteads. The crisis over, Washington went back to Philadelphia, leaving Lee in charge. By mid-November about 150 men had been arrested, including many of the leaders. But with Washington's approval, Lee issued a general pardon "in the wicked and unhappy tumults and disturbances lately existing"—with the exception of those who had committed crimes. A federal grand jury indicted 24 men for treason, but only 2 were found guilty. They were sentenced to hang, but Washington mercifully pardoned them. Several others were convicted of a variety of crimes, mainly assault and rioting, by the Pennsylvania state courts.

Washington's firm actions in putting down the rebellion proved popular throughout the country, and while there were still many battles to be fought in the creation of this nation, this established for the first time the right of the government to enforce federal laws in the individual states and the power of Congress to levy and collect taxes nationally. It marked the

Charles Willson Peale's 1782 portrait of General Henry "Light Horse Harry" Lee, who was appointed by Washington to lead the 1794 expedition against the Whiskey rebels, the first real test of the ability of the federal government to enforce its laws on the individual states.

beginning of a debate that would continue to resonate throughout history and would explode into the Civil War: How do the states and federal government share power?

George Washington served two terms as president and shepherded the nation through often difficult growing pains. There is considerable evidence that Washington actually had wanted to step down after his first term but was convinced to serve again because the bitterness between the Federalists and Democratic-Republicans threatened to rip the country apart. By the time he was truly ready to leave office, the nation was stable and there was a functioning government in place. But there remained one final precedent for Washington to set: the peaceful transition of power. While it is now taken for granted in America, it was not commonplace at that time. Most nations were still monarchies, governed by royals for their lifetimes. Rulers, whatever their title, rarely chose to give up their power. The Constitution did not limit the number of four-year terms an American president could serve. And there is no doubt that Washington easily could have won a third term.

But in September 1796 he published "The Address of General Washington To The People of The United States on his declining of the Presidency of the United States," or as it became known in history, "Washington's Farewell Address," in Philadelphia's *American Daily Advertiser*. It subsequently was reprinted in newspapers throughout the country. This thirty-two-page handwritten document announced, "I should now apprise you of the resolution I have formed, to decline being considered among the number of those out of whom a choice is to be made," and then proceeded to reveal his deepest feelings about the government he had been instrumental in creating. After explaining, often at great length, those things he had learned and what he believed, he concluded by suggesting, humbly, that "these counsels of an old and affectionate friend" might perhaps on occasion be looked to as a guide, "if I may even flatter myself that they may be productive of some partial benefit, some occasional good; that they may now and then recur to moderate the fury of party spirit, to warn against the mischiefs of foreign intrigue, to guard against the impostures of pretended patriotism."

As a result of his decision to step down, the first contested presidential election took place in 1796. Vice President John Adams was the Federalist candidate, and he ran against the Democratic-Republican Thomas Jefferson. The race set the tone for all future elections; in posters and handbills and at rallies Adams was portrayed as the candidate of the wealthy, "the champion of rank, titles, and hereditary distinctions," who would happily establish a titled monarchy if he could, while Jefferson was accused of everything from being an atheist, to displaying cowardice during the Revolution, and, it was whispered, having an affair with one of his female slaves! By three electoral votes John Adams was elected the second president of the United States.

Adams was inaugurated on March 4, 1797. George Washington received a great round of applause when he entered the hall and another when he left to return for the last time to his private life at Mount Vernon. There was no great clamor, no battles or coups. He simply handed to Adams the presidency. It was a remarkable moment, as he reinforced the unique concept that the power to rule this nation did not belong to a person but rather to the office—and it was the American people who would choose the occupant of that office.

Washington left Philadelphia that day to return to Mount Vernon, having fulfilled his constitutional obligations. He would live there for less than three more years, dying on December 14, 1799. His friend Richard Henry Lee delivered his eulogy, which had been written by John Marshall. George Washington, he said, was "first in war, first in peace, and first in the hearts of his countrymen, he was second to none in humble and enduring scenes of private life. Pious, just, humane, temperate, and sincere; uniform, dignified, and commanding; his example was as edifying to all around him as were the effects of that example lasting."

But perhaps James Monroe found a simpler way to characterize Washington, reminding Jefferson, "Be assured his influence carried this government."

CHAPTER 10

Alexander Hamilton AND Aaron Burr

DEADLY DIVISION

A large crowd was gathered in front of the Chester, South Carolina, tavern on that March afternoon in 1807. Those who were there that day recalled it being a happy time, with plenty of music and spirited dancing. They were so absorbed in their merrymaking that at first they didn't notice the nine men riding into town. It was an orderly procession; a bedraggled man in the center was surrounded on all sides by four men. The man had a scraggly beard and was wearing a baggy coat, homespun coarse pantaloons, and a floppy, once-white beaver hat; a tin cup and a knife hung from his cloth belt. Few people paid much heed to him until suddenly, as was reported, "He threw himself from his horse, and exclaimed in a loud voice, 'I am Aaron Burr, under military arrest, and claim the protection of the civil authorities.'"

⌐ Raising the American flag in Louisiana as the state declares its independence from France in 1803.

Their attention now riveted on the spectacle, they watched as a second man dismounted, drew two pistols, and ordered Burr back on his horse. "I will not!" the prisoner responded. Anything could have happened at that moment: Burr's daughter was married to a favored citizen of the state and the former vice president of the United States remained quite popular there. There was a good chance some of the men would take action on his behalf. The guard put down his pistols and, "seizing Burr around the waist with the grasp of a tiger, threw him into his saddle." Before the townspeople could recover from their confusion, "the whole party vanished from their presence."

The riders halted when they safely reached the outskirts of the town. And Burr then burst into tears. One of his guards, "seeing the low condition to which this conspicuous man was now reduced," also started crying. After a brief pause the party continued to Richmond, where the former vice president of the United States was to stand trial for treason.

In popular lore Aaron Burr is most remembered for killing Alexander Hamilton in a duel for honor, but in fact he played a far more important role in the creation of our institutions. He was one of the four remarkable men, along with Hamilton, John Adams, and Thomas Jefferson, whose passions, ambitions, and complex rivalries helped shape our history—and ensured that the fledgling country would survive.

Because of a quirk in our original election laws, Federalist president John Adams's vice president was Democratic-Republican Thomas Jefferson. This was the only time in our history when the president and vice president belonged to different political parties. While the two men had been close friends when serving as President Washington's ambassadors to England and France, their political beliefs had driven them far apart. And during Adams's administration few issues were more contentious than our relationships with those two countries. Britain and France had been at war since 1793, and in 1796 the French had begun raiding and seizing American merchant ships carrying goods to and from England. American sympathies were divided; while officially the country remained neutral, in fact Jefferson's Republicans supported France in gratitude for its assistance in the Revolution, while Adams's Federalists believed the French actions were unacceptable.

Adams dispatched three emissaries to France to try to restore relations, but France's foreign minister, the Marquis de Talleyrand, essentially ignored them, then set terms for peace and threatened to invade America unless Adams agreed to meet those terms. To fight this Quasi-War, as it was known, Congress authorized Adams to raise a ten-thousand-man army; Congress also gave him the "wooden walls" he requested, establishing a Navy Department and commissioning fifteen new cruisers. In June, Adams officially asked George Washington

Once friends, Thomas Jefferson and John Adams became
bitter political rivals. After serving as Adams's vice president,
Jefferson defeated him for the presidency in 1800. Years later
the wounds healed; incredibly they died on the same day,
July 4, 1826, and John Adams's last words were supposedly,
"Thomas Jefferson still survives."

to once again serve as the military's commander in chief, mostly because his name would aid
recruiting. Washington accepted, knowing he would never actually serve, and named Alexander Hamilton his second-in-command. While Adams opposed Hamilton's appointment,
he needed Washington's support, so he had no choice but to accept. In the shifting winds of
power and influence, this was a significant victory for Hamilton.

Perhaps more than anyone, Jefferson was appalled. He believed firmly that Hamilton
secretly had been maneuvering events to reach this outcome. Jefferson remained strongly opposed to taking military action against the French. Supposedly he financed a series of sordid
attacks in the press against Federalist leaders, many of them written by the well-known scandalmonger James Callender. Although Jefferson denied paying for these articles and cartoons,
he certainly appreciated them.

In 1797 Callender had revealed Treasury Secretary Hamilton's adulterous affair with a married woman—for which Hamilton apologized—but then also accused him of attempting to bribe the woman's husband with money and insider information. While Callender practiced the most salacious form of journalism, his explanation for it remained valid, pointing out: "The more that a nation knows about the mode of conducting its business, the better chance has that business of being properly conducted."

As the nation debated going to war against France, the political debate in the House of Representatives turned vicious. On September 30, 1798, Vermont Republican Matthew Lyon

American political debate has always been loud but only occasionally violent. This 1798 etching depicts the fight in the House between Federalist Roger Griswold and Republican Matthew Lyon. It is described in rhyme at the bottom: "He in a trice struck Lyon thrice / Upon his head, enrag'd sir, / Who seiz'd the tongs to ease his wrongs, / And Griswold thus engag'd, sir."

accused the members from Connecticut of putting their own financial interests ahead of the people of their state. That state's Federalist representative, Roger Griswold, responded by calling Lyon a coward, claiming he had been dishonorably discharged during the Revolution. Lyon answered by spitting tobacco juice in Griswold's eyes. The men had to be physically held apart. The members of the House then spent two weeks debating whether or not to expel Lyon for his "gross indecency," but the Federalists were not able to get the two-thirds vote necessary. When the House resumed regular business, Griswold immediately approached Lyon and began bashing him with his hickory stick. Lyon fell back, stunned. He grabbed a set of iron fireplace tongs and began swinging them, knocking the cane from Griswold's hand. Griswold tackled him and the two men crashed to the floor. Any lingering sense of decorum in the people's House was long gone. Other congressmen pulled them apart and held them tightly away from each other.

Their fight served as an apt metaphor for the anger, the bitterness, and the frustration that existed between the two political parties, both of them fully convinced the other was set upon destroying the precarious union. The hostility between the warring parties came to an ugly conclusion, at least temporarily, in what became known as the Alien and Sedition Acts.

Anticipating war with France, the Federalists passed a series of acts that made it far more difficult for immigrants to become voting citizens—for example, increasing the residency requirement from five years to fourteen years—and barred any immigration from "enemy nations." They also permitted the president to deport or imprison immigrants if they were found to be "dangerous to the peace and safety of the United States," especially during wartime. While nominally intended to prepare the country for the war, there was little doubt of the real reason for these new laws: these acts took direct aim at the Republican Party, as much of that party's support came from immigrants. As a Federalist congressman admitted, he saw no reason to "invite hordes of Wild Irishmen, nor the turbulent and disorderly of all the world, to come here with a basic view to distract our tranquility." While the Alien Acts were vaguely threatening, the Sedition Act was a direct challenge to the Bill of Rights. It specifically made it illegal for people to assemble "with intent to oppose any measure . . . of the government" or "print, utter, or publish . . . any false, scandalous and malicious writing . . . against the government." Incredibly, after the long and hard-fought battles for freedom had finally been won, this law made the free expression of thoughts or ideas illegal if they were deemed to be critical of the government, and it allowed the government to fine and imprison people—especially Republicans—who violated these laws.

Because the Federalists completely controlled the Supreme Court, the violation of the First Amendment didn't become a constitutional issue. And while President Adams never used the powers granted to him under the Alien Acts, he brutally applied the Sedition Act for political advantage. In what clearly was one of the darkest moments in our early history, fourteen men were eventually fined or imprisoned for expressing their political beliefs. Perhaps not surprisingly, the first person to be tried was Congressman Lyon, who was indicted in 1800 for an essay published in the *Vermont Journal* in which he had accused Adams's administration of "ridiculous pomp, foolish adulation, and selfish avarice." He was convicted, fined $1,000—a large sum at that time—and served four months in prison. He was reelected to Congress while serving his sentence and later returned to the House.

The scandalmonger Callender was fined $200 and sentenced to nine months for calling President Adams a "repulsive pedant, a gross hypocrite and an unprincipled oppressor," and his administration a "continued tempest of malignant passions."

Both Madison and Jefferson found these acts repugnant and secretly worked with the legislatures of Kentucky and Virginia to pass laws overturning them. As Jefferson said in protest, "Let the honest advocate of confidence read the Alien and Sedition Acts . . . and let him say what the government is, if it not be a tyranny." Madison's Virginia Resolution emphasized that Congress lacked the power to enact these laws, pointing out that enacting them gave Congress "a power not delegated by the Constitution, but on the contrary, expressly and positively forbidden by one of the amendments thereto." Jefferson's Kentucky Resolution argued that every state has the right to nullify, or disobey, federal laws it believes are unconstitutional. It was a strong argument for states' rights. The resolution also warned that the only answer to such repressive legislation was for that state to secede. It was an extraordinarily risky response by Jefferson; if it had become known that the vice president of the United States was calling openly for rebellion, he might well have been arrested for treason. Washington was so incensed by these resolutions that he warned that if those states pursued them it might be sufficient to "dissolve the Union."

Fortunately, it would be another half century before the issue of states' rights actually led to armed revolution—the Civil War. Rather than being settled on a battlefield, this crisis was solved at the ballot box. It turned out to be an amazing display of the power of the people to chart their own course.

In the bitterly fought election of 1800 President John Adams ran against Vice President Thomas Jefferson, the only time in our history that the president and vice president were pitted against each other. The most significant issues of the 1800 election were the Alien and Sedition Acts and a new tax levied to pay for the mobilization of the army and navy. Adams defended them; Jefferson attacked them. In its often-vicious tone, this election set a model for future elections. Among many other slurs, the Republicans attacked the president as a "hideous hermaphroditical character, which has neither the force and firmness of a man, nor the gentleness and sensibility of a woman." The Federalists were no better, calling Jefferson "a mean-spirited, low-lived fellow, the son of a half-breed Indian squaw, sired by a Virginia mulatto father." Even Martha Washington made her opinion known, perhaps intentionally being overheard telling a clergyman that Jefferson was "one of the most detestable of mankind."

The election appeared to be close; Jefferson had strong support in the south but needed to find at least some backing in the north. To appeal to New York's electoral voters, he chose that state's popular former assemblyman and US senator, Aaron Burr, to run with him as vice president. Ironically, Colonel Burr had been a Revolutionary War hero whose leadership during the retreat from New York City had saved an entire brigade—and among those soldiers was Alexander Hamilton.

The Republicans easily won the election, but a quirk in the new electoral voting system that allowed each elector to cast two votes for president led to an unexpected outcome: running mates Jefferson and Burr each received the same number of votes. (To ensure this never happened again, Congress passed the Twelfth Amendment, which created the electoral system still in use today.)

In fact, only a technicality prevented Burr from winning outright and becoming the third president. The election would be decided by the outgoing House of Representatives—in which Federalists held a majority. The votes of nine states were required; the Federalists, loath

John Vanderlyn's 1802 portrait of Aaron Burr, who served as vice president, almost became our third president, eventually was indicted for the killing of Alexander Hamilton, and may have planned a rebellion against the United States.

to put their bitter enemy, Jefferson, in the highest office, instead cast their ballots for Burr. During seven days of debate the House voted thirty-five times—and each time Jefferson fell one vote short of a majority, winning eight states. This stalemate might have continued considerably longer, but Federalist Alexander Hamilton began campaigning for Jefferson, considering him "by far not so dangerous a man" as Burr. Hamilton's disdain for Burr went back to the Revolution, when both men had served on Washington's staff, and had grown in the election of 1791, when Burr had defeated Hamilton's father-in-law, Philip Schuyler, for a seat in the Senate. As Jefferson later explained, "I never indeed thought him [Burr] an honest, frank-dealing man, but considered him as a crooked gun, or other perverted machine, whose aim or stroke you could never be sure of."

Jefferson also was working to ensure that the outcome was in his favor. Unlike most other states, Delaware was represented in the House by one man, James Bayard. Delaware's vote was Bayard's decision alone. Throughout the long impasse Bayard had persistently cast his vote for Burr. Although it was never proved, and Jefferson denied it, Bayard claimed later that Jefferson had made a deal with the Federalists; he agreed not to dismantle Hamilton's financial structure, reduce the size of the navy, or rid the government of Federalists.

Hamilton's efforts, perhaps aided by Jefferson's negotiating skills, eventually proved successful. While Bayard could not bring himself to vote for Jefferson, on the thirty-sixth vote he abstained, making Thomas Jefferson president. But this election also set Hamilton and Burr on a course that would end in disaster.

Among Jefferson's first acts in office was to pardon those men still imprisoned under the Sedition Act, and allow it and most of the Alien Acts to expire. Among those men pardoned was James Callender, who apparently expected to be rewarded for his efforts by being appointed postmaster of Richmond, Virginia. Jefferson, however, wanted nothing to do with him, admitting, "I am really mortified at the base ingratitude of Callender. It presents human nature in a hideous form." Although he refused him that post, Jefferson apparently did give Callender $50.

The furious Callender went to work for the Federalist newspaper, the *Richmond Recorder*, using its pages to attack Jefferson. He claimed that Jefferson had financially supported his efforts against Adams, which caused Abigail Adams to attribute to Jefferson "the blackest calumny and foulest falsehoods." Callender then went much farther, printing for the first time the rumor that has become part of the Jefferson mystique: that Thomas Jefferson had been living in sin for many years with his slave, Sally Hemings, "The African Violet." "By this wench," he wrote, "our president has had several children. There is not an individual in the neighborhood of Charlottesville who does not believe the story, and not a few who know it."

Had that story been printed before the election, it is probable it would have ended his campaign. Jefferson never responded, but historians continue to debate the story. What has been established is that Sally Hemings may have been a half sister of Jefferson's wife, Martha, as Martha's father had taken Sally's mother as his concubine—a not uncommon practice among southern slaveholders. Jefferson had married the widow Martha Wayles Skelton in January 1772, and in the decade they spent together she bore six children. Apparently they were truly devoted to each other and often spent evenings reading poetry together and playing duets, she on the harpsichord or pianoforte and he on the violin. When Martha Jefferson died in 1782 at age thirty-three, several months after giving birth, her husband inherited all of her property, including her five half siblings. And one of them was Sally.

The five Wayles-Hemings children were three-quarters white and one-quarter black. Jefferson never referred to them as his slaves but rather called them servants. In addition to Sally, he also became especially close with James Hemings, who served as his personal assistant and often traveled with him, and who eventually was given his freedom. Tests conducted more than two centuries later confirm that Sally Hemings's descendants share DNA with a male member of the Jefferson family. It would not have been at all unusual for the plantation owner and his servant to have had such a bond. While many historians accept the broad strokes of the story, though, the truth about Thomas Jefferson's relationship with Sally Hemings is likely to remain an unsolved American mystery.

With the Quasi-War with France ended and the American government now firmly in place, Jefferson looked west to see the future. He was aware of how vast the unsettled country was and became determined to expand the nation. His first opportunity came in the south, when Spain ceded the territory of Louisiana to France. Included in that grant was the port of New Orleans, which meant that the mouth of the great Mississippi River, the outlet for almost half of all the crops and goods produced in the western territories, would be controlled by Napoleon. For Jefferson, that was a very troubling situation, "the embryo of a tornado," he warned. As he wrote to the American minister to France, Robert R. Livingston, "Every eye in the U.S. is now fixed on this affair of Louisiana. Perhaps nothing since the Revolutionary War has produced more uneasy sensations through the body of the nation. . . . The day that France takes possession of New Orleans . . . we must marry ourselves to the British fleet and nation." To avoid a future confrontation, Jefferson ordered Livingston to discuss the purchase of "the island of New Orleans" with the French government. In 1803 he also dispatched James Monroe to France, authorizing him to work with Livingston and to offer as much as

$10 million for New Orleans and all or part of the Floridas. If that bid proved unsuccessful, Monroe was instructed to try to buy only New Orleans, supposedly for $6 million, and if that was impossible, he was to take whatever sensible steps necessary to secure permanent access to the port and the river. If the French refused all offers, Monroe was to proceed to London to negotiate an alliance. "All eyes, all hopes, are now fixed on you," Jefferson told Monroe, "for on the event of this mission depends the future destinies of this republic."

The day before Monroe's arrival, France made an extraordinary and completely unexpected counteroffer. Napoleon's adventures in the Americas were not proceeding well, and it appeared another round of war with England was likely. He was advised by his minister of finance, François de Barbé-Marbois, that the country could not afford—and probably would not win—a widespread war in America. Instead, Barbé-Marbois urged Napoleon to abandon his plan to restore the French empire on the North American continent and simply sell the entire Louisiana Territory to the United States.

The offer flabbergasted Monroe. It was far more than anyone had imagined possible. "The purchase of Louisiana in its full extent, tho' not contemplated," Monroe wrote to Livingston, "is received with warm, and in a manner universal approbation. The uses to which it may be turned, render it a truly noble acquisition. Under prudent management it may be made to do much good as well as to prevent much evil." The two men seized the opportunity, eventually agreeing to pay Napoleon $11,250,000 and to assume an additional $3,750,000 in claims American citizens had lodged against France. For $15 million Jefferson had purchased

President Jefferson sent James Monroe (in the engraving at right) to France to try to negotiate the purchase of New Orleans and all or part of Florida. Instead, Monroe successfully bought the entire Louisiana Territory, more than doubling the size of the country, and later became our fifth president in 1817.

Napoleon authorized the sale of the Louisiana Territory (at left) when it became clear France could not afford to restore its North American empire and likely would lose it in a war with England. (Below) John L. Boqueta de Woiseri's colored print of the city of New Orleans in 1803, as seen from a nearby plantation, was dedicated to Thomas Jefferson.

UNDER MY WINGS EVERY THING PROSPERS

828,000 square miles, or about 3 cents an acre, arguably the greatest real estate deal in American history. Stretching from the Gulf of Mexico in the south to the Hudson Bay basin in the north, from the Mississippi River in the east to the Rocky Mountains in the west, this acquisition would more than double the size of the United States. Eventually six states and large areas of three others, as well as smaller portions of two Canadian provinces, were carved out of the land. As Talleyrand admitted, "You have made a noble bargain for yourselves."

When the Louisiana Purchase Treaty was signed on April 30, 1803, Robert Livingston proudly declared, "From this day the United States take their place among the powers of the first rank."

Jefferson's reputation was greatly enhanced by this popular purchase. But among those people who did not share in the celebration was Jefferson's vice president, Aaron Burr. Since taking office, Burr had not been given any work of importance by Jefferson. His patronage suggestions were ignored and he was not consulted on policy decisions; as his political fortunes faded, his resentment grew. Only a few years earlier he had been one of the most respected men in the country, but he quickly had become little more than a shadow lurking in

the background of American politics. When he learned that Jefferson intended to replace him on the Republican ticket with New York governor George Clinton in the 1804 election, he decided to instead run as an Independent—for the governorship of New York. This powerful position, he believed, would allow him to revive his political career.

Alexander Hamilton was horrified by the prospect of Burr winning such an important election. Just as he had four years earlier, Hamilton worked vigorously against him. Burr was soundly defeated by Republican Morgan Lewis. Although it is doubtful that Hamilton's efforts had much impact on the outcome, Burr placed substantial blame on him for his loss. His

Raising the Colours for the Last Time, the Cessation of New Orleans in 1803 shows the French flag flying over the port for the final time before becoming an American possession.

contempt, his anger, and his frustration reached a peak shortly after the election when a letter from Dr. Charles Cooper to Philip Schuyler was published in the *Albany Register*. Relating conversation from a dinner party he had recently attended, Cooper wrote that Hamilton and other Republicans had agreed that Burr was a dangerous man who could not be trusted with "the reins of government." But then, Cooper added, Hamilton had continued ominously that if pressed, he could describe in detail "a still more despicable opinion" of Burr.

No attempt was made to further explain this "despicable opinion." Perhaps it was an allusion to Burr being a well-known womanizer who might have fathered a child out of wedlock. Whatever the inference, Burr took great offense. Whether it was only about this remark or a response to the accumulation of slights, Burr demanded "a prompt and unqualified acknowledgment or denial of the use of any expression which would warrant the assertion of Dr. Cooper."

This was not just an angry exchange of words; Burr had made it a matter of honor. In those days one's honor was not something to be taken lightly: a man's reputation was his greatest possession and needed to be protected, whatever the cost. Hamilton tried to defuse the issue, asserting that he was not responsible for Cooper's interpretation—although he did not deny that he had made the comment. He pointed out that there were "infinite shades" of the meaning of "despicable," an evasion that Burr considered insulting.

Burr persisted, continuing to demand an apology, writing, "Political opposition can never absolve gentlemen from the necessity of a rigid adherence to the laws of honor and the rules of decorum." Hamilton responded through an intermediary, claiming he had truly forgotten the particulars of that conversation "but to the best of his recollection it consisted of comments on the political principles and views of Colonel Burr, and the results that might be expected from them in the event of his election as governor, without reference to any particular instance of past conduct, or to private character."

After a further exchange of letters, Aaron Burr formally challenged Hamilton to a duel of honor. Hamilton had no choice but to accept; a refusal would have been considered an unsightly display of cowardice and likely would have ended his own political career. A secondhand insult had been elevated to a life-and-death confrontation. Duels were not at all uncommon; in fact, a New York newspaper described them as "much in fashion," but they rarely reached the point of gunplay. Most often it would end with an apology or satisfaction, meaning honor had properly been defended. Both men, being high-profile outspoken politicians, had been involved in numerous previous encounters. Hamilton, for example, had been a participant in ten previous duels, including either two or three with Burr—but none of them had ever resulted in a shot being fired. Even those few duels that did end up with two men facing each other with pistols at ten paces only rarely resulted in injury. Often the duelists would *delope*, or intentionally "throw away their fire," usually by shooting directly into the ground. Simply by engaging in the duel, honor was earned.

But Hamilton did fully understand the potentially tragic outcome of such a contest. Only three years earlier, his nineteen-year-old son, Philip, had been shot and killed defending his father's honor in a duel on the heights at Weehawken, New Jersey.

Historians have long speculated—without any resolution—why Hamilton and Burr allowed their feud to reach this point. Most agree that it was not about this last dispute. There are people who believe that Hamilton might have been suicidal, perhaps depressed about his son's death, while Burr required a clear victory over Hamilton to restore his battered reputation.

Whatever the reasons, early in the morning of July 11, 1804, Hamilton and Burr faced each other ten paces apart on the cliffs of Weehawken—on the same grounds where Philip Hamilton had been killed. They had rowed across the Hudson River because, while both New York and New Jersey had outlawed dueling, New Jersey rarely brought criminal action against surviving participants.

No one will ever know precisely what was in the minds of Hamilton and Burr as they faced each other. A week earlier the rivals had attended a Fourth of July reunion of officers who had fought in the Revolution, but there is no record of any conversation between them. A day earlier Hamilton had written his will, making certain all of his affairs were in order, although there is some conjecture that he never intended to fire at Burr but rather planned to retire from the field with both duelists having their honor restored. Only hours before the duel he wrote, "I have resolved, if . . . it pleases God to give me the opportunity, to reserve and throw away my first fire; and I have thoughts even of reserving my second fire."

Burr got there first. Hamilton arrived shortly thereafter. Both men were accompanied by their seconds, friends chosen to ensure that the duel was conducted honorably and to arrange a peaceful resolution if possible. The rules were explained. Considerable tradition dictated the conduct of a duel, and the participants and their seconds were careful to respect it. Hamilton and Burr loaded their .56-caliber dueling pistols. Their seconds measured the distance, ten full paces. Unexpectedly, Hamilton called for a pause. Everyone stopped, curious as to his intentions; he carefully adjusted his spectacles, sighted the barrel of his pistol, and then said he was ready to proceed. As the two seconds, Nathaniel Pendleton for Hamilton, William P. Van Ness for Burr, later agreed in a jointly written statement, "[Pendleton] then asked if they were prepared; being answered in the affirmative, he gave the word 'present,' as had been agreed on, and both parties presented and fired in succession. The intervening time is not expressed, as the seconds do not precisely agree on that point." That disagreement between the seconds is the stuff of history. Only the people on that bluff that morning knew the truth and they would never agree on it. In some tellings, Hamilton shot first, intentionally shooting wide and high into the air above Burr's head, but Burr, startled by the shot in the air rather than into the ground, fired directly at his opponent. Others believe that both men fired at about the same moment or that Burr fired first and his shot threw off Hamilton's aim. Whatever the truth of it, the result was the same, as both seconds agreed: "The fire of Colonel Burr took effect, and General Hamilton almost instantly fell. Colonel Burr then advanced toward General Hamilton with a manner and gesture that appeared to General Hamilton's friend to be expressive of regret, but without speaking, turned about and withdrew, being urged from the field by his friend, as has been subsequently stated, with a view to prevent his being recognized by the surgeon and bargemen, who were then approaching. No further communication took place between the principals, and the barge that carried Colonel Burr immediately returned to the city."

DUEL BETWEEN ALEXANDER HAMILTON AND AARON BURR.

The oft-depicted duel in which Aaron Burr killed Alexander Hamilton on the Weehawken Heights, July 11, 1804.

Hamilton was struck in the lower right abdomen, with the bullet lodging in his spine. His physician, Dr. David Hosack, ran to his aid and immediately understood the severity of the wound. Hamilton said, "This is a mortal wound, Doctor," and lost consciousness. Dr. Hosack later reported, "His pulses were not to be felt; his respiration was entirely suspended; and, upon laying my hand on his heart, and perceiving no motion there, I considered him as irrecoverably gone." Incredibly, though, he revived and in his few words emphasized, "I did not intend to fire at him."

Hamilton was taken back to New York and survived thirty-one hours. Burr, at least initially, seemed remarkably unmoved by the duel. After returning to New York he had breakfast with a relative—and never mentioned the fact that only hours earlier he had shot and presumably killed Alexander Hamilton. The response to the duel seemed to surprise him: rather than having his honor restored, as he had imagined, he was vilified. Any hope he might have had of reviving his political career ended that day. But even more dangerous for him, the New York coroner had convened a grand jury to investigate the shooting. Even though the duel had taken place in New Jersey, meaning New York had no legal jurisdiction, he was indicted in both states for murder. "There is a contention of a singular nature between the two states of New York and New Jersey," he wrote to his daughter. "The subject in dispute is, which shall have the honor of hanging the vice president." Burr never stood trial for the duel; several years later, New Jersey's charges were dismissed and New York failed to take any action to support its indictment.

Although Burr remained confident he had not committed any crimes, he left New York to stay with a friend on Saint Simons Island, Georgia, in order to avoid being arrested. So long as he did not return to New York or New Jersey, he was not in jeopardy. Incredibly, after a brief stay in Georgia he returned to the District of Columbia to complete his term as vice president. President Jefferson, perhaps aware that his own political fortunes might be tainted by any relationship with Burr, stated flatly, "There never had been an intimacy between us, and but little association."

The young nation was then treated to an odd spectacle: a vice president under indictment for murder presiding over the impeachment trial of a Supreme Court justice. Federalist Justice Samuel Chase was impeached by the House for judicial misconduct. Specifically he was accused of eight different articles of impeachment focusing on his conduct during three cases—one of them the Callender sedition trial. There was little question that Chase had remained politically active while sitting on the High Court, and some of his rulings seemed as much political as legal, but it was also clear that Justice Chase had become a problem for the Republicans and they wanted him removed. In his role as president of the Senate, Burr presided over the trial with—according to newspaper reports, "correctness and astonishing dignity." After hearing the testimony of more than fifty witnesses, the thirty-four senators acquitted Chase of all charges and he returned to the bench.

For Aaron Burr, this was to be the last great moment of his once promising career; after finishing his term, he left politics and became embroiled in one of the more curious episodes of early American history. It appears that Burr went west to try to create his own independent nation. Whether he intended to provoke a war with Mexico and annex Spanish territories, lead at least two states to declare independence, or simply develop territories he had already purchased isn't known, but he began traveling up and down both the Ohio and Mississippi Rivers, engaging in land speculation, negotiating to sell parts of the Louisiana Territory to England for half a million dollars, and becoming involved in several other questionable negotiations. In New Orleans he met with Mexican revolutionaries to plan a military expedition into Mexico that a newspaper described as an effort "to form a separate government." He met several times with the British minister to the United States, Anthony Merry, who reported that Burr had told him "the inhabitants of Louisiana . . . prefer having the protection and assistance of Great Britain . . . [and] their design is only delayed by the difficulty of obtaining previously an assurance of protection and assistance from some foreign power." And he met with Spain's minister to the United States, Carlos Martínez de Irujo y Tacón, and supposedly told him that his actual plan was to invade Washington, D.C., kidnap Jefferson and Vice President Chase, and capture the United States Treasury and its arsenal. As his activities grew even more bizarre, he began recruiting an army—it eventually included an estimated eighty men—and storing sufficient weapons and supplies for an invasion of no one was quite certain where.

Burr's primary coconspirator was General James Wilkinson, whom Jefferson had appointed governor of the Louisiana Territory. Wilkinson, who for a time had been commander of the United States Army, had previously tried to separate Kentucky and Tennessee from the Union. But among people who loaned money to Burr during this period was Andrew Jackson, later to be elected president, although there is no evidence that "Old Hickory" knew anything of these plans.

Apparently Jefferson had been informed in 1805 by Joseph Hamilton Daveiss, the federal district attorney in Kentucky, that Burr was "meditating the overthrow of your administration," and intended to foment a rebellion and form an independent nation in the southwest. Jefferson probably found the story difficult to believe, and he took no action. At some point, for unknown reasons, Wilkinson revealed the plot. As evidence, he sent Jefferson a letter he had received from Burr, which read in part, "I, Aaron Burr, have obtained funds and have actually commenced the enterprise. Detachments from different points and under different pretenses, will rendezvous on the Ohio, 1st November. Everything internal and external favors views; protection of England is secured. . . . Navy of the United States are ready to join, and final orders are given to my friends and followers; it will be a host of choice spirits." While the letter did not specifically state that Burr intended to attack New Orleans or set up an independent nation, it did seem to corroborate Wilkinson's story. Finally convinced that this plot was real, if far-fetched, Jefferson informed Congress, alerted federal authorities in

BURR'S TROOPS GOING DOWN THE OHIO.

An 1882 engraving showing Burr's hired troops leaving their camp in 1805 to begin an insurrection.

the west to keep a sharp watch for suspicious activities, and ordered the arrest of Aaron Burr.

Burr was completely unaware that the president was on to him. In November, sixty men and ten flatboats set out down the Ohio River for New Orleans, expecting to meet Wilkinson and a larger force there. Burr himself was two hundred miles away in Kentucky when this expedition was launched. Wilkinson, meanwhile, having completely turned on Burr, declared martial law in New Orleans and arrested most of Burr's followers. Burr was at Bayou Pierre, just outside Natchez, Mississippi, when he discovered he had been betrayed. Months earlier he had been the vice president of the United States; suddenly he was a fugitive on the run, accused of treason.

Apparently outraged by the accusations, Burr declared his innocence and invited the good people of Mississippi to search his boats. While nothing suspicious was found, nonetheless he was arrested. A grand jury found no reason to indict him, but the judge refused to allow him to leave the jurisdiction. Frustrated, Burr escaped. A $2,000 reward was posted for his capture and US marshals were put on his trail.

Abandoning his plans, Burr headed for Pensacola, Florida, purportedly intending to sail to Europe, where he might enlist the support of the British or French to seize Spanish territories in North America. With rumored assistance from Andrew Jackson, Burr made his way into Alabama. He wore old and common clothes, and later his former associates in New York, Philadelphia, and Washington would find great humor in the fact that this elegant man, who had always favored fancy dress and proper manners, would be arrested wearing the mismatched clothes of a bumpkin.

Late on the night of February 18, 1807, a man named Nicholas Perkins was standing outside Sheriff Theodore Brightwell's home in Washington County, then in the Mississippi Territory but eventually to become Huntsville, Alabama, when two men passed slowly. As Perkins, the federal land registrar, later testified, the first man kept his head down and said nothing; the second man paused to ask for directions to Major John Hinson's place. Perkins pointed the way but explained that Hinson wasn't there and besides, getting there meant crossing the creek at the high-water mark in the middle of the night, a very dangerous enterprise.

The man thanked him and the two went on their way. *Well, that's odd*, Perkins must have thought, wondering why they didn't stop to pass the night safely at the inn. It occurred to him that they might be robbers or, even more ominous, the fugitive Aaron Burr and a companion, who were said to be in the area. His suspicions were raised sufficiently for him to wake the sheriff.

They rode over to Hinson's and Sheriff Brightwell conversed with the two men. Something wasn't right about them, Perkins knew, and he galloped to Fort Stoddert to enlist help. He would later testify that Burr's "keen" glance gave away his true identity. Hours later

Perkins and the commandant, Lieutenant Edmund Pendleton Gaines, caught up with Burr and Sheriff Brightwell near the ferry crossing on the Tombigbee River. Apparently he readily admitted his identity and was arrested for the crime of treason against the United States of America. There is no mention of Perkins collecting the bounty.

Eight men escorted the prisoner up to Richmond, where he was to be tried. It was on that long ride that Burr made the Chester, South Carolina, escape attempt that ended in his tears.

Thousands of people from around the country crammed into Richmond in August to witness this spectacular treason trial, the majority of them common folk wearing home-spun clothes and buckskin coats. Those who couldn't afford lodging lived in their wagons or pitched tents. Burr was said to have borrowed as much as $1,000 to purchase his own elegant wardrobe and wore black silk garments throughout the trial; if this was to be Jefferson's show trial, he would show them a man of style and grace.

The former vice president of the United States was arrested in the Mississippi Territory on February 18, 1807, as he attempted to flee into Spanish territory in disguise.

Supreme Court Justice John Marshall was one of two judges presiding, and several of his decisions in this complex legal case set legal precedents that have been respected for two centuries. When picking the jury, it was reported, Burr's attorney selected those men most outwardly hostile to their client, appealing to their honor to render a just decision—but also showing great confidence in Burr's innocence.

Rather than a man on trial for his life, Burr was treated like a celebrity. He was invited to dinner with Justice Marshall at his attorney's home and was given three large rooms in the prison in which to receive visitors of both sexes, who arrived carrying gifts for him. Harman Blennerhassett, the wealthy lawyer and southern politician who had been indicted as a co-conspirator, wrote in his journal, "Burr lives in great style, and sees much company within his gratings, where it is as difficult to get an audience as if he really were an emperor."

The trial lasted several weeks. Justice Marshall and President Jefferson had long been at odds, so Marshall was not at all susceptible to political pressure. If anything, as a strong public supporter of Hamilton's, Marshall might have been accused of bias against Burr. But he insisted on a narrow and specific interpretation of the law. He also ruled that the president could be subpoenaed to provide evidence in his possession, making the important statement that even the president was not above the law. Jefferson rejected that opinion, citing the independent nature of the three branches of government and asking, "But would the executive be independent of the judiciary, if he were subject to the commands of the latter, and to imprisonment for disobedience." He did, however, turn over the requested document.

Wilkinson was the main prosecution witness and Burr's lawyers successfully turned his testimony, showing that his word could not be trusted and that he may well have collaborated with Spanish interests intending to invade Florida in return for the promise that he would lead the new country. The general was thoroughly raked in the media, and the foreman of the grand jury, Congressman John Randolph, colorfully described this very large man as "a mammoth of inequity" and a "most finished scoundrel." The legendary writer Washington Irving, reporting on the trial, described the general's entrance into the courtroom: "Wilkinson strutted into court and took his stand in a parallel line with Burr on his right hand. Here he stood for a moment, swelling like a turkey cock and bracing himself for the encounter of Burr's eye."

Marshall's key ruling was that committing treason required an overt act of war—real steps had to be openly taken—which had to be proved by evidence; intent was not nearly enough. His point was a vitally important one: talking about it, even plotting it, wasn't sufficient to prove guilt. The right of Americans to criticize the government was guaranteed by the Constitution. Burr's lawyers provided evidence that he had been hundreds of miles away when his so-called army left Ohio; as his attorney emphasized, he wasn't even there.

The foreman of the trial jury, Colonel Edward Carrington, read the verdict: "We of the jury say that Aaron Burr is not proved to be guilty under this indictment by any evidence submitted to us." Not guilty. A second trial on a lesser charge had the same result: not guilty. Jefferson, reportedly, was furious, but he had no recourse.

Justice Marshall, in fact, bore the brunt of criticism for the verdict. Jefferson denounced him as "a mountebank, a trickster, a corrupt judge, and worthy of impeachment." He was burned in effigy in Baltimore by Jefferson's supporters and criticized in many newspapers as being a monarchist. While Burr was judged not guilty, the stigma and controversy made it impossible for him to ever again have a normal life in America. He traveled with his schemes first to England, where he tried to find support to instigate revolution in Mexico; when he was ordered to leave that country, he moved throughout Europe to Sweden, Denmark, Germany, and eventually France, still hoping to convince Napoleon to back his dreams. His efforts left him penniless and he returned to America in 1812, rumored to be fleeing a British debtor's prison.

He returned to New York where the murder charges against him were dropped and he resumed his legal career under an assumed name. Eventually he married a wealthy widow, who sued for divorce only four months later when she discovered he was using her money for land speculation. Once the center of the trial of the nineteenth century, he lived out the rest of his life in obscurity.

Jefferson, after finishing his second term, returned to his home, his beloved Monticello. While his popularity at the time was waning, he had long ago assured his rightful place in history by helping to create a nation of laws—and then overseeing its inevitable expansion westward.

The founding fathers had somehow envisioned the possibilities of a great democracy, then gave us the tools necessary to bring that dream to fruition and make it work. But their time was coming to an end, as was Jefferson's. Washington was dead, Hamilton had been killed on that windy New Jersey bluff, and within a few years the rest of the founding fathers would be gone: Adams and Madison, the extraordinary Benjamin Franklin, John Hancock and John Jay, Thomas Paine, Paul Revere and Richard Henry Lee, men who had willingly risked their lives on battlefields time and again to fight for a new nation, a nation founded on a simple and inalienable principle—"that all men are created equal, that they are endowed by their Creator with certain unalienable Rights, that among these are Life, Liberty, and the pursuit of Happiness. That to secure these rights, Governments are instituted among Men, deriving their just powers from the consent of the governed."

Betsy Ross

AND THE

American Flag

On August 3, 1777, Fort Schuyler in upstate New York was besieged by almost two thousand British, Loyalist, and Indian troops commanded by General Barry St. Leger. This was a key battle in the British plan to capture the Mohawk Valley and divide the American colonies. The estimated seven hundred patriots trapped inside the fort waited desperately for reinforcements that might never arrive. At some point that morning, an unknown patriot raised a flag consisting of thirteen alternating red and white stripes with a blue field, or canton, with thirteen white stars. For the first time in history, the American flag had flown.

Ironically, reports that a large relief column led by none other than General Benedict Arnold was approaching caused the British to flee.

There certainly was neither pomp nor circumstance when the flag was raised that day. Nobody cheered with joy; it didn't inspire a surge of patriotism; by all reports few soldiers paid much attention to it if they even knew what it was. While the American flag has become the revered symbol of freedom throughout the world, it was considerably less important during the Revolution. In fact, the Stars and Stripes is considered to be only the third flag to represent a country; until then, most flags represented monarchs, royal families, or military units.

Several variations of American flags had flown before that one. On January 1, 1776, for example, General George Washington, in command of the troops surrounding Boston, ordered the Grand Union flag raised above his headquarters on Prospect Hill. The Continental Colors, as this flag also was known, consisted of thirteen alternating red and white stripes with the British Union Jack in its upper left-hand corner.

According to one of our most cherished legends, Philadelphia seamstress Betsy Ross sewed the first American flag. With her husband, Betsy Ross ran a small upholstery shop not far from the state house. Supposedly Washington would visit often to have his shirt ruffles embroidered and other alterations made. The story told almost a full century later by her family is that Washington and two members of Congress came into the shop on or about June 1, 1776, not long after Betsy Ross had been widowed when her husband was killed in a munitions explosion, and asked her to make a flag based on a pencil drawing they presented. It was said that her late husband's uncle, Colonel George Ross, had recommended her to Washington. She agreed to do it but suggested one change: the stars on the roughly drawn flag had six points and she suggested five-pointed stars. With their approval, she hand-sewed the first American flag.

It is an important story in our history, even if it most probably isn't true. It would be another year, in June 1777, before the Continental Congress would pass an act establishing an official American flag. "Resolved," it read, "that the flag of the thirteen United States be thirteen stripes alternate red and white; that the union be thirteen stars, white in a blue field, representing a new constellation." The resolution, one of many passed the same day, did not further describe the flag, so the actual placement and size of the elements were completely at the whim of the person crafting it. In different early versions of the flag, the stars are placed in a circle, in several stacked lines, or even arranged into a single large star.

Historians generally believe the claim made by New Jersey's Francis Hopkinson, a naval flag designer who had signed the Declaration of Independence, that he designed the basic flag we recognize today, probably adapting it from several different variations. He actually sent a letter and several bills to Congress, requesting a "quarter cask of the public wine" as payment for his work on the flag, the Great Seal of the United States,

Continental currency, and other projects, which was denied because he was a member of Congress and this was seen as part of his duties.

Washington explained the symbolism of the flag, saying, "We take the stars from heaven, the red from our mother country, separating it by white stripes, thus showing that we have separated from her, and the white stripes shall go down to posterity representing liberty." The thirteen stars, obviously, represented the thirteen original colonies. The flag flown in battle over Fort Schuyler apparently was made inside the fort; the white stripes came from soldiers' shirts, the red stripes were made from the red flannel petticoats of officers' wives, and the blue field was cut out of Captain Abraham Swartwout's blue cloth coat. We know for certain Swartwout gave up his coat because a record exists of Congress paying him for it.

But there is no record of who sewed the first flag or what happened to it. The only official mention of Betsy Ross during this period appears in the minutes of Pennsylvania's Navy Board, which paid her "fourteen pounds twelve shillings and two pence" for making the colors for Pennsylvania state ships. But at least three other Philadelphia seamstresses were paid about the same to produce a variety of unidentified standards at this same time. It is known that Ross did eventually sew many variations of the flag; in 1810, for example, she was paid for six eighteen-by-twenty-four-foot garrison flags

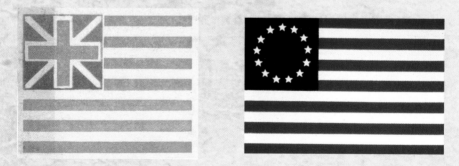

The first true American flag, the 1775 Grand Union flag (at left) or Continental flag eventually evolved into the familiar star-spangled banner that flew over

that were sent to New Orleans and twenty-seven more flags for the Indian Department.

When Betsy Ross died in 1836, at age eighty-four, the flag still had not yet taken its place of honor. While "The Star-Spangled Banner" had been written by Francis Scott Key in 1814 as he watched the flag sewn by another Philadelphia seamstress flying over Fort McHenry, it did not become popular until just before the Civil War when patriotism first began surging, and it was not adopted as our national anthem until 1931.

The historical claim for Betsy Ross sewing the flag actually was made for the first time by her grandson, William Canby, in 1870, ninety-four years after it supposedly took place—and at the same time several other families were asserting that their relatives had produced it. Canby admitted he could not produce any diaries, journals, congressional records, or other documents corroborating his claim, although other members of his family supported him. Canby's story was published in the popular magazine *Harper's New Monthly Magazine* in 1873 and was accepted by elementary school teachers who began including this tale in their history curriculum, giving it the appearance of reality. Over time it took on the appearance of settled truth, even though there is little evidence to support it, and it has become an important part of the American mythology.

 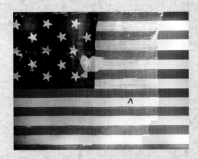

Fort McHenry in September 1814, inspiring Francis Scott Key to write our national anthem.

ACKNOWLEDGMENTS

Writing, illustrating, and publishing a book like this one requires the best work of many people, and I am grateful to everyone who participated. I especially would like to thank the people at the N. S. Bienstock Agency, in particular the founders, Richard Leibner and Carol Cooper, whom I greatly admire for their achievements and the way they work every day, in every way, to make the world a better place. I also greatly appreciate the work of Paul Fedorko, who runs Bienstock's literary department and does so with complete professionalism and the necessary mischievous glint in his eye!

It is always a pleasure to work with Henry Holt's editor in chief, the unflappable and always supportive Gillian Blake, who deals with every one of the many issues involved in this complex project with calmness and wisdom. Editorial Assistant Eleanor Embry successfully keeps all of us on track and does so with a minimum of drama. The design of this book, which personally I love, is the work of Nancy Singer, who successfully re-creates each period with the assistance of Liz Seramur, who collects the images and deals with all the headaches that go with that.

I relied on several people to point me in the right directions, but none more than my friend David Malinsky, who has a passion for this period and has written about it himself. I also relied on Casson Masters's masterful transcription service Scribecorps, as I always do, and I could not recommend them more highly.

I also would especially like to acknowledge the contribution of well respected author Don N. Hagist, Editor, *Journal of the American Revolution*;

the story of the Revolution is replete with heroics, legends, and lies, and separating them can be very difficult, and without his efforts this book would be considerably less accurate.

Finally, as always, my appreciation and my love to my wife, Laura Fisher, who makes the often difficult job of being the wife of a writer seem a lot easier than it actually is. I know what she does for me every single day and I enjoy the opportunity to sing her praises in front of other people. I also need to thank our two boys, Taylor and Beau, for their continued support and for not crashing the cars near deadlines. Finally, our dog Willow Bay, is always there when I need her, and for her I want to thank the North Shore Animal Shelter.

BIBLIOGRAPHY

I have also consulted several websites to gather, compare, and confirm information. The following sites proved to be especially valuable, providing useful material as well as directing me to additional sources:

AllThingsLiberty.com/: Journal of the American Revolution online

AlphaHistory.com/americanrevolution

Biography.com

Books.Google.com

ConstitutionFacts.com

EyeWitnessToHistory.com

History.com

HistoryIsFun.org

HudsonRiverValley.com

MassHist.org: Massachusetts Historical Society

NSA.gov/cryptologichistory: The Center for Cryptologic History (CCH)

OurAmericanRevolution.org

PBS.org

SmithsonianMag.com

USHistory.org

Wikipedia.org

Allbray, Nedda C. *Flatbush: The Heart of Brooklyn*. Charleston, SC: Arcadia Publishing, 2004.

Andrlik, Todd, ed. *Journal of the American Revolution, Annual Volume 2015*. Yardley, PA: Westholme Publishing, 2015.

Arnold, Samuel Greene. *History of the State of Rhode Island and the Providence Plantations, Volume 2*. New York: D. Appleton & Company, 1859.

Barefoot, Daniel W. *Touring South Carolina's Revolutionary War Sites*. Winston-Salem, NC: John F. Blair Publisher, 1999.

Breen, T. H. *American Insurgents, American Patriots: The Revolution of the People*. New York: Hill and Wang, 2010.

Burr, Aaron, and Matthew L. Davis. *Memoirs of Aaron Burr*. New York: Harper & Brothers, 1837.

Carr, J. Revell. *Seeds of Discontent: The Deep Roots of the American Revolution, 1650–1750*. New York: Walker & Company, 2008.

Curran, John J. *Peekskill's African American History: A Hudson Valley Community's Untold Story*. Charleston, SC: History Press, 2008.

Dann, John C., ed. *The Revolution Remembered: Eyewitness Accounts of the War for Independence*. Chicago: University of Chicago Press, 1980.

Ellis, Joseph J. *Founding Brothers: The Revolutionary Generation*. New York: Alfred A. Knopf, 2000.

———. *His Excellency: George Washington*. New York: Alfred A. Knopf, 2004.

Frothingham, Richard. *History of the Siege of Boston, and of the Battles of Lexington, Concord, and Bunker Hill*. Boston: C. C. Little and J. Brown, 1851.

Guthrie, James M. *Campfires of the Afro-American: or, The Colored Man as a Patriot*. Philadelphia: Afro-American Publishing Company, 1899.

Hsiung, David C. "Food, Fuel, and the New England Environment in the War for Independence, 1775–1776." *New England Quarterly* 80, no. 4 (December 2007): 614–54.

Isaacson, Walter. *Benjamin Franklin: An American Life*. New York: Simon & Schuster, 2003.

Kiernan, Denise, and Joseph D'Agnese. *Signing Away Their Lives: The Fame and Misfortune of the Men Who Signed the Declaration of Independence*. Philadelphia: Quirk Books, 2009.

Kozuskanich, Nathan. *Benjamin Franklin: American Founder, Atlantic Citizen*. New York: Routledge, 2015.

Lecky, William E. H. *A History of England in the Eighteenth Century*. New York: D. Appleton, 1892–93.

Malcolm, Joyce L. *Peter's War: A New England Slave Boy and the American Revolution*. New Haven, CT: Yale University Press, 2009.

Mark, Steven Paul. "For Sale: West Point." Journal of the American Revolution Online Magazine, May 2014.

McCullough, David G. *John Adams*. New York: Simon & Schuster, 2001.

Moore, Horatio N. *The Life and Times of Gen. Francis Marion*. Philadelphia: J. B. Perry, 1845.

Nash, Gary B. *The Unknown American Revolution: The Unruly Birth of Democracy and the Struggle to Create America*. New York: Viking, 2005.

Nelson, James L. *With Fire and Sword: The Battle of Bunker Hill and the Beginning of the American Revolution*. New York: Thomas Dunne Books, 2011.

Phelps, M. William. *Nathan Hale: The Life and Death of America's First Spy*. New York: Thomas Dunne Books, 2008.

Puls, Mark. *Samuel Adams: Father of the American Revolution*. New York: Palgrave Macmillan, 2006.

Skemp, Sheila L. *Benjamin and William Franklin: Father and Son, Patriot and Loyalist*. Boston: Bedford Books of St. Martin's Press, 1994.

———. *The Making of a Patriot: Benjamin Franklin at the Cockpit*. New York: Oxford University Press, 2013.

Sparks, Jared. *The Life of Washington*. Boston: Little, Brown, 1852.

Williams, Catherine Read. *Biography of Revolutionary Heroes, Containing the Life of Brigadier Gen. William Barton*. Providence, RI: Published by the author, 1839.

Winfield, Charles H. *History of the County of Hudson, New Jersey: From Its Earliest Settlement to the Present Time*. New York: Kennard & Hay Stationery Manufacturing and Printing Company, 1874.

Winter, Claudia Bell. "The Aaron Burr Trial." PhD diss., University of Richmond, 1967.

Wood, Gordon S. *The American Revolution: A History*. New York: Modern Library, 2002.

INDEX

CREDITS

Page iii: Background and title logo courtesy of FOX NEWS CHANNEL. Page 2: Courtesy of the Library of Congress, LC-DIG-pga-02468. Page 2: Peter Newark American Pictures/Bridgeman Images. Page 6: Stock Montage/Getty Images. Page 9: Historical Society of Pennsylvania. Pages 10–11: Universal History Archive/UIG. Page 13: © Massachusetts Historical Society/Bridgeman Images. Page 13: Museum of Fine Arts, Boston/Carolyn A. and Peter S. Lynch Gallery (Gallery 132)/Bridgeman Images. Page 14: American Antiquarian Society/Bridgeman Images. Page 17: Courtesy of the Library of Congress, LC-DIG-ppmsca-37946. Page 17: American Antiquarian Society/Bridgeman Images. Page 19: Bridgeman Images. Page 22: Peter Newark American Pictures/Bridgeman Images. Page 25: American Antiquarian Society/Bridgeman Images. Page 26: Museum of Fine Arts, Boston/Gift by Subscription and Francis Bartlett Fund/Bridgeman Images. Page 27: Courtesy of the Library of Congress, LC-DIG-ppmsca-01657. Page 28: Granger, NYC—All rights reserved. Page 31: Courtesy of Swann Auction Galleries/Bridgeman Images. Page 32: Courtesy of the Library of Congress, LC-USZ62-45586. Page 37: Peter Newark American Pictures/Bridgeman Images. Page 38: American Antiquarian Society/Bridgeman Images. Page 40: Courtesy of the Library of Congress, LC-DIG-ds-03379. Page 41: National Trust Photographic Library/Bridgeman Images. Page 42: © Philadelphia History Museum at the Atwater Kent/Courtesy of Historical Society of Pennsylvania Collection/Bridgeman. Page 45: Courtesy of the Library of Congress, LC-USZC2-2452. Page 46: Peter Newark American Pictures/Bridgeman Images. Page 49: Courtesy Crocker Art Museum. Page 49: Courtesy of the Evanston History Center. Page 49: John Singleton Copley, American, 1738–1815, *Paul Revere*, 1768 (detail). Photograph © 2016 Museum of Fine Arts, Boston. Page 51: Bridgeman Images. Page 52–53: Granger, NYC—All rights reserved. Page 54: Bridgeman Images. Page 56: © Chicago History Museum, USA/Bridgeman Images. Page 59: Bridgeman Images. Page 61: Peter Newark American Pictures/Bridgeman Images. Page 63: Peter Newark American Pictures/Bridgeman Images. Page 65: Universal History Archive/UIG/Bridgeman Images. Page 67: SuperStock. Page 68: © Massachusetts Historical Society, Boston, MA, USA/Bridgeman Images. Page 69: Bridgeman Images. Page 71: Courtesy of the Library of Congress, G3764.B6S31775.J4. Page 74: Courtesy of the Library of Congress, LC-USZ62-45535. Page 78: Peter Newark American Pictures/Bridgeman Images. Page 82: Courtesy of the Library of Congress, LC-USZ62-78928. Page 84: Yale University Art Gallery, New Haven, CT, USA/Bridgeman Images. Page 87: Pennsylvania Academy of the Fine Arts, Philadelphia, USA/Bridgeman Images. Page 90: Peter Newark Western Americana/Bridgeman Images. Page 92: Photo © PVDE/Bridgeman Images. Page 93: © Collection of the New-York Historical Society, USA/Bridgeman Images. Page 97: Map © 2013 Jeffrey L. Ward. Used by permission. Page 98: Courtesy of the Library of Congress, LC-USZC4-9060. Pages 100–101: Photo © Liszt Collection/Bridgeman Images. Page 103: Peter Newark American Pictures/Bridgeman Images. Page 104: Brown University Library, Providence, RI, USA/Bridgeman Images. Page 106: Peter Newark Pictures/Bridgeman Images. Page 109: © charistoone-images/Alamy Stock Photo. Page 110: akg-images/ullstein bild. Page 112: S Capitol Collection, Washington D.C., USA/Photograph © Boltin Picture Library/Bridgeman Images. Page 115: Granger, NYC—All rights reserved. Page 117: Huntington Library and Art Gallery, San Marino, CA, USA/© The Huntington Library, Art Collections & Botanical Gardens/Bridgeman Images. Page 117: Courtesy of the Library of Congress, E211.J44 E187.C72 vol. 12, no. 2. Page 118: Granger, NYC—All rights reserved. Page 119: Photo © Tarker/Bridgeman Images. Page 120: Granger, NYC—All rights reserved. Page 123: The Heckscher

CREDITS

—////✠////—